parenting
without
fear

parenting
without
fear

*Letting Go of Worry and
Focusing on What Really Matters*

PAUL J. DONAHUE, Ph.D.

ST. MARTIN'S GRIFFIN
NEW YORK

www.stmartins.com

Library of Congress Cataloging-in-Publication Data

Donahue, Paul J.
  Parenting without fear : letting go of worry and focusing on what really matters / Paul J. Donahue.—1st ed.
    p. cm.
  Includes bibliographical references.
  ISBN-13: 978-0-312-35891-4
  ISBN-10: 0-312-35891-1
  1. Parenting. I. Title.

HQ755.8.D655 2007
649'.1—dc22

2007013162

First Edition: August 2007

10 9 8 7 6 5 4 3 2 1

To Jenny, with love.
To Sean, Nora, and Devin,
with hope for what the future will bring.

CONTENTS

part three
Finding Our Way 239

ACKNOWLEDGMENTS

Planning and writing this book has been a long journey, and I have been fortunate enough to receive considerable help from a number of colleagues during the process. Steve Tuber has been a longtime friend and mentor, and his unwavering support and compassion have been instrumental in helping me give voice to my ideas about parents and children. Bob Brooks has generously offered his counsel and guidance, and has supported every phase of this project. Paul Wachtel has taught me to think in positive terms, and that language can be a powerful tool for change.

I have the privilege of having colleagues whom I cherish as much for their friendship as for their clinical wisdom. Andrew Kuhn has always been available for consultations and commiserating, and I am grateful for his insight, wit, and editing skills. In our regular meetings, Beth Falk and Anne Provet have helped me to cast a critical eye on traditional notions of parenting, and to maintain a sense of humor and real-life perspective in work with children and families. Annette Rotter has demonstrated that as professionals we go much further if we approach parents with warmth and understanding, and develop an appreciation for their stress and the dilemmas they face every day. Our discussions helped provide the framework for this book. Jeannie Blaustein was kind enough to read the manuscript with a keen eye for language, and her comments on how to think about worry and how to give parents words they can use echoed in my head every time I sat down to write.

My agent, Matthew Carnicelli, pushed me to think beyond a traditional child-focused approach and to put the spotlight more squarely on the needs of parents. Without his help and gentle prodding, I might have easily gone in another direction. Sheila Curry Oakes, my editor at St. Martin's, understood what I was getting at in a visceral way, and her comments and clarifications have made this a much more readable book. Rodi Rosensweig was an early champion of the cause, and her enthusiasm and pragmatic approach have kept me honest. James Offenhartz was kind enough to offer his ideas on the title and look of the book, and was always ready to share his war stories as a dad in the trenches.

I owe a great debt to the teachers and school administrators who have shared their stories with me, and invited me into their classrooms to learn from them. Cheryl Flood, Lisa Sandhaus, and all the teachers and staff at Rye Presbyterian Nursery School and Rye Play School deserve special mention. Their warmth and respectful approach to families have taught me much about what community building is all about. I could not have felt more welcomed there these past six years.

I want to thank Cheryl Meskin, Jo Kellman, and all the teachers who have attended workshops sponsored by the Board of Jewish Education. These lively forums have helped shape many of the ideas in this book, and I have always left our meetings feeling invigorated. Special thanks also to Debbie Fine and the staff of the Little School, Sharon Hirshik, Wendy Shemer, and Diane Shein.

This book would not exist without the help of the hundreds of parents who have come to me for consultations and attended my lectures and workshops. In many ways, I have merely captured their dilemmas and bottled their collective wisdom. It has been a pleasure and a privilege to sit with them. It rarely felt like work.

I cannot begin to thank my family in a way that would do them justice. My wife, Jennifer Warren, has been my editor in chief and confidante at every stage of this work, and my ideas about mindfulness and compassion are directly linked to hers. My children, Sean, Nora, and Devin, have been more than patient with me during all the times that writing this book prevented me from shooting hoops and playing games with them. They are my main source of wonder and delight, and they have taught me what it means to have humility as a parent. I also want to thank my mother, Collette, for never forgetting the value of play, and my father, John, for showing me what it means to work hard and respect others. A final note of thanks to my brothers, Jay and Michael, who keep me grounded and always help me maintain my sense of humor.

part one

Nothing to Fear but…Parenting

one

Introduction: Thriving Adults, Fearful Parents

Working as a child psychologist is a privileged position. I have the pleasure of hearing compelling stories from parents every day. Many of them are heart-wrenching; some are tragic; others are inspirational and uplifting. By far the most striking tales are those I can't easily unravel. In these cases the stated "problem" does not appear overly serious, yet parents report feeling uneasy, frustrated, or stumped. Sometimes they are more than a little frantic. Curiously, their uncertainty is in high contrast with their outward appearance. Most of these moms and dads are composed, smart, and aware, and a good number are experienced professionals or successful businesspeople. They are nearly all caring and well-intentioned parents.

Take Susan, an attorney in her early forties, who came to my office on an early winter's morning. She had a warm smile, and though she was a little shy, Susan was expressive, self-effacing, and very funny. In the first few minutes I wondered what could have brought her to my door. Yet as she moved beyond the initial pleasantries and began to describe her concerns about her son, Susan appeared weary and dejected. Looking down, she told me she was feeling close to the end of her rope.

Her son Tim was eight years old and in the third grade. He was a smart kid and had breezed through the first three years of elementary school. Now things were changing. Tim had real homework for the first time and Susan couldn't seem to get him to do it on his own. There were also more social pressures, and Susan and her husband were worried about Tim's standing with his peers: Would he make the travel soccer team? Was he having enough playdates? Were kids leaving him off their birthday party lists?

To Susan, Tim appeared vulnerable and anxious much of the time and unsure of his abilities. Often he could not choose whom he wanted to be with or what he wanted to do. Susan had also noticed that Tim was more needy this year, asking for extra toys and games without taking much pleasure in the gifts he did receive. By all accounts Tim was a good kid who often showed compassion for other children and adults. Susan knew he had some great qualities, but could take little solace in this knowledge. Lately she was finding it more and more difficult to feel confident about Tim's future, and she was feeling guilty about contemplating a return to part-time work.

Rene and Ted came in a few days later to ask for help with their four-year-old daughter, Adrienne, who was a real spitfire. Precociously verbal, she had been a fluent talker since she was ten months old. She was beginning to read a little, could count up to one thousand, and loved everything to do with oceans and marine life. Rene admitted that Adrienne did have some difficulty in preschool this year; she was rambunctious at times and did not always follow the rules, nor did she like to share. Ted thought Adrienne was misunderstood by her classmates and perhaps by her teachers as well, although he did admit that sometimes she could become uncooperative and aggressive at home.

Ted and Rene's main reason for coming in was to learn more about how to give Adrienne opportunities to develop her prodigious talents. Should they add on enrichment programs for her? Would a private tutor help? Should she be going to a more challenging school next year? Despite hearing from teachers that Adrienne was always using her imagination and thinking creatively, Ted and Rene worried constantly that they needed to do more to stimulate their daughter. Their first thought was to seek out a team of learning specialists who could assist them in this effort. In our first meeting, they expressed serious doubts that their encouragement and assistance would be enough for Adrienne.

Like Susan, Ted and Rene were capable and successful people who had little difficulty managing most of their responsibilities. They cared deeply about their children and wanted the best for them. Yet when it came to problem solving or making decisions for their kids, they wavered, and lacked the confidence they displayed so readily in other aspects of their lives. They were a bit sheepish about this dilemma and felt considerable despair over not knowing how to "fix" things themselves. Talking about Adrienne's difficult behavior made them uncomfortable, as if they were letting out a secret that they had kept pretty well hidden until that moment. It pained them not to know what course they should take with their daughter, or what resources they might need to call on to keep her on a promising track.

The New Age of Anxiety

Plenty of new parents are anxious. Who doesn't recall coming home from the hospital with a newborn and thinking, "Now what?" Even after we've mastered the feeding routines and diaper-changing, there are many moments of confusion and uncertainty when we are caring for an infant. Things get a little easier as the kids get older. Toddlers look less fragile, and by then most parents are used to the fevers and occasional bumps and bruises. In most cases, the sleep deprivation begins to subside and parents can resume some semblance of normal living.

By the time the child is two or thereabout, parents begin to worry about much more than basic caretaking. Suddenly we wonder if our children are talking enough: Are they social, do they make good eye contact? How do we handle those tantrums? Are they growing, do they move around well, are they going to be coordinated? What about school? Should we sign them up for nursery school or day care? Can they handle the separation? Can we?

The threes and fours bring their own, bigger, challenges. Does he know his numbers and colors and letters? Is she having enough play-dates? Should we join in the soccer and baseball clinics? What about swimming lessons and ballet? Shouldn't they start being exposed to theater and museums and the zoo and musical performances? How come we hear that other kids are reading already? Would math workbooks be helpful?

In the early years of elementary school, the burners are turned up even higher. The academic pressures that parents have only heard about up to this point now hit them head-on. Plenty of kindergarteners struggle to complete their homework, and first graders can have mutiple projects going at school. By second grade the good and not-so-good readers are being tracked and separated. It's no wonder that parents fret over how to give their kids an edge and begin to ask more questions: Are the kids mastering phonetics and getting enough math instruction? The extracurricular menu is ever expanding: Should it be karate or violin lessons or dance? And then there are sports. Parents see second graders are being divided up into A and B soccer teams and can't help wondering if private coaching is needed. How do we build those skills at home? What about our kids' self-confidence? Are they in the popular crowd at school?

Where's the Instruction Manual?

Just thinking about all these choices and pressures can be exhausting and bewildering, and many parents don't know where to turn. As a professional, I often hear about their concerns, which are usually prefaced by: "I've never done this before"; "This is my first time as a parent"; "They don't come with an instruction manual, do they?" It's easy to laugh these off as typical and half-in-jest complaints. I think that is a mistake, because for many parents, particularly the mothers I meet, this confusion goes to the very heart of their dilemma.

Today's parents, especially those who have waited to have children until their thirties or forties, come to their new role with plenty of experience. The trouble is that all their work skills and academic achievements don't translate so easily to child rearing. Leading a professional life is not always the best job training for parenting. Just ask Lily:

As a lawyer I have no problem making decisions; I tell people what to do all the time. Now I don't know if my son is ready for kindergarten and I can't control my two-year-old. They fight all the time and I can't seem to stop them. I feel like I should call Nanny 911. And really, how many activities should a five-year-old have? Do we have to do swimming, soccer, and karate, just because everybody else in town is doing it?

In my experience, parents who left their jobs or downsized considerably to be with their young kids desperately miss work. Things were so much more orderly there. The instructions were clear. And there was no worrying about time-outs or tantrums or arranging playdates or getting the kids down for a nap.

Managing deadlines and multiple clients or projects can be stressful, of course, but in most industries and professions the path to achievement is clearly spelled out: more sales, new clients, and billable hours. Clear rules of the game, including short-term objectives and long-term goals, all appear to be missing in the world of parenthood. And our "clients," no matter how cute or smart, are not always cooperative and reasonable. Entering the realm of young children can be exciting and magical, but for many parents it feels more like they've landed in the Bermuda Triangle. A teacher I know, whose son is a high-tech executive, related this story: "He manages dozens of people but when it came to picking up a group of unruly five-year-olds for soccer practice, he was lost and mildly petrified. He was more than grateful when I volunteered to bail him out."

Little kids are wild, they are provocative, they are chaotic, and they can be lots of fun. They are not usually easily understood, calm, measured, organized, or cooperative. This is not a knock on kids; it just is what it is. But for many parents who have led a fairly structured and reasonably sane life, seeing how kids actually behave can be an unpleasant revelation. As Kate, mother of a three- and a five-year-old son confessed, "A lot of our life is out of control; I feel out of control. I'm running around like a lunatic; nobody listens to me; their dad is never home; I'm wiped out." Kate is not alone, and most of us who have young children can relate to her anguish.

Let's Get Organized!

In a simpler time, if there was such a thing, parents could learn to live with the chaos at home. There wasn't much else they could do. In the 1960s, when some of us were of preschool age, few structured programs existed for kids. It may be hard to fathom, but only 6 percent of four-year-olds were in nursery schools or day-care centers in 1965.[1] Until the 1980s there were no enrichment classes for young children or sports to speak of for kids under age eight or nine in most parts of the country. Before the advent of preschool and other programs, parents had no choice, they had to wing it.

They did have advantages. In our parents' generation adults typically married and had children at a younger age. Many mothers and fathers found it easier to be playful and had the energy and spirit to join in with their kids' craziness. There were also not nearly as many pressures on our parents to keep up with the neighbors. It was perfectly acceptable to let your kids roam around the block and play on their own for hours and hours. Few parents worried about fostering their young children's interests or identifying their passions, or getting down on the floor for "special time" with them. Three square meals and a good washing at day's end were the basic job requirements.

Things have changed. In New York, parents are phoning from the labor room to sign their infants up for the most popular "Mommy and Me" programs.[2] Relax about school? Parents are worried almost from birth about when to start, and programs for two-year-olds are the norm in many urban and suburban neighborhoods. Music, art, creative movement, and language classes are all available for three- and four-year-olds. The ads for many of these have not-so-subtle come-ons with a "Your kids will fail miserably in life if you don't sign them up now" message. Sports classes and coaches who specialize in the under-eight set have sprouted around the country. Reading and math specialists who

i am reminded of a story a friend and colleague told me a few years ago. She and her husband, a writer and academic, were trying to select a preschool for their two-year-old in New York City. They found the process extremely taxing and intimidating, as the competition for spots at the "best" nursery schools was fierce. Their daughter Jamie was accepted at a couple, denied at a few others, including the one they had hoped she'd be admitted to. They met with the director to find out why, and she respectfully told them, "We might have taken Jamie, had we known we were your first choice." My friends beat themselves up for a while. To each other they joked, "We should have known enough to go *early decision!*"

work with first and second graders don't want for business in many communities.

There is a chicken-and-egg debate that exists below the surface. Are we now more knowledgeable and adapting to the new reality of childhood or is there something else that is driving the parenting frenzy? Some parents point to early childhood research that describes "critical periods" for learning and contends that children should be exposed to language and music and mathematics at a younger age. Parents have also heard about the value of early "social competence." Does that inspire their playdate angst and the scheduling treadmill? Aren't they doing the right thing by preparing their kids with rigorous physical training when the local sports teams make their cuts by third grade? Isn't kindergarten much tougher than it used to be and shouldn't kids be starting to read by then?

These are all legitimate questions, and I believe that the changing expectations in our schools and communities and our emerging understanding of young children have fueled much of parents' anxiety and hyperactivity. It is not the whole story. Part of the rush to do more and to sign up our young kids for enrichment classes and lessons comes from the fear of the alternative: having to sit and face them alone, without anyone to assist us. Given this choice, many parents opt to replace the in-house chaos with structure and organized activities outside the home, and get help from people who purport to know more about young kids. At least then we can feel that we are doing something "productive" and our kids are keeping abreast of the competition. We can also enjoy a few more moments of not worrying about how to handle their tantrums and mood swings, their fights with their siblings, their endless questions, their requests to jump on us "just one more time," and their complaints about being *"so bored."*

Organizing a schedule, most seasoned adults can handle that! I know parents who plan playdates for their preschoolers weeks in advance, and have all their children's activities carefully arrayed on their Palm Pilots. At-home time can also take on a structured, preplanned feel: a morning crafts project, a trip to the park after lunch, nap time, art time, and an educational video before dinner. Then there is reading to children, counting games, some ABCs mixed in, all in the service of preparing them for the "real" academics that are coming soon. Sprinkled in between are special outings to the zoo, the circus, or the local nature center, all to give kids exposure to the larger world around them.

It is no surprise that many educated and older parents, especially those who have spent time in the workforce, wish to bring their considerable skills to child rearing. Their efforts usually pay off, and many of our young children today are more verbal, sophisticated, and aware of their environment. Keeping kids busy can be exhausting, but it also allows parents to minimize the potential for conflict and confrontation. There seems to be little point in choosing a more unstructured way of life. Wouldn't that only increase the possibility of unruly behavior at home, raise parents' stress level, and reduce the likelihood that the kids will keep up with their equally advanced peers?

The Risks of Family A-go-go

Despite the apparent benefits of adapting to the new parenting regimen, the busy schedules and organized routines can create havoc in families. Little kids are pretty adaptable, but participating in multiple activities and completing structured brain work at home can make them feel more than a little harried. I know lots of kids who react with enthusiasm when they hear about ballet class or tennis lessons or the minicamp during vacation, but when it comes time to go they are less than enthralled with leaving the house. Kids can become especially resistant to transitioning from one activity to the next. What sounded like a reasonable Saturday schedule with one morning and one afternoon activity, with lunch out in between, may not sit well with them.

We have to remember that young children are not just like their parents. They tire more easily, they may not transition well, and they need lots of downtime to rest and recuperate from school and other activities. They need time to play and relax. Ashley, who was rethinking her schedule for her four- and six-year-old girls, related her misgivings: "I feel like they're living like little adults. We rush to activities; they have no transition time. We expect them all to be multitaskers." In communities where the competition is particularly fierce, the system can easily get out of whack. In many parts of the country, scheduling four or five activities a week for three- and four-year-old children is the norm.

The perils of overscheduling have been well documented,[3] but there is a more subtle and easily overlooked downside to an overly structured childhood that has received much less attention. By focusing most of our energies on the planning and logistics of kids' activities and their education, we have lost sight of our purpose as parents. The real struggle is not how to reduce the kids' activities and lighten their load. It's taking the time to ask ourselves the question, What else should we be doing? If providing extra training to our young children so that they may flourish in school and sports and social settings is not to be our main goal, then what is it? This book is dedicated to answering that question.

A Note on "Expert" Advice

In the last few decades parents have found it more and more difficult to rely on their own insights and wisdom. Ironically, this self-doubt is *more* prevalent in parents who have had considerable life experience and success in their careers. Few mothers and fathers these days believe that their own experiences as children can have bearing on their role as parents. Today's world seems much more complex and more scary, the choices more monumental for kids, the future so uncertain. Many parents feel it is essential to rely on the opinions of child development experts and educators to help provide them with guideposts and a road map to navigate the early years.

In my experience, many resources for parents—books, magazines, Web sites—only add to their anxiety and information overload. Developmental milestones that appeared to follow a more natural course in years past now seem fraught with confusion and worry. Whether it is how to get our infants to sleep, or when to start toilet training, or how to ease separations, parents have a potpourri of advice from which to choose. Although much of it can be helpful, there is usually no absolute, hard-and-fast "right" method and no one parent handbook that they can count on any longer. The more complex issues parents face in the early years, including teaching sharing and empathy, giving children opportunities for independence, and fostering kids' imagination, feel that much more overwhelming, and they do not easily lend themselves to quick fixes or one-size-fits-all strategies.

So where does that leave this book? After all, I'm a child psychologist, and I have strong opinions about raising children. In these pages I offer quite a few strategies and suggestions and some specific words parents can use with their kids. My main concern, however, is not that parents follow my advice to a T, but that they take the time to fully consider the choices they do make. Why, in other words, do we do what we do? Here are a few of the questions to consider: What toys and electronic gadgets should we buy for our kids? How much TV should they watch?

S ome mothers and fathers have grown tired of the pressure to keep up with the latest trends in parenting and have tried to find a way out of the expert cycle. Books like *The Three-Martini PlayDate* by Christie Mellor and *Confessions of a Slacker Mom* by Muffy Mead-Perro[4] have touched a nerve with them, and though short on strategies and substance, they do offer a more lighthearted alternative to the competitive parenting found in many communities.

How do we find a reasonable bedtime for little ones? When should we start sports classes and other activities?

These sound like small decisions, but they each affect larger and more important issues that sometimes go unaddressed, like: How do we teach kids to work hard and value their privileges? When do we have meals together? How much family time should we set aside on weekends? Most parents recognize the significance of these choices, but they often feel that they don't have time to dwell on them. "The kindergarten soccer form and swimming sign-up sheets are due this week. Everyone is doing both; I guess we should too. We'll figure it all out when the time comes." And then it does, and by then time can become a blur of traveling, meals on the run, and just getting through the day.

Becoming a parent is a humbling experience, and it is no less so for those of us who work with children. Nearly all the dilemmas I have described and will go on to discuss are ones I can relate to personally. I struggle all the time to do the right thing by my son and two daughters, and I often come up short. Perhaps I have one advantage as a third party observer to hundreds of families over the past fifteen years. Because I have shared in the frustration, conflicts, and delights parents experience with their children, I have learned that slowing down and stepping back for a moment are the most important strategies for mothers and fathers who want to make thoughtful and informed decisions. I also know that in our own home, in the heat of battle, our well-reasoned plans can go right out the window. Usually my wife and I can reel them back in during the quieter moments that follow. But our shortcomings have made us well aware that staying the course as parents requires confidence and constant vigilance, and the time to set things straight in our own minds.

The Voice of Reason

Much of our anxiety as parents stems from the fact that there are so many things we cannot control in our children's lives. We want answers to our questions and sometimes may be tempted to think we can exert a little extra influence here and there: How tall will he be? Will he be handsome? Will she be a good athlete or musician? Can I count on him being one of the smart kids? Will she be social and enjoy the company of lots of friends? If we are honest, few of us will deny that we wonder about all these things. And who can blame those who wish to give a boost to their children's performance or enhance their social connections?

It is not my intention to criticize parents for wanting to do as much as they can to help their children get ahead. Rather, I would like to encourage a dialogue about what it means to succeed as a parent. What does it really mean to want the best for our kids? Can we reassess our values and our goals without worrying so much about what the neighbors will think, or what the future will bring, or how our children will fare from moment to moment? Can we come to trust our intuition and good judgment in these anxious times? I like to think of it as the search for the voice of reason, one that nearly all adults whom I encounter have within themselves.

To find this voice we have to take the time to step back and to examine our insecurities and fears, and learn how our anxiety about the future obscures our view of the present. When we think about our children, we also have to take particular care not to confuse the end product with the process. Good grades are important, but so is learning to work hard and think independently. We may tend to overlook the longer-term implications for habits attained at a young age in favor of current successes. Competing for attention in the classroom or playing time on the field can be helpful, but so are learning to cooperate with adults and to respect one's peers. Managing a busy schedule filled with activities can be an impressive achievement, yet it may also limit our children's opportunities for quiet reflection, imaginative musings, and creative thinking.

A Mission Statement for Parents

How do our worries and fears get in the way of what really matters for our children? The biggest obstacle for many of us is our preoccupation with long-term and measurable goals. The Holy Grail of parenting, admission to a top college, has clouded our judgment, and too often we put the cart before the developmental horse. When our kids are young we think too much about building their skills rather than focusing on the underlying traits that will be far more likely to ensure their success as they grow older. Encouraging a young soccer player or math student is fine, as long as we are teaching our kids to work hard and have self-discipline, not simply to mimic their teachers and perform rote drills and memorization. Learning a foreign language or how to play an instrument can be a gift to five-year-olds, but only if we are also giving them the time to be alone to use their imagination.

If we spoon-feed our children healthy doses of enrichment, but don't give them time to struggle, to be frustrated, and to fail, they are not likely to put their fledgling talents to full use down the road. Our goal, after all, is to help them become more self-reliant, to think, to imagine, and to do for themselves. They need the time and space to experiment, to be bored, to plan and rehearse their ideas and put them into action. In many ways, the most important prescription I can offer parents is to *do less*, not more. Leave them be, let the kids work things out. Our job is to provide the parameters, and in many cases, the boundaries and limits of their behavior, not to fine-tune their every movement.

Our first job as parents is to care for and love our children, and to provide them the warmth and attention they need. Only through a solid and loving relationship will they feel secure enough to venture out on their own. After that, our job is to be their guides, mentors, and teachers. We are not likely to be as successful if we are their managers, organizers, social secretaries, or their overprotectors. Often I suggest that parents sit back and ask themselves a simple question that they can apply in many situations: "Does this make sense?" Do we really need to plan out their social calendar in great detail? Are we really going to be remiss if they skip the kindergarten T-Ball clinic? Do they need that new educational computer game to keep up with their friends? Are we to be at their beck and call whenever they struggle to make something or try something new? The more we learn to think about our role and to pause before reacting to their requests, the greater the likelihood that we will decide to leave our children to their own devices.

Fears and Lessons for Life

Overcoming fear is a huge hurdle for parents. Fear is contagious, it is insidious, it creeps into all corners of family life, and it rears its head early on in the game. New parents share a host of worries about their infants: What will happen if we don't have the right car seat, if our childproof houses fail us, if our infants eat the wrong thing or sleep the wrong way? Some of these fears are a typical reaction to caring for a newborn taken to a new level by more seasoned and world-weary adults. These early-stage fears gradually diminish, and most of us are freed from their clutches a year or two after becoming parents.

But fear and the day-to-day anxieties of parenting do not go away so easily. They merely morph into a new breed of worry as parents become more focused and goal-oriented during the toddler, preschool, and elementary years. In the following pages we will discuss the most common fears of parents with young children and why so many of us are vulnerable to them. To stop there however, would do little good, and most mothers and fathers would rightly turn away from this work if it were only another chronicle of anxious parenting. My aim instead is to show how these fears prevent parents from identifying their goals and taking on their role as teachers. By unmasking and defanging our fears, we can learn to focus more clearly on giving our children the lessons they will need to live a successful, engaged, and well-examined life.

Overcoming anxiety is the necessary first step for parents who wish to develop a clear game plan for raising their young children. The second phase is coming to an understanding about who we want our kids to become and what kinds of personality traits they will need to thrive in today's world. The core of this book is dedicated to exploring these two themes and helping parents to discover how they are intricately intertwined.

We will see how each of six fears listed below can prevent parents from teaching an essential lesson to their children, and learn what steps they can take to reverse this trend. By overcoming anxiety and uncertainty, parents can regain their confidence and learn to focus on what really matters. Here are the fears we need to combat, and the lessons we can teach our children if we are successful:

FEAR	LESSON
1. Fear of letting go	Independence
2. Fear of not doing enough	Perseverance
3. Fear of taking charge	Cooperation
4. Fear of slowing down	Mindfulness
5. Fear of unstructured time	Exploration
6. Fear of falling behind	Compassion

With these six lessons, parents can provide their young children with the underpinnings for learning and the core values and strength they will need to tackle challenges in the years ahead. Kids who have this foundation are more likely to develop a positive self-image, to gain the confidence to follow their own desires and interests, and to find the will to resist the pull of the crowd when it veers away from their beliefs and goals. Parents who emphasize these lessons recognize that raising resilient, self-aware, and compassionate children is within their reach. In the early years, more than any other time, they have a chance to impart their wisdom and give their sons and daughters the skills that they can rely on for the rest of their lives.

two

What Are We
So Worried About?

many of us remember a time not so long ago when life was simple. Whether it was college or grad school or being single and in our twenties, we didn't have that many worries—complete our schoolwork, work hard in our careers, maintain our friendships, manage a relationship, perhaps—these were the big concerns. A few of us had elderly relatives that needed help, others lost people close to them or had illnesses to contend with. But as young adults, taking care of our own needs was the main concern most of the time.

Now look at us. In our thirties and forties life has become a previously unimaginable web of entanglements, commitments, and responsibilities. "My God, I just realized I have *nine* insurance policies," a colleague lamented to me recently. "How could that be?" There's the college tuition lingering on the horizon, the 401(k) that needs a boost, the late night calls to refinance the mortgage. The sheer volume of information related solely to our financial lives can be daunting. Despite the best-laid plans for the future most of us feel we are on a never-ending spiral with little time to slow down or dream of quieter days ahead. Coming back from vacation gets harder and harder every year.

It's not just financial stress that weighs on most adults. We are now a little closer to having to confront our own mortality, and staying healthy is a more pressing concern. Our bodies have changed. From backaches to knee pains to feeling that a general creakiness is setting in, even the physically fit among us are left with the lingering knowledge that they are no longer in possession of a well-oiled machine ready to go at a moment's notice. It's not so easy to stay up late three or four nights a week anymore, or bounce back from too much celebrating. We have all seen friends and colleagues develop much more serious health conditions, often appearing out of nowhere.

Our awareness of health issues extends well beyond ourselves, of course, and now most of us have parents or other relatives who are facing their own physical limitations. Difficult choices about long-term care are fast approaching. We also worry about our children's health. We hear of kids suffering from resistant infections, physical trauma, serious allergies, learning disabilities, or mental illness, and we can't help but feel like we have dodged a bullet if our children are left relatively unscathed for now. The volumes of available health-related literature only add to our worries, and staying abreast of the latest recommendations for keeping our kids safe and well feels more daunting than ever.

Anxiety in the New Millennium

It's worth taking a moment to reflect on all this worry. It can't be that new, can it? Isn't this what always happens as people get older—they take on more responsibilities, more concerns? The answer is not simple, and a real examination of the relative worries of one generation versus the next is beyond our scope here. Suffice it to say there are key differences today, and chief among them is the heightened anxiety that adults in this country feel about their own safety and security. In the years since September 11, we have had to come to grips with a markedly changing political landscape, and to face constant reminders about the need for more vigilance and more security—in airports, schools, malls, and public buildings.

Suddenly the specter of overseas conflicts, which had always appeared so far away, has come home and created a new kind of fear that most of us have to confront in some form. It's not just the inconveniences at security checkpoints, but the expectation that there will be more attacks that has left many Americans feeling vulnerable, especially those in large urban centers. This has practical implications for people's decisions to move or travel or use public transportation, as well as psychological ramifications. We now must find ways to stay centered and maintain our equilibrium and our focus amid periodic reports of impending danger here and in other parts of the world.

Some of us are pretty successful at blocking it out; after all, we already have so much else to worry about. Yet whether we are conscious of it or not, this new anxiety over safety has affected most adults, not just those with a direct connection to actual events. We now have to adjust to living in a time of marked uncertainty, where "normal" has been redefined to include the possibility of disturbing news reports and terror alerts. Somehow we have to brace ourselves without knowing what form the next attack might take, and it is not uncommon to hear discussions among friends of biological weapons, escape routes, and new hard-to-detect explosive devices. It is difficult to recall a time just a few years back when these would have been the furthest things from our minds and our conversations, encountered only in science fiction novels and disaster movies.

As we mature and grow older, most of us become more realistic and more humble, and understand that some events are beyond our control. The new security realities have accelerated this process and have diminished our ability to provide ourselves and our families with a basic sense of security and well-being. The old stalwarts—a nice home in a safe neighborhood, a solid career, friends and family who care for us—now aren't always enough to assuage these fears. And if we take hits in any of these areas—the loss of a job, the sudden death of a close friend—things can feel like they're unraveling quickly. Combined with the recent spate of catastrophic natural disasters, including hurricanes, earthquakes, and tsunamis, and the reports of global climate changes, even the most impervious and successful adults can find it difficult to cope with the evening news.

Parents Worry, Then and Now

Given the new threats that have permeated our consciousness, it's no surprise that we also worry more about our kids. Yet the increase in parents' fears long predates 9/11. Over the past two to three decades, parents have learned a lot about child development and how to communicate and be more involved at home. During that same time, they have also grown much more anxious about their children. In the late seventies and early eighties, there was considerable publicity surrounding the work of John Bowlby and other attachment theorists who contended that the first twelve to eighteen months were a critical time for mothers to bond with their infants. Some researchers took this a step further, claiming that mothers needed to connect to their babies *immediately* after giving birth.[1] Though later discredited, this study had a profound influence on a generation of new mothers, and positive and negative bonding stories continue to be a staple of parenting magazines and a frequent topic in support groups for mothers.

Anxiety about creating the right environment for attachment sets the tone for a host of worries. Pediatricians report that a quarter of all parents express concern about the vaccinations their kids will be getting, fearing that they might weaken their immune systems or be linked to developmental delays and autism.[2] Despite the advances in play equipment and outdoor matting, parents continue to worry about the risk of injury in the local playgrounds, spurred on by reports of thousands of young children who have been victims of "preventable" accidents.[3] These fears have crept into our living rooms, and "child-proofing" of homes has now become a standard service in many communities.

Concern about the safety of children has become something of a national obsession, fueled by a constant stream of news reports of bad things happening to innocent kids. It's no surprise that parents worried about the reliability of day care after the series of highly publicized trials in the 1980s, but the suspicions and lack of trust have not subsided twenty years later. The advocacy group Public Agenda reports that i n any given year there are a little over one hundred kidnappings of children by strangers in this country. Child abductions are a serious matter but we have to keep the risk in perspective, given that we live in a country with close to three hundred million people. In *Perfect Madness*, Judith Warner compares this to the number of people who are hit by lightning every year in the United States, a figure that stands just above 1,300.[4]

nearly two-thirds of parents have concerns about abuse and neglect in child care centers.[5]

Despite the lack of credible evidence that the threats to children have increased in recent years, we worry much more these days about child predators and kidnappings. Although we can't blame this all on the media, it's not hard to argue that the never-ending reports of breaking news on the latest child abduction help to create a climate of fear in both the cities and small towns in this country. The nature of this coverage leads us to perceive that the real likelihood of threat to any one child, especially our own, is much greater than the reality.

There are signs of abduction worry in our neighborhoods. Few kids are out in their yards, and far fewer roam the sidewalks and streets alone than a generation ago. Unlike our parents, who seemed content to check up on us every hour or so, we maintain a constant vigil and rarely let our young kids out of our sight. Mysterious sightings of cars or vans purported to be on the lookout for vulnerable children spread like wildfire through many communities. Many diligent parents now feel compelled to set up neighborhood watch programs and be extremely careful about who comes into contact with their children.

These specific fears are easily generalized, and we can come to feel that the communities that we have settled in are anything but safe havens. Most of our kids hear a lot about strangers at an early age, as we worry that they need to be well informed if they are to protect themselves against possible harm. On the doors of nice homes in quiet leafy neighborhoods we see "safe house" signs that we hope our children will notice if they are in danger. News reports of disease-carrying mosquitoes set off alarms and sightings of coyotes, bears, and other wild animals roaming through suburban towns make us feel that much more vulnerable. Parents may breathe a sigh of relief if their children want to stay inside and play video games or watch television. As least we know where they are.

We're back to the issue of control again. Life can be stressful and feel random these days, so at least we want to know that we are doing everything to protect our kids. It's hard to argue with this stance. Yet I have heard from many parents who wonder if raising everyone's consciousness about safety has come at a price. If our young children come to see the world as a place where they are likely to encounter bad things or bad people, then they are not going to have much motivation to explore their environment. They may look to adults to lead them where they want to go. I have heard a number of stories of the preschoolers who shrink back at the benign questions from an elderly lady in the grocery store, crying "She's a stranger, Mom!" We may unwittingly be making our kids more anxious if they surmise that we worry a lot about their safety. With danger reportedly lurking around the corner, who can blame them if they're hesitant to take the next few steps out into the yard or on the playground?

Doting but Still Doubting

Whatever misgivings parents might have about safety concerns, at least they feel that they have a clear plan to protect their kids, one that is more or less shared by their friends and neighbors. Beyond the threat of physical harm, parents have come to worry about more insidious threats to their young children. They worry in particular about the limited value of their own good intentions, particularly when they come up short. "I was trying to get the kids to the dinner table, and they wouldn't listen. I held it in as long as I could, but then I just lost it. I feel pretty terrible," reported Tracy, a mother of two preschoolers. After a brief discussion about alternative means of getting them to comply, she looked sheepish. Tracy turned and asked me quietly, "I haven't scarred them for life, have I?"

Self-doubt from moms and dads and the anguish over how to discipline children is not uncommon. Nor is the tendency to look to the future and imagine that these tense parenting moments will lead to a dire outcome for their kids. This anxiety is linked to parents' hearing about "critical periods" for learning in the early years, and the feeling that children's social, emotional, and cognitive development can hinge on just a few interactions with their caretakers. These worries also have a Freudian ring to them. Many parents fear that today's struggles with their little ones will become fodder for therapy in the years to come, and that their children will no doubt lay the blame for all their problems squarely on the parents' doorstep.

In my experience, it is not only discipline issues that spark these fears. Parents have come to view many of their moment-to-moment and day-to-day decisions as having serious consequences for their young children in both the near and long term. Usually parents wonder if they are doing enough, if they are attentive and in tune with their children, aware of their desires, quick to recognize and foster their talents. Are they getting enough socializing opportunities and keeping up with their technologically and academically advanced friends? Few of us escape these nagging questions, and most parents want to be sure they are doing all they can to give their children a head start towards future success.

When I was in graduate school, the child psychology texts were filled with references to the "good enough" mother or parent (a phrase coined by the British psychoanalyst and pediatrician D. W. Winnicott), one who was a fairly consistent, warm presence with her children and attuned to most of their needs. This notion sounds quaint today. In the world of competitive parenting, "good enough" means someone who is not really in the game, who doesn't get it. It may be okay somewhere else, but not where we live, where parents are more savvy and up-to-date on the latest trends in child development and education. "Good enough" implies a more relaxed attitude that few parents I know can relate to. We don't usually feel like we'll have another chance; if we don't get it right today there may be no tomorrow. The time is now. Our kids have so much to learn and so much to experience. We don't want to be slackers or selfishly focus on our own needs. It's the children who matter.

The Roots of Fear

How did this fear take hold? Why are today's parents more hesitant, self-critical, and afraid? How did we become such a child-focused culture? Since when did parenting take on such importance that many adults are ready to drop their own interests and pursuits in order to tend to their children's needs? The answer to these questions can be traced to changes in the political and social climate, the surge in the advice industry, the media's focus on children, increasing economic pressures, and the explosion of technology and the consumer culture in the past three decades.

The loosening of social structures in the sixties and seventies has profoundly influenced the beliefs of many of today's parents, who view themselves in stark contrast to their own rigid or authoritarian parents and vow to parent differently. Despite the obvious limitations of the "seen but not heard" view of childhood popular a generation ago, our parents had a clearer sense of boundaries and expectations regarding their children, one that was largely shared by their neighbors. Few of them worried about taking charge in their own homes.

Today's parents face a different challenge. Many of them view openness and communication with their children as the hallmarks of good parenting. They encourage their kids to express themselves, to speak their own minds and, not infrequently, to "question authority." Men in particular are wary of being forced into the role of disciplinarian, and want to avoid becoming a feared presence to their kids during the limited time they are home. Often parents believe they can reason out their difficulties with their young children, and expect that their kids will live up to their end of the bargain. When they do not, things can go awry quickly. From a very young age kids can intuitively sense their parents' ambivalence to using firmer methods of discipline, and they quickly learn to take full advantage of their hesitation or lack of will.

Wishing for closeness and for more open communication is not a bad thing, of course, and most parents that I know try hard to balance their roles. They want to be good listeners and teach their children how to problem-solve. They also know they have to step in and take a tougher stance once in a while. Yet a lot of mothers and fathers worry about creating too much frustration for their kids, and fear that they might squelch their spirit or curtail their will if they come on too strong. They also long to have good times with their children, to do fun things together, and to not make their family life any more stressful by enforcing stricter rules at home.

As a result we send some mixed signals. Yes, we want our kids to cooperate with us, but as the psychologist Wendy Mogel and others have pointed out, we don't always act as if we deserve their respect.[6] Sometimes the kids see us as their "friends" and have not learned that there are any discernible differences in how one treats adults and children. When it comes to defining responsibilities in the home for our children, or tying these to their privileges, parents often do not have a clear playbook. Young kids are happy to step into the void, of course, and they tell us loudly, in their own words, that those privileges—the handheld gadgets, the video systems, the candy and ice cream—are actually *entitlements*, and rightfully theirs! In the face of their determination and boundless energy, it is not easy for us to put up a good fight.

What Do the Experts Say?

Confronted with these predicaments, few mothers and fathers today feel completely grounded, and many are hesitant to rely on their parents' child-rearing model. They are not as likely to have brothers and sisters and cousins around to observe and bounce things off, and it often feels like there are few local role models who can take their place. Whatever success they have in their careers appears to be of little use when it comes to raising the kids. The work model doesn't apply so well at home.

We don't want to be stuck like this, so we do what we have learned to do in many other aspects of our lives: We turn to the experts. Parenting has come to feel like a monumental and ever-changing task, and we feel compelled to keep up with the latest technology and techniques. This requires research and analysis, and a careful weighing of the opinions of highly regarded educators, pediatricians, and child psychologists. Not surprisingly, the advice industry has taken off in the past two decades, as parents, and mothers in particular, have become more educated, affluent, and goal-oriented.

This search for answers has proved to be a tricky one, however. As Ann Hulbert has pointed out in her revealing book *Raising America*, parents have heard markedly inconsistent advice from childhood experts in the past several decades.[7] Don't spare the rod; reward, don't punish. Leave them alone and they'll prosper; "floor time" and special moments are essential to bonding. Put infants on their backs, no, on their stomachs, perhaps their sides. (Soon we'll have them sleeping on their heads!) Parenting has become a professional pursuit, but unlike law or medicine, the texts and reference manuals have shifted rapidly in short periods of time and offer dramatically different counsel (the family bed or Ferberize?). There is no shortage of good books for parents, and I will mention several in these pages, but the trend reversals have left many parents feeling helpless and at sea and not knowing whom to trust. They can't count on a single voice, and for better or worse they

i t is instructive to revisit some of the early tried-and-true recommendations to see how much things have changed. In the first edition of his seminal parenting book, *The Common Sense Book of Baby and Child Care*, Dr. Spock "liberally" announced that parents should not push children too early toward toilet training, or not until they can "at least sit up steadily alone, which will be *around 7 to 9 months*" (!)[8] He understood the burden on mothers, who had to wash loads of cloth diapers, often by hand, and their need to have their kids trained by the time they were two years old, rather than the age of three or four that is the conventional wisdom today. The "when they are ready" approach currently adopted in most pediatricians' offices presupposes the availability of disposable diapers at a reasonable cost, and parents' willingness to wait for nature to take its course.

don't have the same old reliable and well-worn copy of Dr. Spock that the previous generation so often used to answer their questions.

Media Mania

Confounding the issue, the media has fed into parents' fears and served them a steady diet of home remedies certified by the experts du jour. From the now-debunked "Mozart effect" that expounded on the virtues of classical music for babies to the well-intended reporting on brain research in the early years, magazines and news programs have often misrepresented the "latest scientific findings" in early childhood development and left parents with muddled impressions about how to apply these in the nursery. And the "studies have shown . . ." mystique that lends weightiness and a measure of certainty to these reports holds many parents' attention.

These snippets and sound bites can seem harmless enough, but I have heard parents repeat small threads of ideas and advice that have become very much unraveled from their original source and meaning. For example, there have been several news reports on adopted children that have focused on their difficulty forming attachments to their parents. These stories can be interpreted as a call for a new mother to spend more time with her infant and to postpone the separation process, but taken too far, this line of thinking can create an undue amount of dependency and more than the usual amount of anxiety for both of them. Reports on the learning benefits of television[9] or links between teenage video-game playing and improved visual tracking skills[10] may sound innocuous, but they can lead to confusion for parents who are trying to limit screen time. They can also be used to counter arguments for an "hour a day" that other experts prescribe.

In a more global sense, the culture of experts and the media's reliance on the latest findings have posed a serious threat to parents' ability and willingness to trust their own instincts. This despite the fact that there are few indications of any emerging fault lines in parents' intuition or judgment. The vast majority of parents I meet have solid and well-reasoned positions on important child-rearing issues, and they often draw liberally from their own early experiences. Yet for many parents this is no longer enough to justify their actions. They feel compelled to compare themselves to their neighbors and other parents (often through the Internet, on sites like urbanbaby.com), and to check their own thought processes against those of the childhood gurus.

This trend towards second-guessing by parents is part of a larger social movement in which parents, and mothers in particular, have come to face ever higher standards and loftier expectations. The new "mommy mystique," chronicled by Judith Warner in *Perfect Madness* and Susan Douglas and Meredith Michael in *The Mommy Myth*,[11] preaches that mothers should devote themselves fully to their children at the expense of their own interests and adult pursuits. Well-publicized reports of the harm that can come to children of working mothers or those who do not fully dedicate themselves to bonding with their children and satisfying their needs has created an onslaught of guilt and anxiety for women in this country. Nobody seems to be doing it right or following the inspired examples of celebrity moms and the television mavens of healthy domestic and family life. Instead many mothers and fathers end up feeling exhausted, depleted, and in despair at their perceived failings. It is no wonder that they have little energy left over for their spouses, their hobbies, and their own intellectual pursuits.

The Status Game

In less competitive times, the choices parents made or didn't make for their children were seen largely as matters of personal taste or family tradition. There has always been a certain pressure to keep up with the Joneses, of course, but most parents were not faced with the constant scrutiny and interest in their *child-rearing* decisions that have infiltrated most middle-class communities today. More than ever before, parents appear to look to their children to provide a measure of self-esteem, fulfillment, and social status. Adult dinner party conversation can now easily turn to how we handle allowance in our homes, how many extracurricular activities our kids have, or what musical instruments they will begin next year. Who among us is not concerned about where our kids fall in the academic, athletic, and social hierarchy at school?

Even preschool children are subject to scrutiny over their accomplishments. We fret about their physical and social prowess and whether they are living up to their potential. Too often we focus on specific achievements: Can our child draw well? Recite the alphabet? Kick the soccer ball with reasonable accuracy? We can easily forget that the early years are about growing and trying, not succeeding or failing. We might also miss something more important. In all the hustle and bustle and the race to measure, we may take little time to step back and ask ourselves a few basic questions: Are our kids nice people? Do they play well

with others? Do they cooperate and listen to adults? Do they know how
to have fun?

The Shrinking Pie

It's worth looking further at what's driving all this competition and focus
on achievement. I don't think it is simply parents looking to feel better
about themselves or worrying what the neighbors will think. Most of the
parents who come to my office are motivated to give their kids a leg up
from an early age because they worry about what the future will hold for
them. We see the current financial realities of maintaining a middle-
class lifestyle in this country and the prospect of diminishing opportunities for our children to succeed and remain upwardly mobile, and it's
pretty scary. In today's fast-paced and uncertain economic climate, the
decision by parents about when to introduce kids to the computer, or
buy an educational video, or join the kindergarten soccer club can
seem to have profound implications. There is a lingering fear among
many mothers and fathers that making the wrong choices or waiting too
long to get started could lead to serious consequences in the long run.

By now we are familiar with the high school rat race and the pressure to build an impressive portfolio to present to top-notch colleges
that has become an all-consuming effort for many teenagers. The multiple advance placement classes, the sports achievements, the right volunteer jobs, the identifiable "passion" in art or music, have all become
the new standards for a certain segment of the adolescent population.
However, the downward push of academic pressure driven by the per-
ception of limited opportunities and worry over children's financial future has now reached a new frontier. As one mother in affluent
Westchester County noted, "I've heard parents say that their first or second grader is taking Mandarin because China is the next global super-
power, and they want their kids to be competitive in that world, so they
are choosing activities that will give them an edge."[12]

This may sound like an extreme example, but these days few middle-
and upper-middle-class parents are immune to the pressure to get their

little kids to do something productive, something that will make a bold statement. "Have them learn the oboe," I have heard more than once or twice in casual conversation, "college orchestras are always looking for kids who can play the oboe." "Try fencing, I hear you can still get a scholarship in *that*." These days even preschool parents feel they must get going, and the thought of breezily enjoying the early years without actively programming their children, jump-starting their learning, and setting attainable goals sounds like a fantasy.

The Price of Success

Having discovered young children and their anxious parents, mass advertisers have volunteered to assuage their fears. The five and under set are the latest consumer group targeted by commercials during the Saturday morning cartoon marathons. Their parents are now besieged by claims that Mozart CDs and Baby Einstein videos will help their toddlers develop their brains and their academic skills. Apparently we need just the right stroller, car seat, and baby monitor to keep our infants safe. Technology's latest proponents, the manufacturers of gadgets, computers, and toys for preschoolers, hail the learning advantages of their products. Not surprisingly, they pay little attention in their advertising to the studies that suggest that passive screen time is detrimental to young children's mental and physical health, and research that questions the impact of media saturation on their independence, attention, and imagination.[13]

Parents who have grown up with the fast pace of advances in technology can be easily susceptible to the lure of the newest educational products. It can seem reasonable enough that the computers, cell phones, and BlackBerrys that have made our lives more convenient and organized must have junior replicas that can offer our kids a head start on the digital age. With a little coaxing from Madison Avenue and the parenting press, we can come to believe that the "smart toys" and latest inventions are necessities for our children. After all, we don't want them to be left behind by their more sophisticated, plugged-in peers.

Some of us claim to know better, but we are still susceptible to feelings of guilt and can easily project our hopes and aspirations for our children into the things we buy for them. When our son was born I wanted to buy him an appropriate first gift. On the day he came home from the hospital, I went out with my "Right Start" catalog in hand and proudly returned with a stuffed animal, a little Dalmatian with a red bow. I thought I had found the perfect color scheme for a newborn just as the catalog had suggested, black and white and red, all in one toy!

Of course I know, and teach, that if infants want to look at one image more than any particular color it is the human face, and they are predisposed from birth to engage and interact with people. This stuffed animal, tucked away in our attic, always reminds me of the vulnerability of parents, and how easily we can be lured into the sights of those seeking to sell us what we cannot buy: peace of mind and reassurance that we are good parents. It is not just the recommendations of the experts, but the sheer volume and diversity of consumer products for young children that have made parents' task that much more difficult. We must now wade through and determine what the necessities are, what the neighbors have, and what might be the next big thing to nurture our child's talents and brain power.

How to Stop the Madness

No parents want their kids to be left behind while the other little boys and girls enjoy the fruits of their labor. The recitals, the travel team jackets, the "gifted and talented" designation—who among us would dismiss that we yearn for our kids to attain these markers of achievement? In our country competing for the top slots is as natural as craving apple pie, and pushing young children to achieve and accomplish more just seems to make sense. Besides, what choice do we really have? Isn't everybody in town doing the same thing? Aren't all the kids programmed? Isn't every family organized around the kids' schedules? To argue that things could be otherwise sounds foolhardy and hopelessly out of date.

Despite the widespread acceptance of this new and "normal" family life, many parents feel that they have lost control over their children, and they long for the power to make *individual* decisions for their kids and their families as they see fit. More than a few mothers and fathers want to rid themselves of the nagging anxiety that they are not doing all they can for their kids. However strong this longing may be, they also realize that fighting the tide is no small undertaking. If parents decide that they want to set out on a different path and teach their children different things, they will inevitably have to ask themselves if they have what it takes to separate from the crowd.

three

The Tools to Combat Fear:
Endurance, Confidence, and Courage

I magine we could divide up all the sources of stress and anxiety in our lives. How many pieces of the pie would there be, what would they look like, and how big a slice would each command? For me, it might go something like this: I worry about the health of my family, my career, my relationship with my wife, our financial security, how to balance work and family time, and about the prospects for peace in the world, threats to the environment, the impact of disasters, the racial and economic imbalances in our country. I worry about our children: about their being well liked, doing well in school, staying healthy and safe, finding hobbies and passions, having enough downtime, and learning to cope with the increasingly complex demands of growing up.

For most of us, worries about work, family, and our children take up the lion's share of the pie. And the kids' portion seems to be the fastest growing and least in our control. Who can keep up with the notes and announcements that come home from school every day? The logistics of planning a calendar for preschoolers and elementary school children can be daunting. With playdates, homework, sports, music lessons, cultural outings, it can seem like we're on an endless treadmill during the school year. It's not only the daily hassles of carting our kids around, but the fear of what will happen if we jump off the well-traveled path that creates a lot of our anxiety. Despite how many of us bristle at the labels, the "soccer moms" and "minivan dads" who chauffeur their kids from one activity to the next are the norm, taken for granted by advertisers, political pollsters, and the majority of middle-class parents in this country.

Compared to many species, we humans are pretty adaptive creatures, and we have adjusted well to the fast-paced lifestyle and demands of modern parenting. From multitasking to eating on the run to cutting back on sleep, we do whatever it takes to keep up. Many parents pride themselves on surviving their daily and weekly schedule, and it's hard not to be impressed by how much can get packed into a seven-day cycle in some homes. Yet this adapting has come at a price. Not only are many of us exhausted and more stressed than ever, but we can also feel trapped by our children's commitments. How many parents relish the guilty pleasure of a rainy fall Saturday, knowing they can sleep a little later and not trudge over to the soccer field at 9:00 A.M.?

Look Who's Not Coming to Dinner

Missing out on rest is one thing, but we may be sacrificing more important things in our attempt to keep up our frenzied lifestyle. I recently came across a poem written by a fifteen-year-old girl who had just returned with her family from their annual vacation at an old-fashioned New England resort. She warmly recited the fun times they had together, the games they had played, the meals they shared, and the family activities they had participated in. At the end of the poem, she struck a wistful and resigned note, and concluded simply, "Now we are back to eating alone."

We have to ask ourselves if we can afford to wait for vacations to reduce the frantic pace of our lives and share evening meals with our kids. In many ways, dinnertime is the best opportunity for parents to hang out with their children, to talk to them, to hear about their ideas and answer their questions. That doesn't mean that it's always going to be easy or relaxing or that the kids will love the idea of sitting down at the table together. There is compelling evidence that we need to get them used to it from an early age. Researchers at Columbia University have recently found that having a regular family dinner is one of the most important protective factors for adolescents and is linked with a reduced risk of becoming involved with drugs and alcohol, lower stress levels in teens, and higher academic performance.[1] This report should give us a reason to pause and consider what place meals and family time should occupy in our homes now, *well before* our younger kids become adolescents.

Family dinners are not only for children. Parents also need a break and a chance to feel more connected. They need time to be home, to relax and refuel. After all, what is the point of rushing around and trying desperately to get everything done if we can never find the time to sit down at the table with our kids? And what have we come to when we have to make eating dinner at home an occasion for an annual holiday each September? To make dinnertime a priority we have to be more willing to write it into our schedules, to actively plan to set aside the dinner hour a few times a week no matter what else is pressing at the moment.

Searching for Control

Have dinner together, spend more time at home, and reduce the kids' activities—all sound reasonable. But many parents are likely to find it easier to climb Mount Everest than to adopt these changes. In the current economic climate, many working- and middle-class families are finding it harder than ever to stay ahead financially, and plenty of moms and dads are working extended hours or multiple jobs to keep up with the bills. Family meals and leisure time may sound great in theory, but many parents have little choice but to forgo time with their kids in order to take more work or more shifts. By default their young children are in more activities because they need to be supervised when their parents are not at home.

This feeling of having little control is not limited to parents who are struggling financially. Even those in the best-paying jobs often feel hamstrung by their work schedules and unable to reduce their com-

amily Day: A Day to Eat Dinner with Your Children was established in 2001. It is sponsored and promoted by the National Center on Addiction and Substance Abuse (CASA) at Columbia University.

mitments outside the home. The explicit and implicit pressure to go the extra mile for the good of the company, to put in face time and work as many hours as everyone else, limits the maneuverability of all but the most senior executives in most industries. Despite the push for a more family-friendly workplace, few businesses are willing to grant flexible schedules, make long-term commitments to their employees, or reward years of loyal and devoted service. As skilled workers and professionals age, they feel that much more vulnerable to the vagaries of corporate hiring and firing. This nagging anxiety keeps them beholden to the workplace and feeling like they should always be available and on call. Now more than ever, everyone wants to be viewed as a team player.

In my experience, parents who are older and comparatively well off also feel more pressure to create the right environment for their children, both in and outside the home, and to create opportunities for them to succeed. Many of us earn enough to more than adequately provide for our family's needs and do not feel the constant pressure to make ends meet that can tear families apart. Few parents find solace in this achievement, and we give ourselves little credit for providing our kids the old basics—food, shelter, and clothing. Instead we feel the pull to adapt to the ever-increasing expectations of family life and the financial obligations that go along with them. We also remain susceptible to the "breakthroughs" in child rearing we hear about in the media and in dinner conversations with other parents. From the latest software and videos, to foreign language instruction and math tutoring, to music lessons and extra batting practice, parents feel compelled to give their kids every advantage from an early age so that they can compete on equal footing with their similarly enriched peers.

Do we have to accept this state of family affairs? Should parents with young children get used to the reality of long, stress-inducing days and mind-numbing logistics for the next ten to fifteen years? Should they buckle down and do their best to keep up with the latest trends in parenting, despite the nagging feeling that staying on top of the game is harder than ever?

If we ask therapists who treat anxiety and stress problems for advice, they might respond along these lines: "Learn to control the things you can control, and let go of the rest." These are pretty familiar words to many of us, but at first glance, they offer little comfort. Control doesn't seem to be an option. We work longer hours and aren't home as much, school is more demanding, and our kids' extracurricular and social lives are much more complex that ours ever were. That's just the way it is.

If we look more closely, however, we may find that the choice is not so stark. Most of us cannot simply decide to opt out of the frantic lifestyle, and advice books that counsel us to let it all go, whether tongue in cheek or not, are of limited use in the long run. Maybe there are ways to slow down and feel more in control. It could be that the typical kids' activity regimen works fine for one family but not for another. I have seen time and again how parents who rethink their schedules—planning for more family meals, limiting their children's activities, and giving their kids and themselves added downtime—have come to feel more in charge of their lives.

This is just the beginning of the story, not the end. In this book we are not only going to be talking about having more family time and less frenzy. Other authors have made that case. Scheduling and logistics matter, of course, but only if we believe that there are other ways to focus our attention as parents. What else are we going to do with the kids, after all? How are we going to spend this time with them and why? What do young children really need to learn from their parents? What are reasonable limits on the attention we give our kids? How do we take measures to restore balance in our lives and maintain our own interests?

The Path to Stress Relief

Knowing where we can take more control and exert our influence is an important first step in overcoming anxiety. Next we have to find some concrete ways to reduce our stress levels. Stress is unhealthy, as we all know. It increases our risk of heart disease and a host of other physical ills. It can sap our energy, limit our motivation, and make it difficult to concentrate. When we are stressed we have much less patience for our kids and spouses, and often for ourselves as well.

The first task for reducing our stress levels involves a leap of faith. We have to believe that we can make changes and that we will feel better because we do. That seems simple enough, but it is not only small shifts in behavior that matter. Let's take our caffeine intake as an example. If we drank less coffee we might feel less agitated. But why do we drink coffee in the first place? It tastes good, it's warm and comforting. It also gives us a jolt, and helps us get through a busy day with a little more energy and alertness. For many parents it's hard to imagine surviving a crazy week without those pick-me-ups, and we don't find ourselves expecting less than crazy weeks anytime soon. As we get older, we need more high-test fuel to keep up. What's the problem with that?

There's a fine line between keeping up and going over the edge. We can easily feel too revved up and strained and out of control. This is not just a parenting issue or dilemma for mothers, of course. Most successful adults, men and women, live and work at a fevered pitch, and many of us feel like we thrive on this regimen. To de-stress we have to challenge some of our basic assumptions. Maybe *we* should slow down; maybe we cannot get all our work done in the time we've allotted; perhaps we should be a little less demanding; maybe our age is becoming more of a factor (heaven forbid!). These are all issues that I have personally struggled with in recent years, as have most of my friends and colleagues. It's not easy to acknowledge the wish to be less hard-charging, much less to follow through on this desire. Cutting back our coffee consumption to one or two cups a day, and avoiding caffeine in the afternoon and evening, can be one small step in this direction and can help lower our overall level of anxiety.

R & R for Parents

Whether we want to or not we cannot do it all without rest. This is a simple equation that sounds reasonable enough, but in our culture rest and relaxation are not the easiest variables to manipulate. In this country there is a lot more attention paid to those who rest less, not more. We hear of those go-getting executives who survive on five or four or three hours of sleep a night, and who wake in the middle of the night to get a head start on the business day. It may be easy to dismiss these claims as the extreme behaviors of the not so few, or of a work ethic gone slightly mad. But how many of us send and receive e-mails at 12:00 or 1:00 A.M. or awake at dawn to get organized for the day? I'm often amazed by the time stamp I see on the e-mails I receive in the morning from parents who wish to reschedule appointments or give me an update on the day's events. We have so many things to catch up on and precious few hours to do it, and our days can easily extend long into the night.

Some of us might also look back fondly on our days as night owls, and many of us still do work productively into the evening. However, like many of my contemporaries, I notice a significant dip in my energy and focus by six or seven at night, and the idea of my putting meaningful thoughts on paper much later than that now seems absurd. I wish it were not so and I long for the energy I had ten or twenty years ago. I also know now that I approach my work, my wife, and my kids very differently if I have had a good night's sleep—I can feel the tension level in my body when I do not.

Working at the computer into the evening hours puts us in bed later and it also interferes with our ability to sleep well. Most people, and this includes kids and adolescents, cannot easily transition from intense brain activity to a restful state in a short period of time. The caffeine we have in the late afternoon or the glass or two of wine after dinner can also disrupt our sleep patterns, and prevent us from getting the most out

S leep deprivation has become a national health issue in the past few decades. The National Institutes of Health (NIH) reports that forty million Americans suffer from chronic sleep disorders, and that another twenty million have frequent sleep problems that affect their day-time functioning. According to the National Sleep Foundation (www.sleepfoundation.org), 71 percent of adults sleep less than eight hours a night during the week, an amount that remains the gold standard for a healthy night's rest; 40 percent get less than seven hours of sleep on a regular basis.

of the time we do set aside to rest. We all know from experience that there is a noticeable difference between how we function and feel on seven or eight hours of sleep versus five or six. If we had any doubts, researchers at the University of Pennsylvania have found that sleeping for four to six hours a night for two weeks straight is akin to going without sleep for three nights in a row.[2]

Lack of sleep can take a serious toll on us physically and mentally. When we rest at night we relax our muscles, but we also restore energy and balance to our nervous and immune systems. This recharging helps us to feel sharp and responsive, and allows us to problem-solve and retain our critical thinking and decision-making powers. It also allows us to ward off illness and disease. Adults who are fatigued are not only less likely to be healthy, but are also less apt to have a clear frame of mind or to communicate effectively. We don't have to extrapolate far to see how this can impair our ability to function as parents, a role in which we are regularly required to quickly assess situations, make decisions on the fly, and to explain our reasoning to a less-than-forgiving audience.

Sleep is critical, but there are other ways we can tend to our bodies to build our resilience. We hear about the benefits of *exercise* all the time, but usually those reports do not focus on how physical activity plays a key role in stress reduction. Strenuous exercise elevates the endorphin levels in the brain that can give us a sustained feeling of pleasure or "runner's high." For a lot of people, playing sports and being physically active is a shortcut to connecting to the more carefree days of our youth or young adulthood, and these recollections often add to the pleasant physical sensations we feel while working out. Exercise can also open up our minds, and provide a clarity and a singular sense of purpose that can be so fleeting in other parts of our lives. All we have to do is hit the tennis ball, make the shot, or get over the next hill. As an added bonus, we also sleep better at night when we exercise during the day.

There are other ways we can soothe and restore our bodies. Warm baths, massage, or a little *pampering* can go a long way toward making the week's tensions melt away. Listening to good music, eating sumptuous meals, and relaxing with friends can also help restore balance amid the frenzy. These feel-good experiences can help sustain us in the long run. In his book *Happiness*, the British psychologist Daniel Nettle reports that one of the keys to maintaining a sense of well-being and pleasure is, not surprisingly, building into our lives the things we like to do.[3]

Last, but by no means least, maintaining a healthy sex life and reserving time for intimate moments with our spouses is critical to helping us recharge and renew our sense of selves as adults with our own needs and desires. Yes, I realize it's the ultimate catch-22. We're all too tired for that. But if we can manage to set aside the time (Be careful how you mark it on the family calendar!), making love can go a long way toward helping us remember why we decided to get into this together in the first place.

The Endurance Test

Why does a parenting book concern itself with rest and exercise and the physical well-being of parents? Lowering our day-to-day anxiety and overall stress level is one reason. Parents who take good care of themselves have another distinct advantage over their contemporaries: the energy to outlast their kids. In a sense, "parenting without fear" means having the will and the resolve not to be outdone by our children. While I don't want to portray parents and children as adversaries, in a way we must gird ourselves for battle. Without the strength to stand up and command attention, parents have little hope of advancing their ideas and values, and they risk being overrun by the little infidels in their midst!

Even the best parents find it hard to hold the line. Take Mary, the mother of one of my son's friends. Not long ago she and I were traveling to the boys' basketball game together. We were talking about the usual stuff, scheduling and practices, fitting it all in, and the homework hassles. At one point Mary turned to me and said softly, "It's just so hard to keep up. All the reminders to my kids to wash up, to get upstairs to brush their teeth, to use their table manners, to speak reasonably to each other and to us, it's a constant battle." I was a little taken aback. Mary is a proud and hardworking mother of three well-behaved and pleasant kids. I had always admired her resolve and consistency, and I guess I did not expect her to be feeling the strain so much. If Mary was having a hard time, how was everyone else holding up?

The answer, I'm afraid, is not too well. Most parents I meet have good instincts and try hard to be positive role models for their children. They have heard time and again that consistency is the key to good parenting and they wholeheartedly embrace this idea. Yet the proof is still in the pudding, and I hear the same stories over and over: "I try hard, but at the end of the day, when I'm tired, that's when I give in to the kids"; "Sometimes I just can't take it anymore, and I give them what they want to get some peace and quiet."

No parent is perfect, and we all relent when we know we should not. But in order to earn our children's respect we have to show them that we mean business most of the time. This follow-through requires a level of energy that many parents, especially those past their midtwenties, find daunting. Usually parents can muster their resolve for the big issues ("No hitting other children"; "Listen to your teachers") but find that the daily routine of parenting is hard to maintain: "Clean up your toys";

"Clear your plates"; "Ask in a nice way for more juice." Sometimes it is easier to do it for them, and to postpone the "teachable moment" for a later date. As we tire, the lines we have drawn in the sand can start to fade. Fluctuating limits on TV time and video games are prime examples of this phenomenon. We may rationalize the benefits of giving in ("There are lots of good educational programs on TV") to prevent us from feeling more anxious and defeated.

We have heard it before but it bears repeating. *Parenting is exhausting!* There are no two ways around it. The best intentions, the latest child development concepts, the consistency we all strive for, they can go right out the window at 3:00 A.M. when our three-year-old crawls into bed with us, especially when we have to catch the seven o'clock train for work. Do we put our child back to bed and deal with the fallout or do we roll over and try to catch a few more hours of desperately needed sleep? This is parenting in the trenches, and to maintain our equilibrium and our sanity, we have to be well fortified for the task at hand.

First and foremost, parenting is about *endurance*. Most parents care deeply about their kids and want what's best for them. Too often, however, the mind is willing and the flesh is weak! I am not suggesting that we need to be perfect; nobody is going to deliver on their promises and intentions 100 percent of the time. But if we can manage things four times out of five, and follow through with our kids 80 percent of the time, that's pretty darn good. So if we acquiesce to our children's whininess occasionally, and don't correct their rudeness once in a while, and give in now and then to their request for an extra video, and let them into our beds once during the work week, we are not bad parents. We have to be realistic, but we also have to be physically and mentally prepared to say no and to go the distance most of the time if our children are going to take us seriously.

It's by no means an original metaphor, but it still holds true: Parenting is a marathon not a sprint. The finish line, or the end of the first long leg, is eighteen years away! And the daily grind can be unbelievably taxing. It takes a lot of energy to maintain a reasonable pace day to day and week to week, and the notion of keeping things going for months and years can be awe inspiring and ego deflating. When we give in, when we lose our resolve with our kids, it's generally because it is the less painful option at that moment.

Rebecca, a thirtysomething mother, explained her faltering efforts to teach her five-year-old self-discipline: "I know I shouldn't, but I usually clean up after him; I just can't deal with an argument after a long day at work." This is not an uncommon sentiment by any means. Sometimes I meet parents who are geared up to solve a specific problem, to master their nighttime routines for example, but are crestfallen when things don't change quickly, and they lose their momentum if they do not see steady and unwavering progress toward their goal. Or they might be dismayed by the next hurdle that presents itself so soon after the first was overcome.

Sleepless in the Suburbs

Unlike our targets for productivity in the working world, which can at least appear to have an underlying logic and predictability, children do not always respond to our well-reasoned and well-researched plans for change. Let's get back to the 3:00 A.M. dilemma for a moment. Let's assume these parents have decided they want their son (let's call him Sam) to stay in his own bed. They have read the sleep books their pediatrician recommended, and have tried to establish a consistent routine in which they leave Sam in his room to fall asleep on his own and return him there with minimal intervention and comforting whenever he comes out in the early evening. So far so good, and after a few weeks and much coaxing and gnashing of teeth, he begins to fall asleep on his own.

Yet Sam still wakes up pretty consistently at three or four in the morning, comes into his parents' room, and climbs into bed with them. So his parents consult with me and ask for advice. I take a brief history of the problem and ask Sam's parents a few simple questions: How frequently is Sam waking up? How often do they put him back into his own bed? Do they lie down with Sam then? Do they ever fall asleep in his bed? Do they feel guilty when he cries for them? Does he have a "blanky" or special stuffed animal to comfort him in his bed? Are both parents on the same page, and do the routines change when Dad or Mom is out of town? We might chat a little while longer and then Sam's parents ask me what I think.

I used to try to be diplomatic in those moments, or take a dramatic pause to try to add gravity to my conclusions. Now I try to keep it simple: "I think you should put Sam back into his bed when he gets up in the middle of the night. It will probably help him if he knows you are going to be consistent and follow the same plan most of the time. Decide on a reasonable waking time when he could come in and cuddle (say six or seven in the morning), but before that do what you can to put him back. Try to be calm and matter-of-fact about it, and let him know you will not be swayed even if he gets upset." I ask one more question: "Are you up for this?"

It is very easy for me to tell parents to be consistent, to put their son back in his bed no matter the hour, and for us to all nod our heads in agreement at such a reasonable, if not novel, idea. I know all about the best-laid plans to get kids to sleep, and I have seen them collapse in our own house in the wee hours. I appreciate when parents are honest with me, and shared a laugh recently with one mother when she said in a high-pitched tone: "Well, it can't get any worse. Right now I'm going out of my mind with delirium!"

Sam's parents have to do a little mental reckoning, and consider if they have the ability in the next few weeks to devote the necessary energy and sacrifice of their own sleep that it will take to get him to learn to stay in his bed through the night. Ultimately, they have to make a not-so-simple decision: Will it be more painful to confront Sam's sleep problem head on now or deal with the lingering discomfort and anxiety of waiting, knowing that sooner or later they will have to bite the bullet and that there will be no ideal time to begin this plan.

I also know that there are no guarantees that a few weeks will resolve the issue. Sleep problems that have developed over a few years are rarely overcome easily, and there are usually several back-and-forth steps before the battle is won. Those who promise a quick fix do a disservice to parents, as do those who optimistically declare that a good plan and a couple of intense weekends should "solve that sleep problem."[4] Experts and media coverage can also cloud the issue for parents with stories on the "family bed controversy," the merits of having children sleep on the floor of their parents' room or the separation problems of the waking toddler.

I do not typically debate other approaches to sleep with parents unless they seem genuinely confused as to which direction they want to go. In my experience, this is pretty rare. Most, like Jim and Laura, have a pretty good sense of what they want to do: "We love our daughter and enjoy having her close to us but now she is bigger and she should be in her own bed. Plus we need our sleep." "Okay," I say, "let's talk about how to get there." Half the battle is having Dad present and willing to help. It's too much to ask one parent to get up with a preschooler every single night. So we look for a time when the demands of work and home are a little lighter for both parents. My job is to get the parents to gear up for the struggle that lies ahead, and to commit to the plan to put their daughter back in her own bed without a lot of fanfare. If they are rested and motivated and armed with the 80 percent rule, chances are they will, eventually, get to the other side of the sleepless night abyss.

To follow the method outlined above, parents have to have a firm belief that today's intervention will bring dividends down the road, and that in the long term it will be worth the considerable effort they will have to exert in the upcoming weeks or months. Whether it's overcoming sleep problems or getting children to the dinner table or helping them learn to do more on their own, I use the same adage with parents, borrowed from an old oil filter commercial: "You pay now, or you pay later." Silly as it sounds, it gets to the point. We can't suddenly wake up when our kids are seven or nine or twelve years old and decide we want to start teaching them self-discipline and respect for others or the value of learning to be calm and focused on their work. Far too frequently, I have another phrase going through my head when parents bring their older children to my office. After hearing about their current concerns and the years of struggling leading up to that moment, I find myself thinking, "I wish I had known these parents when their child was four or five years old."

Mind Over Minors

In addition to the physical challenges in raising children, there is also the mental challenge to become more mindful parents. "Mindfulness" is a concept used frequently these days in the treatment of stress and anxiety. As the psychologist Jon Kabat-Zinn describes it:

> *Mindfulness means moment-to-moment, nonjudgmental aware-*
> *ness. It is cultivated by refining our capacity to pay attention, in-*
> *tentionally, in the present moment, and then sustaining our*
> *attention over time the best we can.*[5]

In other words, mindfulness means staying focused on what is happening here and now, in the conversation you are having, in the book you are reading, in the report you are writing. It requires us to tune out extraneous information, to not get caught up in the bills we have to pay, the deadlines we might miss, or the phone calls or e-mails we have to return, when they are not of central concern to the task at hand. Mindfulness has gained credence as a tool to resist the pressures of our increasingly complex lifestyles. It can help us cope with the demands of multitasking and hyper-scheduling that can easily overwhelm our capacity to sort through and make sense of volumes of information in a meaningful way. Mindfulness is similar in spirit to meditation and other forms of enhanced self-awareness, but it is meant as a more practical application that can be honed and used on a day-to-day and moment-to-moment basis to increase our capacity to stay connected to what we are doing and to the people we are doing it with.

Intuitively, kids know mindfulness when they see it. Or, I should say, they know when adults are not being mindful of them. Take our use of the telephone. Kids are so used to phone calls disrupting their conversa-

mindfulness can seem a little too New Age or Zen, and I can understand the resistance to a concept that sounds so ethereal. But the real difficulty many of us have is in imagining that we could actually make use of mindfulness as a technique. On the eve of a lecture I was giving on stress reduction a few years back, my wife and I were discussing how she uses mindfulness in her work with anxious adults. I was busily taking notes on my laptop as she spoke, staring at the computer screen while trying to carry on our conversation, when she stopped me: "You are not being mindful!" she said teasingly. I realized how difficult it was for me to stop and focus on just one thing, whether at home or at work. I have tried hard to use her mantra, "stay in the moment," since then, and it is still a constant struggle.

tions and time with adults that they are shocked when I don't pick up the phone in my office during my meetings with them. Almost every day I hear kids complain that their moms and dads never really listen to them or talk to them because they are too busy chatting on their cell phones. Frequently parents admit that they struggle to follow through on their requests, like calling the kids to the dinner table, because they are distracted by a call or a pressing e-mail message they have to return. Parents generally feel torn and anxious in these moments because they are not fully tuned in to either situation and are not doing justice to their kids or their friends and colleagues on the other line.

So what happens? The kids resist or they act out as a way of being heard, of getting us to pay attention to *them*. More than anything children want to know that they are our first priority, that we are keeping them in mind when we are in their presence. A few ways we can demonstrate that we are mindful of their needs are by sitting close to them, making eye contact, using simple language and short phrases, and waiting for them to respond to our questions. Not answering the phone during dinnertime or bedtime and staying faithful to these evening rituals also lets kids know that we are committed to being with them. These gestures show our children that we are actively working to stay in the moment and that our time with them is important.

Mindfulness is more than just concentrating on one thing or blocking out all the background noise. It also describes a conscious effort to focus on what really matters in any given interaction. As Kabat-Zinn tells it, "Mindful parenting involves keeping in mind what is truly important as we go about the activities of daily living with our children." It requires a delicate mental balancing act, between staying involved in the immediate moment with our kids and considering how today's dilemma fits in with our overarching values or the lessons we are trying to teach them.

For example, lots of parents worry about their kids eating healthy and nutritious meals and do their best to restrict snacks and sweets in the house. If six-year-old Tim asks his mother for ice cream after lunch, and he has had only a few bites of his sandwich, she has a decision to make. Should she give Tim the ice cream despite his limited appetite for what she has already prepared, or should she put her foot down and link his dessert directly to eating a healthy portion of his meal? To answer the question, she has to first consider what she is trying to accomplish at mealtime. Let's assume she wants Tim to learn to eat a balanced lunch and that she doesn't want to see his meals become a shortcut to sweets. Tim's mom might say, "You can have the ice cream but only if you finish a few more bites of your sandwich."

Her approach sounds reasonable enough, but the problem with this response is that this sets up a "dessert for bites" bargain that she should try to avoid. I often hear how these simple standoffs become protracted, tense exchanges. Parents sometimes admit that despite their better judgment, they can't help but stand over their kids and force them to eat "just one more bite!" If Tim's mom were to give him the ice cream at that moment, but make a mental note to forgo ice cream and other desserts in the house for the next few weeks, she might "lose" today's battle, but avoid escalating to a war that she probably will not win. She knows that from now on, she will approach the lunch/dessert dilemma with a different attitude. Maybe there will be ice cream and maybe not, but Tim will no longer be able to use food as a negotiating tool, and his mother will not have to try to bargain with him to get him to eat.

The Confidence Game

Being mindful can help us stay connected to our children and it can also help us feel like we have a game plan for how to deal with them in different situations. Few of us would enter business negotiations without a clear strategy of how to achieve our goals, or prepare a lecture or a meal for that matter, without an image in our head of how we want it to turn out. Parenting is not so given to logic and linear reasoning, of course, but our kids are well aware if we have a sense of purpose with them and if we know how to get them to be helpful or cooperative in any given moment. From a young age, they can smell fear and indecision. We often underestimate the brilliance of two- and three-year-olds, who can sense hesitation in our voices or read ambivalence in our facial expressions, and are poised to go for the jugular at just that very moment!

Having a plan helps us feel confident as parents, and along with endurance, *confidence* is the key to successful parenting. Being confident doesn't mean we have all the answers. Nor are we all going to be like Alexander the Great, who accomplished so much at a young age because he bravely led his troops into battle and never showed fear or weakness to his men. We can learn to speak with authority and let our kids see that we do, indeed, have things to teach them, and that we expect them to listen and learn from us, most of the time. We can also deliver the message in a tone that says we believe we deserve their respect and attention.

It sounds as if I am advocating a return to a more rigid or authoritarian household structure. That is not my intent, but I do think parents could benefit from a little corrective adjustment from a more child-centered, gentle approach to one that reasserts their role as teachers. In fact, we have a lot to learn from our children's teachers, and I believe that most parents can benefit if they listen in on their child's preschool or kindergarten classroom routines.

Most nursery school teachers are lovely and nurturing, but the best ones also know how to switch gears fairly quickly. Cleanup time might begin with a nice song, but in most classes the children's help in picking up toys is not an option but a requirement. The children are expected to pitch in before they move on to the next activity. Although many parents struggle to get their kids to wear reasonable clothing in the morning, this is not usually an issue at school. If the kids want to go outside they have to wear their coats, period. There is not a lot of room for argument and negotiation. It is true that teachers benefit from peer pressure and the fact that most of the group conforms to what is expected, which helps with the more recalcitrant or obstinate children in class. Yet I am convinced that the key to teachers' success in getting young children to comply has more to do with the nonnegotiable way that they frame their requests.

Most parents are not always so clear. Many struggle because of their ambivalence about taking charge. We want our kids to listen, but we also want to be nice to them and not hurt their feelings. We worry about the harm we might do by raising our voices. Parents also know that they risk increasing their own stress levels if they directly confront their children's resistance. They often try a more gentle approach first, despite ample evidence that this has not been effective in the past.

Here's a typical, nagging situation that occurs in many families. Mom calls the kids to the dinner table and four-year-old Johnny remains glued to the television. Johnny's mom tries to remain calm and says nicely, "Johnny, please come to the dinner table." Johnny gives no indication that he has heard her request and does not budge, so for the second time his mother calls out to him. Still there is no response from Johnny. Mom makes a third request and then a fourth, and is starting to feel exasperated. We can all guess what happens next. On the fifth time, Johnny's mother screams at him in a very loud voice, *"Johnny, come to the table now!"* Johnny comes to the table looking a little shell-shocked and bewildered, and his mother feels frustrated and upset for losing her cool.

Let's examine this situation from Johnny's perspective. He vaguely hears a request from his mother the first time, but if it's delivered in a sweet tone he might think to himself, "Well, I know my mother said something, I'm not sure what, but she was so nice about it I don't think I have to pay much attention to her." And on the second and third and then fourth occasion he reacts similarly: "I guess she needs me, oh, yeah, maybe it's dinnertime, but I really want to watch this show and she doesn't *really* seem that concerned if I do." Finally, Johnny hears an explosion from his mother. That gets his attention, but it's puzzling to him. "Boy, she was just so nice, and now what's this?" And if he goes to the next diagnostic step, he might conclude: "My mom is a lunatic!"

We have all been there, and done exactly what Johnny's mother has done. To undo this pattern, we have to be clearer and more up-front with our kids. We also have to be less ambivalent about taking a firm stand and not worry so much about staying *perfectly calm*. Johnny's mother could have walked in and turned off the television the first time, or told him she would come back in five more minutes to escort him to the table. Perhaps she will decide that for Johnny, TV before dinner is not a good combination, because he often has trouble with transitions. Maybe Johnny also needs a signal that his mother is serious, some words or gestures (like counting "One, two, three . . ." in an exaggerated manner) that lets him know she is not messing around.

Dinnertime is part of the "business" that is conducted in the house each day, along with getting up and getting dressed, brushing teeth, doing homework, preparing for bed, and completing chores. When we conduct business with adults or with children, we have to show some resolve and adopt a different tone of voice. We would never dispute a credit card bill by saying, "Oh, by the way, I'm not sure, but there may have been a mistake here, could you check into this charge when you have time?" If we did, our request would likely end up on the bottom of the pile or in the "don't have to call them back" category.

With kids it's no different. If we are too timid or overly nice all the time, they do not learn to take us seriously. And if we go from zero to sixty miles an hour as Johnny's mother did, they may feel hurt or stunned by our outbursts of anger, and we are likely to feel guilty and ineffective. If we can find thirty miles per hour, and raise our tone as a signal that we mean business the first time, we are more likely to get our children to comply and to reinforce the fact that we are their parents and deserve their respect.

Confident parenting is not just about getting children to comply or conform to rules and routines. When we are clear and show resolve with our kids, we give them the reassurance that we are in charge and capable of handling their ups and downs. For most children it is a relief to know that their parents are not going to be thrown by their tantrums or their anger, and that they do not need to negotiate every task or requirement presented to them at home. Young kids naturally express a wish to be in control and they do need room to assert their independence and voice their opinions. They are also comforted by the fact that at the end of the day they can count on their parents to help them do the right thing.

A Few Brave Moms and Dads

Once parents have learned to manage their own children, they still need to contend with other parents and how they are raising their kids. Even if we believe that we have established good routines and expectations in our own homes, we still feel the pull from other families nearby who have different rules about outside activities, staying up late, or access to television, video games, and computers. Saying no to children is one thing, but in the age of competitive parenting, deviating from the group can bring its own challenges. I hear a familiar lament from parents: "I wish we lived where I grew up," which is typically a less affluent community or neighborhood where children had fewer advantages, and where the adults did not feel as compelled to answer to each other about their child-rearing habits.

Taking a stand that differs from the norm is not easy in any endeavor and parenting is no exception. It takes a lot of *courage* for parents to stick by their values and their decisions and to resist prevailing trends in their community. I do not use this word lightly. In my experience, parents worry about being criticized for making different choices and wonder if their kids will suffer if they do not have the same privileges as other children in the neighborhood. Establishing rules about bedtime, family meals, playdates, and weekend activities can be complicated by how these standards will be received by neighbors and friends. Many of us dread being seen as old-fashioned, behind the times, or stuffy and overly demanding.

Karen, the mother of a four-year-old girl, consulted me about her daughter Amy's busy schedule. She had decided to cut out Amy's afternoon ballet lessons, only to feel pangs of anxiety and regret when her friends remarked casually, "We don't see you at the gym anymore." Karen did not doubt that discontinuing the class was the right choice for her daughter, but she worried about disappointing her friends and fretted about what it meant to take a different path from her peers in their small, insular town.

I often speak to groups of parents about finding their own way and not feeling swayed by the "norm." Occasionally during one of these workshops, someone will turn to me and say, "So what do you do in your house?" This happened not long ago in a roundtable discussion about children's access to technology and media. I explained that my kids did not watch much television during the week and that despite my eight-year-old son's repeated requests, we had decided not to purchase a video game system. He and my daughters did have access to computer games, but we also tried to limit these during the week.

The woman on my right turned to me, and perhaps before she could catch herself, called out, "Sounds like *Little House on the Prairie!*" Everyone laughed, and it was clear that many of the mothers in the room had similar thoughts. I have repeatedly mentioned that moment in other evenings with parents. To me, her comment implies two very different messages. It sounds kind of nice, that image of Laura in the Big

Woods, a sort of sweet and simplified family life. But it also sounds so hopelessly out-of-date and old-fashioned!

Not many parents want to be seen this way. We want to be cool and make sure our kids are up-to-date on the latest shows and fashions and games. We worry that they might be left out or left behind if they do not have all the cultural lingo down at a young age, or if they are slow to demonstrate the technological prowess and computer abilities that their four- and five-year-old friends have mastered already. We want our kids to see the latest movies—Harry Potter springs to mind—even though many "family films" are not really appropriate for kids under the age of eight. Despite what we see on the fields in town on Saturday mornings, we are concerned that our kids might not learn the game-breaking techniques if they do not join the local soccer league in kindergarten. And there are music lessons, language classes, and enrichment programs that all hint that our children's "critical period" for learning is slipping by right before our eyes.

Dealing with discipline or sleep deprivation is one thing, but coming to terms with the pressure to keep up with our friends and neighbors causes a completely different level of stress for parents. Thoughtful mothers and fathers often have to choose whether they want to pursue a more independent course that will, at times, put them at odds with their contemporaries. Having friends with similar values can help, but many parents still feel a sense of isolation: "We're the only family on the block who doesn't let our kids have Game Boy; it's tough to go it alone." Ironically, I often hear this refrain from parents living in the same town, and sometimes in the same neighborhood.

Feeling alone and in uncharted waters can cause tremendous strain on a couple and can compound the anxiety mothers and fathers already experience in raising young children. Parents who have the courage to establish their own way, and the confidence and endurance to stick with it, are far more likely to cope with the stress of raising children and not as apt to succumb to the fear and anxiety that torments so many parents. Those who can recognize and appreciate the relative privilege their

i n chapter 11 we will discuss how parents can make connections with each other and form their own mini-communities, which can provide a buffer for their children against the pervasive demands of early academic pressures, social competition, and scheduled activities.

children enjoy and the value of their own good instincts may even find the rare moments when they can count their blessings, and take pride in the fact that they are working hard to provide a solid foundation for their children, and to teach them the lessons they will rely on well into the future.

part two

Fear Not, Teach Them Well

four

Fear of Letting Go: Independence

Parents often decide to consult with me when their children begin to have academic difficulties. Susan and Bill came to my office recently to talk about their ten-year-old son Andy's homework problem. Andy had just entered the fifth grade, and his parents were concerned about his work habits: "For the first time, Andy has to apply himself, and we cannot seem to get him to focus or do his work by himself."

I reviewed Andy's history and found that he had no serious learning or emotional difficulties. Two things struck me, however: Despite his previous academic success and keen intelligence, Andy had never learned to work independently at home or to develop confidence in his own ideas. His study skills were lacking and he almost always needed adult prompting to complete his work. An avid video game player, computer whiz, and a three-season soccer player, Andy was on the go from morning to night, and he had few opportunities for quiet reflection or time alone without some stimulation. He was tired when he sat down to do homework, and always needed his mother by his side.

Andy's story is not an unusual one. I see many older children who are bright and capable, but are not comfortable being on their own. They sometimes have trouble thinking for themselves, independently solving problems, or simply being alone. They often appear anxious and not well grounded. Like Andy, the extent of their struggles is revealed when they are asked to do something challenging, such as homework in middle school. This task requires children to be attentive, organized, and to plan their time efficiently. It also demands something more of them; to be physically alone doing their work, and to be alone with their own thoughts and ideas. For many middle school students, these expectations represent a monumental shift for which they received little training in their early years.

To understand why some children have more trouble separating and becoming independent, we first have to explore a fear that is prevalent among parents in this country: the fear of letting go. As much as we all take pride in our children's first steps, their early babblings, and their venturing away from us, the joy we feel is often tempered by anxiety. We worry what the world will hold for them, whether they can survive on their own, and how we will fare when they begin to leave us. These are normal concerns and not usually cause for alarm, but somehow they have come to creep into parents' consciousness in ways that have led to subtle and not so subtle changes in our behavior.

The Bonding Years

Today's world seems to be a pretty scary place. We are confronted by frightening images on a daily basis: war, terrorism, natural disasters, outbreaks of incurable diseases, and child abductions. Disturbing stories populate the nightly news and fill the local newspapers and it feels as if we all need to be more watchful, wary of strangers, and careful to be on the lookout for any harm that might come our children's way.

For many of us, these external dangers dovetail with our internal fears. Parents who are a bit older, and those who have waited to have children or have struggled to become pregnant, often feel that their newborns have a magical presence. It is not unusual for parents to refer to their "miracle baby," conceived and delivered after years of trying and repeated disappointments and loss. We naturally feel an intense longing for and connection to our infants, and any delays or disruptions in their arrival only serve to heighten these feelings. The bonds we have with our children can carry us through some rocky times, especially in the early years when their demands are greatest (and we are most sleep deprived!). The attachment we feel toward our infants also makes us feel protective, and we keep a close watch over them lest they stray too far from us and get hurt. With older parents, this protective instinct can become intensified, and many parents come to feel that only they are fit to watch over their young ones, and that their keen eye and touch is necessary to keep them safe.

Who can blame parents for wanting to stay close to their children? Many have heard of the importance of the attachment phase and how infants gain a sense of security in the first year or two by maintaining a close connection with their parents or other caretakers. Child development experts widely agree that a "securely attached" infant is more likely to be capable of learning, developing friendships, and forming relationships with other trusted adults. The key for parents is staying attuned to their infants, responding to their needs, and remaining in the moment during their time together. There seems to be little downside to enjoying this phase, or prolonging it a little. At its best, it feels so good. The smell of a baby fresh out of the bath, the feel of chubby legs, the sound of the infectious little chortle, can all be pretty irresistible. For many parents who are not sure if this first or second child will be their last, there is a temptation to keep the baby years going as long as possible.

This desire begs the question: Doesn't extending the baby or toddler period also create more work for parents? The answer is not so simple. It is true that when children are more dependent, parents must care for them that much more, and changing diapers, bathing, dressing, and feeding children is hard work. Despite these hardships, I often hear interesting comments from parents when their child is becoming more independent. As one mother remarked recently, "I like my two-year-old to clear his dishes, but I'm a neat freak, and it makes me a little crazy when he misses the garbage." The other mothers present nodded at her dilemma, one that felt pretty familiar to them. Sometimes, like when we're rushing out the door, it's easier if we wash our children's faces, dress them, and put on their coats. And the family-style eating that they practice and preach in nursery school sounds great in theory, but who has to clean up the crumbs all over the floor every day?

There are a number of small decision-making moments for parents that can be missed opportunities for encouraging independence. We know children should be doing more on their own, but sometimes it is just easier to do it for them. In many of these situations parents wrestle with two issues: giving up control, and giving in to exhaustion. If we keep our three-year-olds in a stroller for that walk down the block to the park, we can more easily keep them safe and under our watchful eye, and we won't have to chase them. By doing so, we may be losing a chance for them to move about and explore on their own, and learn to be a little more responsible for their own safety.

If a four-year-old comes into the parents' bed after midnight it can be that much tougher to handle, because we're not going to be thinking so clearly. Plans to teach her how to be more secure in her own room and how to soothe herself can easily go right out the window at this time of night. It's all too tempting to keep the peace and move aside so that everyone can get some rest. How many of us have kept our children in nighttime pull-ups into kindergarten and beyond, knowing that the extra push necessary to get them into underwear at night will inevitably be accompanied by a few weeks of wet sheets and midnight awakenings?

Life on the Fast Track

The struggle to help children learn to be comfortable on their own is often obscured by another demand felt by parents. Today, more than ever, they feel the pressure to be the academic, athletic, and social instructors, to hone their children's talents and skills from an early age. Encouraging more independence often takes a backseat in this debate, as parents feel that their first order of business is to raise well-prepared children. It's easy to poke fun at the French lessons for two-year-olds or the violins in the nursery, but we all feel pressure to make sure our children are keeping up. So we get them on the computer at age two or three, we buy "smart" toys and videos to help them learn colors, and maybe have them listen to classical music or visit the local art museum. As children enter preschool there are games to learn, puzzles to master, and songs to sing. Some parents introduce workbooks at home, because it seems that it can't hurt to have a head start on counting or letter writing.

In many communities, the push to provide activities outside the home begins in earnest at age three or four. There are tennis lessons, dance classes, and soccer clinics designed exclusively for preschoolers. Sometimes parents go along with these against their better judgment, because, to put it simply, "everybody's doing it." The pressure to keep up with the crowd can be intense. In our first meeting, Nancy reported that her four-year-old daughter, Amanda, was tired much of the time, and struggling with going to school many days. After we talked of giving her a chance to rest and spend quiet time alone, Nancy decided to pull Amanda out of her weekly swim classes, only to repeatedly hear the swim coach ask when they would be returning. Nancy felt guilty each time she heard this, and wondered if she had made a decision that would have a lasting negative impact on her daughter.

The Effects of Holding On

For most children, the process of separation goes pretty smoothly. As a toddler develops more of a sense of security, she can venture forth into the world, armed with the image of her parents in her head (and perhaps a blanket or other object to remember them by) and the knowledge that they will be there upon her return. Although there is a good deal of variability in this process, and almost always a dose of tears and heartache to go with it, most children are well into the separation phase by the age of three. During this time, children become capable of entering preschool and remaining with other trusted adults, namely their teachers.

Parents' fears can have a significant influence over the process and delay children's ability to seek ties with other adults. If children sense that their parents are not comfortable with other caretakers, or worry about what dangers might be lurking in the playground, they can cling more closely and grow wary of venturing out on their own. Tales of preschoolers admonishing their mothers for talking to strangers in the grocery store or the post office are not uncommon. Some little kids will develop an "insecure attachment," and feel the need to stay close at all times or risk disappointment or despair. In a small number of cases, this can progress to a more serious separation anxiety that prevents children from leaving their parents for any extended period and interferes with their transitioning to nursery school.

Most parents do their best to contain their fears, however, and I do not see too many families in which things have progressed to this point. Yet there are more subtle signs that parents' fear of letting go is having an impact. Often I hear parents' voices drop in the consultation room when they are about to deliver a piece of news that they think I won't want to hear. "Well, I know Sam is three, but he still needs a bottle to fall asleep," Beth admitted sheepishly. "I know, I know, we need to fix it, but we haven't been able to find the right time. Besides, I thought he would stop on his own like his sister did when she turned two." "Why do you think it's different with Sam?" I asked. "I'm not sure, but you know, he may be our last and I love giving him his bottle and snuggling with him at night. I'll miss it."

Parents are almost always nervous about telling these stories, worried that I will judge them or that somehow other parents will find out their secrets. This wish to keep children close to us, and to baby them, is not unusual, nor is it a bad thing. Nobody would deny snuggle time to a mother of a toddler or preschooler or a first grader, for that matter. The problem is when this wish to stay close prevents us from giving children the nudge they need to move on, to give up the bottle or the pacifier, to sleep in their own beds, or to transition out of diapers. These days, it's not unusual to hear about parents feeding their four-year-old son, the six-year-olds in Mom and Dad's bed, or the three-and-a-half-year-old with the nightly bottle. In fact, I hear these stories from parents and teachers on a regular basis.

In many families children get the message that hanging on to their baby experiences will assure that their parents remain close to them. Kids crave the kind of attention they receive when we tend to them in the bathroom or sleep next to them in bed. Our job is to find reasonable substitutes for these moments of closeness as they get a little older. We may play games with our three- and four-year-olds, read to them, and find other "special time" activities that they enjoy. We can also show our kids that we can still regress alongside them; we can laugh and be silly, tickle them, hug them, throw them up in the air, and carry them up the stairs just like a baby.

Coaxing Kids from One Phase to the Next

Sometimes with or without these replacements children's baby habits drop off naturally and parents do not have to actively intervene to help them move on. Yet in many instances it makes sense for us to set limits and decide on a concrete timetable for the phase to end. It may help if we have a plan that includes incentives for accomplishing this goal. Often just bringing up the issue more directly can help. "We need to think about that pacifier; you know you are three years old now," Dina explained to her son Max. He would have none of it, for a time. But two weeks later Max volunteered, "Mom, I think I'm ready to put my pacifier in the garbage."

Few children are as brave as Max, and we usually need a more customized plan for a pacifier removal. I usually suggest that parents pick a date a few weeks away when they will have a "good-bye to Pacy" ceremony. On the appointed day, they wrap up the pacifier and put it in a safe place in the attic or in an out-of-reach cubby. We don't have to make any big statements about becoming a "big girl" or "big boy" (these can easily backfire), but we can let our kids know in a confident voice that the time has come to move on. They can survive just fine without their pacifier. Having a plan and a timetable helps relieve some of the children's anxiety and parents' guilt, and in most cases the deadline does not precipitate a major confrontation.

Not all transitional objects have to be relinquished in this way. Young children who have a special blanket or teddy bear can hold on to them for many years, and continue to rely on them for comfort and to soothe themselves well into elementary school and beyond. The trick here is to get the kids to think about the appropriate time and place to use their favored object. After the age of two or three, they may not need to take their special stuffed animal everywhere, and it can be reserved for nap time and bedtime, or for long rides in the car. Other situations become judgment calls for parents. Transitional objects may not be necessary at the family dinner table, but they may help kids get through a long or formal dinner outing or church service.

Toilet training can be problematic for many families, but parents who can find a similar sense of resolve can help their children to move forward on this front. The "when they are ready" approach to toileting that is recommended by most pediatricians today has its merits, but can lead to unnecessary delays for older preschoolers. For Maggie, three and a half, who was using the toilet about half the time and had clearly established pretty good control, an extra nudge was all she needed.

I encouraged Maggie's mom, Debbie, to buy only one more pack of diapers, and to count down with Maggie the ten or so days that it would take to go through them. With some coaxing, Debbie told her daughter, "Dad and I think you are ready to use the toilet all the time. In a couple of days, there will be no more diapers, and you can now use the bathroom whenever you need to. We will remind you to go a few times each day." I asked Debbie to try to be nonchalant about toileting and try not to react too strongly if Maggie had accidents (easy, of course, for *me* to say).

Maggie protested at first, but her complaints diminished when she saw that her mother was standing firm. She was also excited about going to a new camp that summer where she had to be toilet-trained, and the fact that the plan would finish a week before camp started gave her an extra incentive. Maggie did have a few slips in the first week, and after having to change her clothes two or three times, Debbie admitted she was getting frustrated with the process. But she and her husband stuck with the plan, and within a week Maggie was using the toilet without incident.

This timetable wasn't too rigid. If Maggie had not responded, I would have suggested that her mother wait for a time before returning to the plan, perhaps until the start of the next school year. Some kids take longer to have full control of their bladder and their bowels. Others worry about letting go in the bathroom, and feel that they risk losing a part of themselves down the toilet. These difficulties may become more apparent after putting a toilet-training plan like this in place. It is worth persevering for at least two weeks to see if the kids can overcome their fears and learn to regulate themselves more fully. If the situation does not improve, we may need to take a closer look at the child's resistance, or parents may decide to wait a few more months to let nature do its work.

For bedtime routines to take hold, parents have to be ready to take the plunge. As we discussed in the last chapter, despite wondrous tales to the contrary, toddler or preschool sleep problems do not go away overnight (and with older kids, breaking bad sleep habits can be that much harder). I usually advise parents to find a two- or three-week period when everybody is in their routines and they will not be facing any major stresses at home or at work. The effort to make the necessary changes will be tiring enough. More importantly, we have to steel ourselves to resist kids' demands to have us by their sides at night, and not give in to the crying that ensues when we turn away from them. This sounds straightforward, but if we are ambivalent about taking a strong stand or are struggling with our own feelings of abandonment, letting our kids stay alone in their beds can be a monumental battle.

The first step is putting kids to bed on their own without sitting or lying with them until they fall asleep. The key here is letting them have the experience of going down without assistance. If they succeed they are more likely to feel secure and let go of some of their worries about monsters and strange things that go "boo!" in the night. They may also learn how to go back to sleep when they wake up in the middle of the night, which little kids, like the rest of us, inevitably do. This doesn't mean that we can't read stories and sing lullabies, and cuddle for a moment before tucking them in. These rituals are all designed to smooth the transition to sleep. Usually it's best to keep them short and simple, and in the early stages not to prolong the bedtime stories and songs for more than fifteen or twenty minutes.

There is no real substitute for parents putting children back in their beds in the middle of the night if they want them to learn to be comfortable sleeping on their own. In my experience, kids respond pretty well to a clear statement from their moms and dads ("You need to stay in your bed from now on"), but only if they back it up. If we manage to adopt a consistent approach to bedtime and nighttime wakings, our children will probably give up the fight sooner than later. We may finally be able to approach the evenings with less anxiety and less fear about the complaints and battles we will encounter. The message should be a pretty simple one: "Mom and Dad have made sure your room is safe and sound" and we are going to demonstrate our confidence in that statement by putting you back in there!

The Value of Alone Time

In some families, there are less recognizable signs of difficulties with separation or the transition to independence. The children may appear confident, eagerly running off to school, enjoying playdates, and actively participating in sports programs. But they are not left on their own too often, and in the house they stick close to Mom or their babysitter. They may enjoy watching television or videos, or exploring on the computer, but without these they are at a loss as to how to entertain themselves. Temperament, of course, plays a big role here. Some children are naturally more reserved and cling to their parents, and are slow to warm up to new environments. Others are more natural explorers and driven to take the initiative; they love setting out on their own in and out of the home.

The tone parents set matters. If we welcome our kids being close by us, and feel more comfortable monitoring their movements most of the time, they are apt to become used to this state of affairs and feel our absence is a potential cause for worry. Six-year-old James was brought to my office by his parents because of frequent tantrums and his nervous habits, including constantly biting his fingernails. During our first meeting I asked him about his earliest memory. He responded eagerly, "When I was two and three, I followed my mom everywhere, and my mom always followed me around." It was clearly a memory he cherished, and James was frustrated that he could no longer have his way at home all the time. He had managed, however, to get his mother or babysitter to sit right next to him when he was doing his homework, a habit we were eventually able to break.

Children may not only come to rely on their parents' being right by their sides, but they may also like the perks that come with it. If kids sense that their moms and dads are continually available to tend to them or to do things for them, they are likely to take advantage of the situation. Complaints by parents of being ordered about ("Get me a glass of milk!"; "Bring me my shoes") by their preschoolers are not unusual. But who can blame the children? If out of the interest of keeping on schedule, keeping things neat, or keeping the peace, parents do what they are told, kids can learn to enjoy sitting back and ordering them about. After all, as I like to remind parents, "It's good to be the king!"

Again, it's easy to point a finger at other parents, but we all have to be reminded at times to let young children take care of themselves. "Grab your coat"; "Put on your shoes"; "Toss your clothes in the hamper"; "You get the milk out!" are reasonable exhortations for three- and four-year-olds to hear on a daily basis. When we see that our kids are capable of meeting these expectations, we will be more comfortable asking them to chip in and do more. We may, in the process, start to feel okay with doing less.

We also need to give children room, to let them color and play, to wander around the house, to smell and taste new foods, to listen to the sounds and rhythms of their families. Let them begin to make a few decisions: "I prefer cereal to eggs"; "The blue shirt will do today"; "Can I hear that book again?" They also benefit from alone time to play, to make their own imaginary worlds where they can be kings and queens. Free playtime in school is essential to this process, as children learn to explore their environment, to be curious, to take the initiative, to size up their classmates. They learn to make choices, to like and dislike toys and activities, to express themselves, and to learn, as so many do, "all about me."

At home there is not always that same built-in period of exploration. Parents are often anxious that their newly mobile toddlers will get hurt, and the thought of leaving them alone seems counterintuitive. We also worry about three- and four-year-olds being up to no good, or making a huge mess if unsupervised for too long. Sometimes we use the television or the computer as a distraction, so we can at least count on our children's whereabouts when we are showering and a little peace and quiet when we are preparing dinner. It is hard to argue with this logic, especially when parents are otherwise judicious in their young children's exposure to television and videos. But if we don't give kids over age two time to fend for themselves and hold them accountable for their actions during these periods, they may not learn how to play on their own effectively or how to behave responsibly without an adult monitor.

Private Time for Everyone

Many parents today, especially mothers, feel the pressure to be "doing good"; to read to their children, to play games with them, to work on art projects. These are all, of course, important ways to maintain connections and have special time with young children. But if our kids come to expect that during much of their time at home they will be entertained by us, they don't have to think for themselves or plan their own diversions. They may also have little respect for the fact that both of their parents have work to do, in and out of the house, and cannot always be right next to them. Whether it's paying bills, doing laundry, preparing meals, catching up on the newspaper or the mail, fixing things in the house, returning phone calls, exercising or, heaven forbid, relaxing for a while, mothers and fathers have a lot to do. Our kids do not always welcome this revelation, but they can come to appreciate that although their needs are important, they have to be balanced with the realities of family life.

If preschoolers or elementary-age children rarely have opportunities to be on their own and don't naturally seek them out, they may come to view being alone as a punishment or a rejection by their parents. In my experience, it is not unusual for a mother to introduce the notion of a set-aside time for her child to be on her own, and to hear back, "You mean, you don't want to play with me?" which leads to a healthy dose of guilt for Mom. If we look at this time as a gift to our kids (granted it may not be one they want to unwrap!) or as a learning experience, it might be easier to enforce this rule.

I do not mean to be glib here when I talk about learning to play. Many young children these days seem not to know how to go about it. Some three- and four- and five-year-olds come into my office and see action figures, dolls, building toys, cars and trucks, drawing paper and paint, and get right down to work. But many others look a bit befuddled and are not sure how to get started. They usually turn to me to pick out something to do. It may be a lack of confidence, or a feeling of doubt that they can create something interesting. Yet many of these kids come to recognize that they do, indeed, have some pretty good ideas once I encourage them to take the lead. The first task is to give them room to make these choices, and not to step in if they seem hesitant or complain of being bored.

Time for Play

The pressures to be involved in activities outside the home can also limit young children's desire for independence. If four-year-old Emma goes from preschool to dance class to a playdate and comes home at four or five in the afternoon, she is not likely to have much energy left to devote to pretend play and creative alone time. She will probably need downtime, and will perhaps ask for a video or story from her mother or her sitter to unwind from her busy day. Next it is time for dinner and preparations for the bath and then bedtime routines. If this process is repeated two or three days a week, Emma may go through most of the school week without spending much time on her own. If her weekend is as packed, as it is in most homes, with family obligations and more planned activities, she may not get much alone time then either. Her parents may feel that they are giving Emma the chance to develop her interests and talents, but are they ones of her choosing? Does she have a chance to give them shape and structure?

The anxiety parents feel over providing the right experiences for their children so that they will be prepared to strike out on their own can have a paradoxical effect. At a fairly young age, children may sense that they can learn about the world only at the discretion of grown-ups, who are there to instruct them and help them cope with mistakes and disappointments. They might learn specific skills (how to kick a ball, to dance with a group, to stay afloat, etc.), but not how to think and solve problems for themselves, and apply the knowledge they have learned.

Take seven-year-old Teddy, who excelled at karate and soccer, and could go on at great length about what he had learned in these activities. He was terrific at playing games with his mother and sister. But when I asked him what he liked to do on his downtime, he protested loudly: "I hate being alone; there's nothing I can think of doing. It's boring!" Then there are the stories of older children who are drilled in sports like baseball in year-round camps and academies, but when interviewed cannot fathom making up their own pickup games, choosing sides, and making the rules. They have never had *that* experience.[1]

Learning How to Let Go

The first step in helping children to move forward is for parents to step back. In the blur of child-care duties and the exhaustion that comes with raising young children, it is not easy for us to take time to contemplate the ways we would like to guide our kids. It is even tougher to try to peer into the future, to envision what things might look like three or five years down the road (think of Andy's homework problem). But in order to help children separate and learn to do more on their own, we need to have some sense that this is leading somewhere, and that we are not just pushing them out the door for our own purposes. We have to believe that learning to spend time on their own and to chart their own course is good for our kids, essential, in fact, to their learning to problem-solve, to develop confidence in their ideas, and to think for themselves.

Secondly, parents have to assess the risks and benefits of keeping their children free from danger. That is a strange statement, as none of us want to put our kids in harm's way. Yet part of allowing children to move on is accepting that they might get hurt; scrapes and scratches come with the territory when children set out to explore on their own. Things can also get a little chaotic, and messy. Crumbs will land on the floor, milk will be spilled, and we must try not to cry (that saying has not been around for decades for nothing!). We may also feel that things are a little out of control, and for many of us, not just the neat freaks in the crowd, this can be tough to accept.

In the early years children are by nature a little wild, more than a tad impulsive, and not totally in control of their bodies. I sometimes ask a room full of parents to imagine trading places with their preschoolers, who would be left alone in the conference room for a half hour or so. Worried gazes meet mine. "They would trash this place," I usually hear back. "Exactly right," I respond, but not because they are bad kids. While running around, touching everything to see how it works, jockeying for position, they would turn things topsy-turvy. That is their job. Our role as parents is to balance giving them room to explore with keeping them safe (and everything in the house more or less in one piece), and to recognize that these goals have equal merit.

The path to independence is a back-and-forth process, not an even road forward. We expect, of course, that young children will also need the time to be *dependent*, to be cared for, babied, and loved with no particular purpose in mind. Balancing this back-and-forth can be a delicate task for parents. The key is not to confuse or blend the two. Some parents find it helpful to think of ways they can encourage their children's separation while still leaving time for them to *just be* little kids. We should give them time to regress and be cuddled, but not when they have work to do. I often encourage parents to get up a few minutes earlier to snuggle their preschoolers in the morning, but to leave enough time so they can get dressed on their own. Likewise, there is no problem with young children wanting to be held and babied and gushed over, but not when they have to eat their dinner.

One way to solve this dilemma is to provide separate "baby time," a specified pretend playtime when parents can allow their children to regress in healthy ways. Reading picture books, playing toddler games (e.g. peekaboo and pop-up toys), and carrying a preschooler up the stairs in the rocking position are all popular and bring squeals of delight from many four- and five-year-olds. I sometimes recommend that parents provide each of their children with their own small baby photograph album, which they can use to tell stories of the earliest days and milestone moments that may seem a bit distant already to a child in kindergarten or first or second grade. Although some kids balk at the "baby time" label, they almost universally love these moments with their parents.[2]

These times are healthy and essential for us parents as much as they are for our children. None of us want to see our kids grow up too soon, and we can treasure being needed by them. It also makes us feel good. The wildness, silliness, and pure elation that come from their squeals are unlike anything else in our life, and these moments can make the rest of our stressful and hectic lives fall away for a bit. We all need time to regress, to be held, to laugh out loud, and at their best young kids can elicit these feelings in ways that are unmatched. Being conscious of helping our children spread their wings does not prevent us from still enjoying these cozy moments in the nest.

Reversing the Trend

Once we accept the challenge to look at our own needs for safety, control, and closeness with our children, and the costs and benefits of each, we can begin to reassess how we are helping our children separate and be on their own. Sometimes I will help parents rethink their goals and encourage them to include nurturing their children's independence and capacity to be alone near the top of the list. Next we review ways they can alter their schedule and their approach. Usually the harder part is deciding which activities to forgo to leave more downtime for quiet, solitary play.

Let's take the case of Anne, a working mom, and her daughter Sarah. During her visit to my office, Anne reported that Sarah had been doing pretty well in kindergarten. No longer afraid of school, she now went off willingly. Sarah was beginning to read and enjoying math, and her parents had decided to provide extra workbooks for her at home. Sarah also appeared to be managing her impressive schedule: full time at school plus gymnastics, ballet, sports class, skating, and swimming every week.

Yet lately Sarah was displaying signs of anxiety—biting her nails, twisting her hair, and weeping when she made mistakes. Anne was growing exasperated and she could not understand why Sarah did not work to her full potential on all her class projects. Sometimes, Anne admitted nervously, she could not resist stepping in and doing Sarah's work for her. "What can we do," she asked in a worried tone, "to get Sarah back on track?"

First we talked of the importance of helping Sarah feel more secure and confident. Sarah was a bright child who was already doing quite well in school. I suggested that her mother drop the workbooks for a while, as she might implicitly be suggesting that Sarah needed to work harder on her studies. Despite her apparent interest in all her activities, Sarah also clearly needed more time at home and unstructured opportunities to play on her own. After my consultation with both Anne and her husband, Ted, they decided to reduce Sarah's schedule to one activity during the week and one on the weekend. That was the easy part, and Sarah was clearly excited by the changes. "You mean I can have two more hours of pajama time on Sunday?" she asked her mom excitedly.

Sarah was less enthused with her mother's other new plan: "Every day we are all going to have private time, and you will have a chance to play alone for a while." Sarah's reluctance was not surprising. Since she was a baby, she had spent little time away from her mother or sitter when she was home, and did not easily gravitate toward imaginative play or other solo pursuits. Her father was worried Sarah would see private time as a rejection, as she often sulked and grew angry when he was working at home and unable to play with her, and would yell at him, "You don't love me!" Sarah did enjoy drawing and looking at books, and Anne and Ted agreed that these would do for now. I also encouraged her parents to introduce other low-structure building toys, like Legos or blocks, and dramatic play items that she might use as props, and assured them it was okay if Sarah coaxed her three-year-old brother to play, too.

Sarah gradually accepted the concept of alone time, and over a period of months she was able to increase play by herself to twenty or thirty minutes once or twice a day. Despite her reluctance and admitted need to see things done "perfectly," Anne pulled back from Sarah's schoolwork and allowed her to do her activities on her own. Sarah knew things were a bit messier now, but seemed proud that the work was hers alone. She never asked for her workbooks back, and seemed more content at school and at home. Although she was still somewhat anxious, her hair twisting and nail biting were much less frequent. Anne and Ted continued to be impressed by how much Sarah relished her downtime, and how they, too, had come to enjoy not rushing about so much on the weekends. They also found a few quiet moments to step back and recognize that Sarah and her brother were smart, good kids, and that they had a lot to be thankful for.

At the end of my last meeting with Sarah's parents, Anne turned to thank me and then stopped. "So what am I supposed to do now?" she asked plaintively. Anne explained that for so long when she was not working she had devoted herself completely to her children. She, too, had to get used to the idea of private time and the possibility that she might feel lonely and a little lost. I assured Anne that this was not unusual for parents of children emerging from their early years, and that she might also take this time as an opportunity to think of other interests and playful pursuits for herself. Though the idea that she had a right to more personal time, away from work, took some getting used to, she soon came to find that being alone was an invaluable stress reliever, a chance to focus on some of her hobbies, like cooking and reading.

Anne's dilemma is not an uncommon one, especially for mothers with young children. If they do not have to be so attentive all the time, especially as their children move beyond infancy and the toddler years, how do they fill their days and find a substitute for the physical demands and emotional needs of their children? Few find solace in increasing their household chores or adopting an idealized, retro version of the mother who does it all. Some consider returning to work part-time or volunteering in their schools or in the community or, like Anne, set aside time for pursuing other interests.

This dilemma has been well documented of late (by Judith Warner in *Perfect Madness* and others), and unfortunately, satirized to the point of appearing trivial (think *Desperate Housewives*). But for many mothers and some fathers, this struggle to rethink their role, and to reestablish a separate and more independent self, mirrors the process they are trying to support in their young children. If they stay determined to push through this transitional period and to establish an identity that includes more alone time and personal interests, they can provide a model for their children to emulate. And with other demands on her, it can be easier for a mom to tell her kids, "I'm taking care of my business right now, you take care of yours."

mothers who begin to expand their interests and to define themselves beyond their role as a parent are more likely to be happier. As the British psychologist Daniel Nettle explains in *Happiness: The Science Behind Your Smile*,[3] adults who are able to see themselves having multiple roles and interests are more able to withstand setbacks in any one area, and to have a more generally positive outlook on their situation. For many mothers, this sense of happiness and resilience will no doubt have a salutary effect on their interactions with their children.

Staying on Track/Teaching Independence at Home

Set Aside Alone Time

Seeking moments when children can be on their own takes a conscious effort by parents. In many families, scheduling demands, social commitments, and school-related activities can take precedence, leaving little time or energy for kids to play alone. But as was true for Sarah's family, this is often more by default than design. Few parents would dismiss the notion that raising independent children is important, but unlike the lessons or practices available for other pursuits, there is no clear blueprint for most of them to follow to achieve this goal.

Each family instead needs to create their own plan. "Monday and Thursday are now downtime days, no playdates and no activities," one mother of two preschoolers announced during one of our meetings. "The kids are free to do what they like, but I'm not going to be by their side the whole afternoon." It sounds simple and maybe even a little stilted to plan this kind of downtime, but in most busy families, if it's not on the schedule, it's not going to happen. With the constant pull of organized sports and enrichment programs, parents have to decide how they set their priorities and what message they send to their kids about the value of being on their own.

Build in Time to Think

We have been focusing mostly on alone time, on children having time set aside for exploring and imagining. But these are not the only ways that children can be given time to think and do for themselves. Most of us can do a better job of providing kids space throughout the day. Take car rides, for instance. I don't begrudge parents entertaining kids with DVDs or games on extended trips, say for a few hours or more. What troubles me is when I see families riding about town on short errands with movies playing for the kids. It's no big deal, we might say, and why not grab a few moments of quiet (though I am not sure most Disney sound tracks qualify) and keep the kids calm.

The problem is that children can come to expect that all time and space must be filled and that they are entitled to be entertained or amused wherever they go. If we turn off the videos, and turn down the *Barney* tapes, they are forced to fend for themselves a little. Maybe they will look out the window and recognize the changes in the passing scenery. They might make up a pretend story about the people in the car next to them. Perhaps they will rework some of the day's experiences in their minds, and try to make sense of who did what to whom. There are an infinite number of trips kids can take in their heads, but if we fill them with a series of images, they have little room for visualizing on their own.

Let Them Roam

Physical space is just as important as mental reckoning. Children need places to roam and explore without us right by their sides. The backyard is a good starting point, but many parents find it hard to leave their young ones alone there for more than a few minutes. I am not suggesting we ignore our kids, but we can stay out of view for a while and let them check out the swing set, the trees, and the mud piles.

The local park is another place that children can run free and establish a little more distance between themselves and their parents. They can also try out some more challenging physical equipment in the playground. If we worry too much about keeping them safe and free from harm at the park, they will sense our anxiety and will stay that much closer to us. Just as babies often look back after they take their first steps, slightly older children usually take their first tentative steps in public with one eye locked on their parents. If they see us wave back and reassure them, they are more likely to keep going.

For my wife and me, the beach at low tide has long been a favorite spot to give our kids room to roam. All three of them learned to really walk and run there, without fear of falling down and getting hurt. We have fond memories of our daughter at age two holding her arms behind her and pretending to fly as she charged across the sand. For them, the water, sand, and rocks provided hours of amusement and the material for building forts, canals, and bridges by themselves. As they have gotten older they can wander off to the ice-cream truck on their own, and to the snack bar at the end of the beach.

Not that we never get nervous. Sometimes they seem too close to the water or a bit too far away from us, or they strike up conversations with other kids and parents we do not know. Over time it has become easier for us to check the urge to go to them, and usually a quick visual assessment reassures us that there is nothing much to worry about. All parents face these moments on a regular basis, when we mentally check out the risks involved in our kids' activities and decide if they need to be supervised more closely. If we choose not to always err on the side of caution, we can give our children the sense that they can feel safe and secure on their own, and that the world is not such a dangerous place.

Teach Kids to Take Care of Their Business

In addition to giving young children time to play alone, parents can also teach them to care for themselves. By the end of preschool kids should have learned how to dress themselves, to brush their teeth, to put away their clothes and their toys. They can do it, and they do at school every day. More importantly, children *want* to be helpful and independent. It makes them feel confident and more grown up to know they can be helpers and not just rely on their mothers and fathers to meet all their needs.

The Value of Work

We can also expect kids to help out in the house. When I speak with nursery and elementary school parents I often hand out a job chart, with a list of helpful things children can do at home. Some are traditional (making their beds, setting the table), some quirky (give Mom a back rub, take care of the compost bucket) and a few are admittedly a little far-fetched (put gas in the car, help bring in firewood). But what I like most about this particular list is not the specific jobs, but that it begins at *eighteen months!*[4]

Some parents gasp at the idea of their toddlers being asked to do work. But even before the age of two, many children can and want to pitch in with family chores. Each of our children was expected by that age to pick up the morning paper off the front stoop, shake it out of its little plastic bag, and bring it to the kitchen table, a task they all enjoyed. Many three- and four-year-olds love helping in the kitchen, and relish the idea that they are doing their part to nourish their family. Older children may like to help out in the garden or yard. In these ways, parents can create a family life in which children are active participants from an early age, not passive recipients of adult caretaking. If we put this into practice on a daily basis, helping out can become second nature to our kids, and we will be less likely to be faced with constant demands that we take care of everything for them.

The Payoff

How will this foundation of independent play, creative thinking, and self-sufficiency help children? Ask your local kindergarten teachers, and they will tell you. Despite increasing academic pressures in the early grades—and I have heard experienced educators say that today's kindergarten is more like second grade twenty years ago—most teachers will not list reading, writing, or counting as the most important prerequisites for kindergarten. Instead, they talk about children being ready to learn; to sit still, to listen, to pay attention, to take the initiative, to explore, to take risks, to tolerate mistakes, and to cooperate with their peers and the adults who are there to help them.

Young children who have learned to quietly play alone and to create their own stories and their own ideas are far more likely to enter elementary school feeling confident in their abilities to handle new tasks and challenges. Many have been solving problems and riddles in their heads for years already, and can remain focused and attentive without any external stimulation or adult instruction. Independent play almost always includes a natural process of trial and error, a skill that many children can draw on when learning the alphabet or early arithmetic. All true learning, after all, involves making mistakes and coping with frustration, and children who have learned to play on their own will have crossed that bridge innumerable times by kindergarten or first grade.

Parents who ask children to care for themselves and pitch in at home are also teaching them how to be cooperative and helpful members of a community. The teachers that I know are thankful for children who respond to their requests, who listen the first time they are asked to do a job, and who look for ways to be helpful with other students. Like some of their classmates, these children get labeled, but in a way their parents might cherish: "Good kid," "A real thinker," "Works well on his own," "She's a pleasure." No grades or ribbons or trophies can make parents as proud as these accolades. The teacher's feedback may also be the first real validation that parents have been on the right track, and that their struggle to resist the activities and social commitments that would have deprived their children of time for independent play was well worth the effort.

five

Fear of Not Doing Enough: Perseverance

Rachel came to my office to discuss how to handle her four-year-old daughter's tantrums and outbursts. After a short time on this topic, the conversation veered in another direction, and she spoke of her life as the mother of three small children:

> It's so hard to keep up. With their playdates, ballet classes, Gymboree, and preschool, we barely have time for anything else. I try to spend time with them in the basement each day; we have an art room filled with supplies and do projects together as often as we can. . . . Mealtimes are tough. I feel like a short-order cook, preparing three or four things for them to eat so they're all happy. I'm always picking up after them; it feels like it never stops. Tell me it's going to get better!

Rachel's laments are pretty common. I hear many similar stories from parents who are doing all they can to make sure their young children are happy. They know about the importance of the early years, and they work hard to provide a cozy and stimulating environment at home. They have made sure that books and educational materials are in plentiful supply. Creative playthings are readily available for their young ones, along with computer software and games to teach early reading and counting skills. From a young age, their children have the opportunities to take art and dance classes, join sports teams, and hone their musical talents.

The pressure on parents to provide enrichment to their children at a young age has drawn considerable attention in the media, but another trend that has flourished alongside it has gone less noticed. We are working harder to jump-start our kids' learning and creativity, but we are also working overtime to provide them with near-perfect environments. We know kids can become stressed at a young age and we really don't want to struggle with them. So we do everything for them. We dress them, clean up after them, and pick up their clothes. We make sure that they have foods that they like and that their music is on in the car. We arrange their playdates and make sure that they are not behind the crowd when it comes to the latest toys, video games, and technology.

Faye embraced this style of parenting. A former marketer who left her job to become a full-time mother after the birth of her second child, she was always second-guessing herself. Though a smart and engaging woman, she had largely ignored her own interests since becoming a mom. As she confessed, "My philosophy of parenting was always my kids' needs first; I tried to do everything I could for them to avoid a confrontation." Faye became pretty adept at anticipating the needs of her five-year-old son and three-year-old daughter, but she admitted that she felt like she was "walking on eggshells" most of the time, and lived in fear of things getting out of control.

In many ways, parents in this country have become the *givers*. We feel tremendous pressure to set our kids on the right path, and many of us vow to do whatever it takes to get there. If that means one more trip in the car each day to take tennis lessons or an early morning wakeup each day to practice violin, so be it. If it means parents have to work harder around the house (or in most families, that mothers have to work harder) and clean and cook a little more than expected, well, that must go with the territory. For many parents, the energy and effort of the early years is sustained in part by a wistful notion that in time the kids will be more able to take care of themselves.

Although working hard to protect our children from getting frustrated and making sure they have the right early experiences can seem like a reasonable game plan, in the process many of us are losing the chance to teach our kids how to work hard and to let them learn from their own mistakes. Focusing too much on encouraging our children's talents and boosting their self-esteem can prevent us from expecting our kids to care for themselves and to come up with their own solutions to problems.

First Have Fun

Parenting has always included sacrifice. The groans and workload of today's parents echo those of previous generations in many ways. Without the labor-saving devices we take for granted—the dishwasher, washing machine, and microwave, to name a few—motherhood in the early- and mid-twentieth century was in many ways a more physically demanding job. Yet the psychological burden on parents was somewhat different. Though child-rearing experts had made inroads by the middle of the last century in this country, few parents believed that they carried primary responsibility for developing their children's intelligence and creativity. Until the past twenty or thirty years, most families expected their children to pitch in when they were able, and parents were generally not overcome by guilt over providing the right kind of experiences for their little ones.[1]

The current anxiety parents experience over not doing enough for their children is driven by two related trends. Parents are working more hours outside the home than ever before, and far more mothers are in the workforce either full or part time than a generation ago.[2] With fewer hours at home, we want to maximize our time with our kids. We make sure they are well fed, entertained, and read to during the precious hours that we have together each evening. And we arrange for family outings, cultural activities, and dinners together on the weekend when dads are more available.

In the interest of time and preserving these fun occasions, we may find ourselves doing more than we want for our kids. We may toss their clothes in the hamper, clear their plates, ignore sassy behaviors, and give in to requests for treats. It's not that most parents don't see the value in saying no or getting their children to help, but in that moment when we decide whether to ask one more time or keep the peace and do it ourselves, the latter often feels like the more compelling and, to be honest, the easier option. In this subtle way, the goal of family togetherness and quality time can come to take precedence over expectations that our children learn to behave and do their fair share at home.

The Achievement Wars

Another reason we have come to expect more of ourselves and less of our children is that many parents view the early years as the prime time to identify and foster their children's nascent talents. This push goes well beyond the local soccer clinics or preschool dance recitals. I have heard from parents about their three-year-old son's fascination with astronomy and their search for the right science program for him. Bill, a first grader, talked to me recently about his wish to publish a book, and I then listened as his parents discussed their frustration with the limited intellectual pursuits available in the highly rated local public school for an advanced child like him.

Rather than a time of play and imagination, the preschool and early elementary years have become a time to hone skills and optimize achievements. In many towns, the sports "stars" emerge by age six or seven, and are then shuttled off to travel with all-star teams to compete against similar aspiring athletes from other cities or counties. Many of the highly regarded dance, gymnastics, and music programs also reflect this trend, and offer a similar level of specialization and tracking from an early age. The resurgence of educational programs for "gifted and talented" children around the country taps into a widespread concern among parents that schools are not providing a challenging enough curriculum for their young children and that critical periods of learning are passing them by.

There are compelling reasons why the rush to identify talent at a young age may turn out to be a shortsighted goal. As we have often heard, children's unique abilities do not always present themselves at a young age. For every child prodigy in athletics, music, or mathematics, there are many more Michael Jordans, who famously failed to make his high school basketball team on his first attempt. Our science competitions may point us toward the next genius in physics, but it is just as likely that he or she will follow the path of Albert Einstein, who was not always a diligent student and failed to pass his engineering exams before he settled on his ultimate course of study.

If we try to select out the best and brightest in the early years we are likely to discourage the slower to develop and the less competitive children from testing their mettle. I remember a recent session with five-year-old Teddy, who responded to my request to draw a house by filling his paper with scribbles. When I asked him what it was, he said slyly, "It's abstract art." He and I shared a laugh, but it was apparent that he was a bright kid whose fine motor skills had not yet caught up with his overall intelligence. Instead of plugging away with crayons and markers, he did what a lot of boys learn to do from a young age. He had given up on drawing and pronounced it not for him, albeit in his own clever and engaging way.

Many young children I meet are simply not ready for the level of commitment and training that we expect of them. In towns where many preschoolers have two or three after-school activities, twice a week swim classes for our four-year-old may not feel like anything unusual. But many preschoolers cannot handle this load, both physically and emotionally, especially if they have more than a few hours of school each day. This doesn't mean that they can't come back to formal lessons in swimming or soccer or chess in a few years, but they might be better off with more casual exposure for now. "Yes," parents often reply when I suggest this course of action, "but by then everyone else will have a few years of practice under their belts." True, perhaps, but if our kids are not ready now, what is the point of pushing them ahead?

The Perils of Early Success

What about the kids who do stick it out and those who naturally excel from an early age? In my experience, signs of precociousness can come to haunt kids and their families. First of all it can be quite a burden for a four- or five-year-old to be labeled "gifted." I have met kids who have heard many adults toss out the term "genius" in their presence and have come to embrace their precocious displays of intelligence. One seven-year-old boy proudly informed me that his principal had announced to him, "Boy, you really are a genius." When I asked Emma how second grade was going after two months, she tossed her head back and stated proudly, "I already know everything there is to know in second grade." Yet both of these children were referred to me because they were beginning to have doubts about their abilities and feared losing ground to the rest of the class.

The scientific fact remains that no matter what the ability under study, eventually we will see a "regression to the mean." If a child starts out at the 90th percentile in height, he may well be in the taller group a few years later, but he is likely to have come back down the scale a few notches. In much the same vein, children who are quick-witted and verbal in preschool are likely to be fine students in a few years, but may not be at the top of the class in all subjects. Early coordination is perhaps the best example of this. Some little kids are awkward and ill at ease in their bodies while others seem to be natural runners and climbers. It makes sense to wait a while before we try to predict who will be the varsity athletes in the crowd, because many children physically mature and grow at a much slower rate than their peers.

Not surprisingly, many kids fight to hold on to their exalted status. Who wouldn't want to be number one all the time? But as they get older, many suffer through a cruel realization that they now have peers who can keep up. Despite their continued high level of performance, being very good does not always feel like enough. Chris, a fifth grader I had known off and on for many years, was growing nervous about his travel basketball tryouts. His growth had slowed some, and though he was still relatively tall and a skilled player, he knew he was at risk of not starting and perhaps not even making the team. The thought was galling to him, and he glumly told me, "I have always been the best; I couldn't handle not making the cut."

For many of our early achievers, we risk setting up a situation in which they must perform at a high level or risk bitter disappointment. Given their early prowess at sports or academics or music, they might also limit their interests and only focus their attention on activities at which they feel assured of success. So a kindergarten boy might avoid drawing, and another might not try climbing the monkey bars if he thought he was not likely to master them immediately. Bill was serious about writing his book, but would not join in with the other boys kicking a soccer ball at recess. He already felt he could not keep up, and that his short stature would always be a serious detriment to his athletic success. Despite his wish to be accepted and join in with his peers, he chose to sit out the games, lest he risk feeling humiliated by his less than average ability to kick a ball.

True Grit

For all their considerable skills, many of our bright young children are not learning to persevere and handle frustration. They may do one or two things very well, but they often have not learned to handle adversity and new challenges. Ultimately, it is just these qualities that we should be encouraging, not specialized training in one discipline. As Ann Hulbert has noted, efforts to "discover" geniuses have been hampered by the fact that those who achieve greatness almost always possess a knack for persistence and a confidence in their abilities, two traits that are not easily identified on standardized tests.[3] In fact, the early identification of a particular talent and the lavish praise that usually comes along with it can actually reduce the likelihood that children will learn to push forward and test the limits of their abilities. At a young age, they can learn that maintaining their standing is of utmost importance, not breaking new ground or branching out and trying new endeavors.

Researchers who have studied high-achieving kids have found that intelligence is not really the key factor in their success. Andrea Duckworth and Martin Seligman, psychologists at the University of Pennsylvania, have come to very different conclusions. They found that middle school children with the best grades were the ones who had the most *self-discipline*. These kids could control their impulses, were more apt to follow the rules in class, and could delay gratification. As Duckworth explains, a lot of the children in their study "were not a genius in any way but were really tenacious." She and Seligman have come to call this tenacity "grit," a dogged determination to hold off on immediate rewards (like playing video games instead of studying) to accomplish more difficult, long-term goals.[4]

Like most good research, there is something about this study that makes intuitive sense. Think of the successful, hardworking people we know. Usually what impresses is their determination and ambition (in other words, their grit), not their whiz-bang intelligence or wit. Most people who have risen in their careers or have made a mark in business have been willing to put out the sweat and grind it takes, and have not been deterred by the setbacks along the way. This is evident in the corporate world and no less true for enterprising painters or carpenters or shopkeepers. These men and women are willing to put in the time and effort to get where they want to be, no matter what or who tries to lure them away from their goals.

The question is how do we help our kids develop their self-discipline and grit? First we shouldn't overemphasize their intelligence, but we should praise their *efforts*. Carol Dweck and her colleagues at Stanford University have studied the difference, and she explains why we need to make this distinction:

> When you praise kids' intelligence and then they fail, they think they're not smart anymore, and they lose interest in their work. In contrast, kids praised for effort show no impairment and are often energized in the face of difficulty.[5]

the belief that hard work is what really matters has always been a fundamental aspect of the American character. Ben Franklin summed it up best in *Poor Richard's Almanack*: "Diligence is the mother of good luck."

Telling children that they are smart doesn't cut it, and may set up expectations that they can't meet. We do much better if we talk about their persistence, as in, "I really appreciate how you cleaned up all your toys, that was *hard work*. I'm going to tell Mom about that when she gets home." If we can help our kids identify with the idea of persistence, and pushing through or solving problems on their own, they are more likely to develop values like determination and self-discipline, which are the underpinnings of academic success and other achievements.

Lessons in Resilience

Recognizing and praising our kids' efforts is half the battle. First we have to give them real work to do. If we tread too lightly and don't expect too much of our children at home (or at school, for that matter), then we won't have examples of their hard work and times they pitched in. Given this logic, we shouldn't pick up after our children so much; maybe three-year-olds should be putting their clothes in the hamper and dressing themselves. Perhaps we don't have to intervene every time the blocks get knocked over or our kids get stumped by a puzzle. In each case, if we stop and think twice, we may choose to do less for our children.

To accomplish this we have to believe that children are tough, that they can handle more responsibility, and that ultimately learning to do more on their own is good for them. We can look to case studies of childhood resilience for evidence. Beginning in the 1970s, researchers began looking more closely at the effects of trauma on young children. The pioneering work of the child psychiatrist Lenore Terr, who studied children who had suffered through acute traumatic situations, including accidents and natural disasters, helped others begin to identify the short- and long-term effects of trauma.[6]

On a parallel course were a number of researchers studying other types of trauma in childhood—loss of a parent to death or mental illness, major injuries or medical procedures, and firsthand experience with war among them. This second group, which included the British psychiatrist Michael Rutter and his colleague, Norman Garmezy, made a somewhat startling discovery that they had not predicted.[7] They found that a certain subset of children was seemingly immune to trauma, and that some, in fact, performed at a higher level after their loss than they had previously. The psychoanalyst E. J. Anthony used the term the "invulnerable child" to describe this group, who seemed impervious to trauma and capable of rising above their perilous circumstances.[8]

Subsequent studies tempered their optimism somewhat, and for children subject to extreme poverty, abuse, and violence, such positive outcomes remain the rare finding. Nonetheless, these early trauma researchers made great strides in identifying the potential coping mechanisms for children under stress. The resilient children they identified felt secure and in control of their lives, even when surrounded by chaos. They were generally cooperative and had good social skills, and could delay gratification of their own needs and desires when the circumstances demanded. Children who fared well under stress also proved to be capable of planning ahead and relied on their own capacity for mental trial and error.[9] Many also turned out to have rich fantasy lives, and were able to turn away from their personal tragedies and escape into more benign worlds of their own making. Many of the biographers of the leaders in the arts and sciences and business in the last century have focused considerable attention on their ability to overcome adversity.

The Case for Struggle

What can we learn from this research and how does it apply to our own young children? Obviously we don't want to expose our kids to traumatic situations hoping something good will come of it. But as we look to build our children's resilience, we might consider if some more modest exposure to difficult situations might not be in their best interest. Colleagues of mine at the Jewish Board of Family and Children's Services in New York have recently coined the term "optimal struggle," and have tried to define some reasonable rites of passage in childhood that might help bolster our children's capacity for self-reliance and help them cope with more significant challenges down the road. They recommend that parents think carefully before seeking professional help for young children with mild delays or offering tutoring to a child without significant learning problems who is struggling for the first time in elementary school.[10]

With a little creative thinking and planning, it is not too hard to imagine how we can create similar challenges at home for our children. Letting kids do their own homework, giving them more chores, or limiting their opportunities to have toys or candy are just a few of the practical ways we can let them "struggle" without risking any harm. If we choose instead to indulge their wishes and let them off easy, we can't really expect our kids to develop self-discipline. It's not fair to call them "lazy" or "spoiled." After all, these labels say more about parents than they do about kids. But with a concerted effort to stem the tide, we can teach kids that they have to work for what they get and make do with what they have. Sometimes it helps to put it in simple language to kids: "You get what you get, and you don't get upset."

Why does the concept of struggle seem so foreign to us today? It's not as if today's parents didn't hear those words in their own houses growing up. Others endured a lot worse. Many of the most successful parents I meet in my office are walking examples of resilience. Having overcome family instability, difficult living environments, or poverty, they have surged to the tops of their professions and are now enjoying the fruits of their labor. These same mothers and fathers often struggle when it comes to passing along the lessons they learned. They do not wish the same fate upon their own children, and in many cases they have devoted their lives to staying as far away from their former circumstances as possible.

Sometimes they do stop and wonder. One single mother I met angrily threatened to drop off her teenage son in her old Brooklyn neighborhood, hoping, perhaps, that he would acquire by brief exposure the determination and drive that had led her to a successful academic career and medical practice. Jim, a thoughtful and caring father, admitted half in jest, "Sometimes I wish my kids had the same disadvantages I had." After we shared that lighthearted moment, we did some serious thinking about how Jim could begin to expect more from his young son and daughter.

Besides the obvious wish to shield children from pain, parents avoid looking for ways their children can struggle because they believe this is not their job. From as far back as most of us can remember, we have heard about the importance of children's self-esteem. Most parents firmly believe that helping children feel good about themselves is their primary mission. In his insightful review of recent trends in parenting, the historian Peter Stearns noted that despite research to the contrary, popular lore in the latter part of the last century stated that "children needed help and latitude in living up to standards, less chance to feel guilty about failure, and more opportunity to express the self in the process."[11] As a society, we gradually moved away from expecting children to adapt and meet adult expectations and became more attuned to their vulnerability and individuality. In the process, parents came to feel that their main role was to nurture their children's self-image, praise their achievements, and protect them from harm.

In my experience, parents of young children often take this to the next level, and view themselves as the chief protectors of their children's potentially fragile psyche. They are readily available to their preschoolers and do not hesitate to dress them, put on their coats, help them in

i t is ironic that the self-esteem movement and the research on resilience grew up alongside each other during the 1970s and 1980s. They apparently were never introduced to one another, but if they had met they might have formed a formidable collaboration that might have anticipated and diffused many of the dilemmas parents face today.

the bathroom, and prepare them meals on request. Slightly older children sometimes get the same treatment, and often get considerable assistance with their schoolwork and constant reassurance that they are performing at a high level. Many of these well-intentioned efforts come from parents who share the same two goals: to avoid conflict with their children and to bolster their self-esteem.

These attempts to make our children feel more secure can easily backfire. If we think back to our own early experiences and try to identify the valuable lessons we learned as kids, we might recall our parents' affection and praise, but we will not likely pinpoint moments when we received extra help or tending to. It is more likely we will have memories of times when we took some initiative or tried something new and were rewarded for a job well done. The resilience research suggests that if we want to strengthen our children's resolve and nurture their ambition, we should not be overly helpful nor should we always avoid difficult situations where they have to fend for themselves. This can sound silly and out of place when we are talking about making our three-year-olds breakfast or helping them on with their coats, but the small goal of having kids do more and parents do less presents itself in a number of these moments every day.

Tying Laces: A Lesson for Life

Let's take a simple example: learning to tie shoelaces. For many parents the invention of Velcro and slip-on sneakers and shoes has been a joy. They no longer have to fight with their young ones to get over that final hurdle in the morning, because presto, flap over, and tight, they're off and ready to go. When pressed for time, as we often are on the way to school or work, we don't wait for our kids to put their shoes on; it's easier to do it for them.

Our kids don't complain, of course; they are usually happy when things are made a little easier for them. If they do wear tie-up shoes for sports or other occasions, they rely on us to get them snug and tight the way they like. This pattern can repeat itself well into grade school, and many children remain dependent on their parents' ministrations long after they are physically capable of mastering this task.

Let's weigh the pros and cons of the new shoe styles. They definitely cut down on the fuss and frustration and allow us to move without much extra time or effort. All of us welcome that. Men's and women's loafers and clogs have been popular for a long time. Our kids can have the freedom to put shoes on by themselves from a fairly young age, and leave the house without hesitation.

But there is a downside. If our kids simply slip on and go they miss out on something important. Tying shoes is a complex transaction. It requires concentration, fine and gross motor skills, cooperation with an adult, tremendous patience, and ultimately, lots of practice. It is also inherently frustrating for the average four- or five- or six-year-old child. And that is the point. If we are trying to teach our children to work hard, to persevere when things get a little challenging, learning to tie shoes is a good first step. Gentle praise ("Good job, you have the cross and one loop down") and encouragement ("Let's try that second loop again") from parents, along with recognition for their child's effort and hard work ("Wait till Dad sees what you did today!"), can set the stage for future success at overcoming difficult obstacles.

During workshops for parents, I often ask for a show of hands from those who can recall when they learned to tie their shoes as children. Almost always the majority of the hands spring up. Adults of a certain age have vivid memories of that milestone. A generation ago, learning to tie your shoes was the next best thing to getting your driver's license. You had the freedom then to run outdoors, to keep up with the older kids in the neighborhood, to be independent. You felt like you had really mastered something important. This may sound like an overly romanticized version of childhood in the sixties and seventies, but it's hard to see how the slip-on shoes convey the same feelings of accomplishment. It is remarkable to see how many older elementary-age children still have not mastered the art of tying their own shoes. Loose laces might be the current style, but in this case it appears that fashion has been led by poorly developed form.

The Tantrum Blues

We have all heard stories of the "terrible twos." We know they are coming. Like the Gremlins in that movie, the little terrors can seem to appear out of nowhere. A quick reprimand or a denied request may be all it takes to set off a fit of previously unmatched intensity that can be shocking for mothers and fathers, especially if it's their first time around. For many parents, temper tantrums present the first big challenge with letting their children struggle. Nancy told the story of her daughter Claire's outbursts:

> She's only two and a half and I hate to see her scream like that. It can go on for forty-five minutes! I feel so guilty. I want to go in and comfort her but I think maybe I shouldn't. Sometimes I do go, and I try to be calm, but after a while I tell her just to "stop it, stop your screaming!" That usually only makes things worse. I asked her about it and Claire told me, "I can't stop when I start screaming," and I think she's probably right. She seems so out of control. I wish I could help her.

By any measure, Nancy qualified as a good mother. She was kind, thoughtful, and sensitive to her daughter's needs. Claire's tantrums were usually set off by her mother reprimanding her for being overly physical with her eleven-month-old sister. Nancy had little choice but to call Claire on this behavior, even when she did volunteer her apologies to her sister. I had a few recommendations for her: "Try to stay calm in the face of her outbursts"; "Wait until the tantrum is over before you soothe Claire"; "Avoid undue confrontations when she is sleepy or hungry." I also gave her words she could use with Claire: "I know you're frustrated, but it will be okay in a while"; "You're upset and angry; we'll talk about it more when you calm down." Nancy thought this might help some. She also understood that she needed to be more forgiving of herself, and to not hold herself to such high standards each time Claire had a meltdown. Still she felt guilty much of the time.

In our two meetings held six months apart, Nancy was able to acknowledge how desperate she felt, and how painful it was for her to watch Claire while she appeared to be in such agony, knowing all the while that there was little she could do for her daughter. She worried a lot about what would happen to Claire if she followed through on plans to go back to work in a few months, and was also concerned about how she would adjust to her new part-time babysitter. In my experience, many mothers can relate to Nancy's anxiety and grieving at the loss of the halcyon days with her daughter. It's common for these feelings to remain hidden from even close friends and family members, for fear that they will be dismissed by casual reassurances that it's "just a phase." Many new parents, in particular, are tormented by their children's tantrums and feel a tremendous responsibility to set things right with them.

The Good News About Tantrums

If there is one thing I try to offer to Nancy and other mothers it is a firmly held belief that tantrums are a healthy and necessary part of every child's early years. They are, in other words, a good thing! Well before they can learn to do for themselves, children first need to learn how to manage their feelings. This is no small task for toddlers and preschoolers, who can sometimes feel pretty overwhelmed by the intensity of their emotions.

Tantrums present a chance for children to learn to cope with frustration and disappointment. This can be a bitter pill for them to swallow, particularly as they realize that they cannot have everything just to their liking and that they cannot control their parents all the time. We expect them to be unhappy and to show their displeasure at these revelations, not in a calm and verbal way that we adults may do (or at least *try* to do) but within their own limited repertoire: screaming, kicking, stomping their feet, flailing about. This is all par for the course, and not usually cause for worry.

I am reminded of the written Chinese word for crisis. It combines two characters, the symbols for danger and opportunity. For many parents, tantrums qualify as the first experience with any kind of crisis involving their children. And there is danger present, or at least it appears that our kids are at risk for physically harming themselves or others nearby during these moments. It also feels like they may suffer lasting psychological damage if they keep up with the screaming and carrying on without any intervention on our part. At some point in meetings to discuss tantrums, parents almost always ask the question that speaks to their biggest fear, as Tess did in our second session together: "It's not too traumatic, is it? To let her cry like that I mean? My beautiful child is not going to be scarred for life, is she?" The answer they hear from me is clear: "As long as you keep her safe and out of harm's way, you are not going to traumatize your child," but I know that the risk of causing emotional pain to a child can continue to feel like an enormous burden to parents.

This is one of the major dilemmas for parents. Do we try to rescue children from their obvious distress or do we give them the opportunity to come out of it on their own? If Nancy tried to soothe Claire when she screamed, and picked her up and comforted her the moment she expressed any upset, she might have negated her immediate pain, but she would also have prevented her from learning to tolerate and work through her frustration. If we jump through hoops and give in to unreasonable requests to avoid conflicts with our kids, we are not helping them to learn the limits of their own desires and how to delay gratification of their impulses or wishes. In many respects, these are the most important achievements for a two-year-old child.

Tantrums and the Older Child

It's not unusual for the twos to pass pretty uneventfully, only to be followed by the "thrashing threes" or the "fierce fours." For a variety of reasons, tantrums and struggles with frustration can appear to be a nonissue until the later preschool years, and in some cases, they do not appear until a child is five or six. This delay can wreak havoc for parents. First, they may not be prepared for the sudden turn of events, and after a few years of cooperative behavior from their kids it can be a real shock to have to confront their anger and intensity. Four-year-olds are bigger and stronger and can appear to be at a much greater risk for hurting themselves or doing damage to others, including their parents!

Perhaps the biggest difference in older children is their ability to verbalize their frustration. This has advantages, and many older kids can relate to and readily adapt the word "frustration" to describe their feelings. It has a visceral quality to it that they understand. Unfortunately, they also tend to direct their verbal attacks at their parents. "You're a bad mommy"; "You don't care about me"; You're the meanest dad ever"; "You don't love me anymore"; and perhaps the kicker, "I hate you!" are part of the angry preschooler's lexicon (along with a few other early curses, like "stupid" and "idiot"), and it's not just for those who are new to tantrums. These words can sting and cut to the quick when they are fired off by raging three- and four-year-olds, and leave many parents feeling like they have ruptured their ties with their kids forever by setting limits on their behavior.

Parents have to work that much harder to stay the course when older children express their frustration for the first time. We can't bear to see them so unhappy, especially when we thought we would be in the throes of the "magic years" by now. And their verbal darts can make us shudder, and once again lead us to feel that we are causing undue pain or trauma. On some level children know that their moms and dads have this weakness and want to rescue them. Kids want to feel better or get what they want right now, and they will try all the tricks at their disposal to get us to acquiesce. This is their job, and as parents our job is to teach them they have to wait, and that they cannot always get what they want when they want it. Life is filled with frustration, and giving in sets up unrealistic expectation that it is not.

On paper this sounds pretty reasonable. But even as adults, most of us have our own conflicts with delaying gratification. This is partly due to our culture's fascination with acquiring new things, and the siren song of the newest and latest consumer goods that entice our desires. Many parents can relate to how much their children want and the wish to feel good sooner rather than later. We also avoid moments of frustration with our children because they make us feel bad. When we set limits or say no to requests, we not only have to deal with our children's upset feelings, but we also have to cope with our own limited tolerance for pain and discomfort. It is natural to want to banish these feelings, and to find a quick solution to whatever problem has aroused them in our children and in us.

What happens when this phase goes awry and parents give in to the fear that they are doing harm by saying no to their children and letting them express their anger? I hear many stories like Tina's, who worried about her four-year-old son, Andrew. He would cry intensely if she did not drive past the fire station on his way home, and she arranged all her travels with him around passing this local landmark. Three-year-old Frances announced to her teacher, "I only have to wait for toys from Santa Claus, I get everything I want from my Mom and Dad right away!" Sometimes it's apparent that older kids have never learned to handle frustration or delay gratification. Take Darren, a bright and capable fifth grader. His parents reported that all Darren thought about were new toys and electronics, but that he quickly discarded each new purchase and moved on to the next object of burning desire. For him, everything needed to be bigger, newer, and more expensive.

It is easy to dismiss these children as overindulged or unappreciative of their good fortune. Their parents are also an easy target. We have all read the op-ed pieces on declining respect and the surge in rude behavior among children, and the "problem with today's parents" who don't teach their children good manners and who give them too much. These are real issues, and we will address them further in the next chapter. Yet lumping all of parents' or children's behavior into one basket is misguided and hints at a moralizing crusade (which few child-rearing critics would admit joining).

Children are not "spoiled" or "entitled." Many have simply not learned how to wait for what they want and how to accept no for an answer, because they have not had enough experience with limits. A few mothers and fathers are carefree and indulgent materialists. Yet the majority of parents I meet are driven more by fear, not excess. I know all the parents in the above examples and though reasonably comfortable, they are decent, hardworking people trying to do right by their kids. They did not want to see their little children struggle and they wanted to avoid conflict with them. Mainly they wanted their kids to be happy.

The real issue for them and many other parents is learning how to visualize how helping kids to endure today's frustration and tantrums can lead to a more settled and lasting sense of well-being down the line. Our job as parents is, in a sense, to postpone our children's happiness and to let them struggle now so they can learn to overcome small doses of hardship and discover their own capacity to make themselves feel better. If we can teach them to work hard, to tolerate disappointment, and to bounce back from adversity when they are young, they will be that much better equipped for the struggles that lie ahead.

Frustration and the Intense Child

Parents of a certain type of child with a less easygoing temperament are likely to encounter more significant obstacles during this phase and be-

i n his review of research of what constitutes happiness, David Nettle is careful to distinguish short-term feelings of pleasure and joy from a more enduring sense of satisfaction and well-being that lead to a fulfilling life. Though he is focusing primarily on adults, parents might do well to remember that the different levels of happiness that he describes apply to children as well. Helping kids to learn to delay gratification and deal with frustration when they are young can prepare them to focus on long-term goals that will give them a more lasting sense of accomplishment.

yond. We have different labels for these kids: "the difficult child," "strong willed," "out of sync," "hyperactive," "explosive." Parents have their own descriptions: "high maintenance," "frustrating beyond belief," "a thorn between two roses." Often these children are bright and precociously verbal. As one mother joked about her four-year-old daughter, "Before the tidal wave of emotion hits, she's very articulate." These kids are generally capable and fast-charging, but when they hit a roadblock they can burst with frustration and rage, and look to lash out at anything or anyone in their sights. Their parents usually bear the brunt of these outbursts, which can last for an hour or more.

I like to refer to these children in a slightly different way. I simply call them *intense* kids. I chose this word not because it is particularly descriptive or implies any diagnostic or clinical significance. "Intense" is a neutral word. An intense flame can bring warmth and light; an intense fire can burn out of control. I often find that the same kids who are so difficult are also the most enthusiastic. They are filled with energy and bring tremendous determination and concentration to bear when they are engaged in an activity. They often seek out adventure and new experiences; they may love to travel. I'll admit that I have a soft spot for intense kids and the challenges they present; they have provided many of the fondest memories of my work in the office and in the classroom.

I know that intense children are not always the easiest to live with. When Cynthia came to see me she was at her wit's end. Her daughter Maggie, a first grader, had been having intense tantrums since she was three, and they hadn't diminished much. She was bright and doing well in school for the most part, but as soon as she encountered difficulties with reading or another subject, she would lash out, usually at herself: "I'm dumb"; "I'm so stupid; why don't you give me away!"

Five-year-old Geoffrey confessed to me that it was "so hard to wait, I get so angry when I have to listen to my mom or when she says no to me." And we recall two-year-old Claire's assertion that she just could not stop screaming once she started, a contention her mother would not dispute.

Watching these children struggle is much more of a challenge for parents. Sarah evoked a scene from *The Exorcist* to describe the experience with her three-year-old daughter, whose tantrums often lasted from forty-five to sixty minutes: "Well, at least her head hasn't spun all the way around yet!" All kidding aside, the rage and thrashing behaviors of intense kids can be downright scary, and evoke painful images of a future tinged with fury. The adolescent years loom large in these moments. Parents are often ashamed to admit to their worst fears; that something has gone terribly wrong with their child and that they are part of the problem. They ask for advice hoping they can remake what feels like a tortured and exhausting existence for both of them.

It is tempting to tell parents to let things play out or let nature take its course and their kids will be fine in the long run. This line of reasoning, which has some merit, does little to assuage parents' anxiety about the future, nor does it give them any tools for the present. We sometimes have to do it differently with intense kids. We may use humor more readily with them, and try to nip their outbursts before they get so out of control. Their screaming and rage may be too much to bear at any one moment for both the child and parent, and at that time we may have to give in to their desire and comfort them more directly. Parents of intense children often benefit from having regular consults with their pediatrician or another professional who can help them manage these storms.

From my vantage point, the most important goal for parents is to recognize that their children are not destined for a life of torment and misery. If we think of the successful adults whom we know, many of them have the same traits as intense kids: They are hard-charging, hyperfocused, enthusiastic, energetic, demanding. It can be helpful for intense kids to hear their parents talk about this positive side of their personality, and in calmer moments, to use humor about the times they get carried away with excitement. "You can be so much fun, but sometimes you do drive us a little crazy!"

For now these children need help from their parents to understand that it is hard work for them to listen and to hear no, to manage their feelings, and to curb their enthusiasm. I usually suggest parents say something like this: "We all have work to do. Your older brother is learning to read, your little sister is starting to use the toilet. You have to work hard to control yourself when we tell you that you can't have what you want. Don't worry, we'll get there." If parents can muster the confidence to utter these last few words, they can reassure their children and themselves that life will not always be so frustrating, and that they can expect that in the not too distant future things will start to get better. In my experience, when parents have a pretty clear plan and can learn to surf the rough waters of the first few years, things almost always do.

Teaching Kids to Persevere

Set Realistic Goals

The early years can be a time when we take enormous pride in our offspring's accomplishments. If we have children who are among the first in the neighborhood to speak in sentences, hit a baseball, or read without assistance, we can feel tempted to congratulate ourselves on our parenting techniques or at least on passing along their unique gifts through our genetic heritage. Feeling flush and proud is part of the joy of parenting. All of us hope to have these feelings once in a while.

Yet these moments of satisfaction can also lead to a mind-set that quick and easy victories will come readily to our children. Whether we are conscious of it or not, we may set up an expectation for ourselves and our kids that this is the only way to go, that less than the head of the pack is not good enough. When they fail to get over this high bar, we may feel our anxiety increase and give off subtle messages that they need to do better for us all to feel okay. We might find ourselves in a place we thought we would avoid, where disappointment and regret follow on the heels of every missed opportunity or average showing. Our kids might learn that perfection is the goal, and if they are intense and demanding to begin with, they are likely to wholeheartedly embrace competition to be the best at all they do.

Parents can avoid this trap by putting less stock in where their kids stand in relation to their friends and classmates. If we instead compare kids' accomplishments today to their own earlier efforts ("You swam a little farther today in camp"; "You are doing a good job now with forming your letters"), they will have a better sense that we care more about trying hard than their absolute performance or being the best in the group. We can also praise kids in a realistic way for what they *do* without labeling them a star (or genius or fabulous athlete) and setting up unrealistic expectations that they may soon struggle to meet.

Don't Overdo Praise

Kids naturally feel good when they perform well. Research shows that this is the real key to self-esteem, that children's feelings of confidence and satisfaction are based on their own appraisal of their performance, not being told that they are special or unique.[12] If we stick to the facts and acknowledge a job well done they are apt to want to push themselves further. It is important for kids to know that they have our support and that we recognize their accomplishments, but we have to be careful not to overplay their success or take too much pride in our own contribution ("All that pitching I did really helped you!").

Sometimes in an attempt to make our children feel good, we praise them effusively even when they have exerted little effort. A colleague of mine recalled a time he had taken his kids sledding at the local hill. He and the other dads waited at the bottom while their five- and six-year-olds went up and down merrily. One dad proudly yelled, "Great job!" every time his son came down the hill. My friend thought to himself, "Hmm, I thought it was gravity!"

We all want our kids to know we care about them and are there to cheer them on, but we have to be careful to be genuine in our praise. Otherwise it will start to sound like background noise to them, and they will not be able to distinguish when we are truly pleased and proud of what they have done. From a young age our kids can read us well, and they know if we are being disingenuous or overly complimentary.

Focus on the Process, Not the End Product

At the beginning of this chapter we looked at the perils of focusing on singular achievements at an early age. I am especially concerned about "gifted" kids who avoid challenging situations and learn to steer clear of risk. If we focus too intently on the end products—the dazzling art project, the triumphant dance recital, the perfect score on the spelling quiz—we can also lose sight of the process that got our kids to that point. Most importantly, we want our kids to learn to *persevere*, to know what it means to work hard and overcome challenges. Teaching our kids to push themselves, to plug along even when tired or bored or when an activity is not in their bailiwick, is an invaluable gift, one they can rely on for much of their lives.

Think back to Teddy, the little abstract artist. He comes to mind when I walk into a preschool classroom and see the paintings and drawings hung across the room. Often the most accomplished pictures are front and center, drawn with deft hands and filled with imaginative arrays of color and shapes. I like to go to the fringes and find the drawings tucked away at the end of the line. There may be a little stick figure man or an oddly shaped house or animal.

I know that many of these artists, the realists in the crowd, have worked extremely hard to create compositions that at first glance pale in relation to the neighboring Picassos and Renoirs. But I try to encourage their parents to look beyond the relative merits of the canvass and think of what it took for their children to get to where they did. Many of them probably would have liked to scribble something or give up or find a clever retort like Teddy, but they kept at it and produced something to hang alongside their peers who were more advanced in their fine motor skills. These are the moments when parents should beam with pride and praise their kids for the effort they have exerted, and not get caught up in the ribbons that may elude them right now.

Give Kids Opportunities to Practice

We know that for any skilled athlete, his performance on game day comes only after hours of repetition and practice out of the spotlight. Larry Bird and Michael Jordan clearly had physical gifts, but their ability to sink a ball through a hoop came only after hundreds and thousands of attempts, and lots of misses along the way.

I am not advocating that we make our little kids sports junkies. But we can teach them at a young age the value of practicing. For a three-year-old, it might be learning to put on a shirt and pants. A four-year-old boy can practice cutting with scissors. A kindergartener might spend time learning to tie her shoes and button her coat. A second grader can plug along and master a chapter book. When children balk at continuing, we want to be there with words to coax them: "Just try one more time to snap the button"; "Two more pages and then you can take a break." We can be available to help our kids with any of these tasks, of course, but we should get in the habit of letting them fiddle and struggle awhile before we intervene.

Learning to ice skate and ride a bicycle are among the activities that naturally require practice and ultimately deliver a sense of accomplishment when kids can move on their own without falling. It usually takes a lot of patience and frustration tolerance to get over the hump. In both of these examples children have the opportunity to learn from adults, to gradually feel more independent, and to see the value of working over time to achieve a desired outcome.

This is not a seamless process. Our kids will get frustrated as they struggle with putting on their clothes or learning to read or staying upright on a bike. They will make plenty of mistakes. Our job as their parents is to step back and resist the urge to shield them from these experiences or make it all better for them. As my colleague Robert Brooks has written, "When youngsters view mistakes as temporary setbacks and as opportunities for learning, we as parents will have helped them develop a resilient mind-set filled with hope and problem-solving skills."[13]

"Hope" is a key word here. Children will not be diminished by their mistakes if they use them as motivation to try harder the next time around. After a tough day on the ice, we can offer words of support: "You fell down a few times out there, but I saw that you kept getting back up. Way to go." If we are overly reassuring or too sympathetic with their plight ("Boy, that must have really hurt"), they are more likely to focus on their disappointment and see their failings in bold relief.

Mistakes Are Okay

The best way to give children license to make mistakes is to find ways to demonstrate to them that their parents make errors. Our kids don't often see our mistakes. Believe it or not they may still believe we are supercompetent! I'm not suggesting that Dad come home and tell his six-year-old son he lost a million dollars in the market, but we might share a few more practical stories that they can understand. My kids love to hear stories of silly things I do. Sometimes I wear a sock inside out. When I have little time and lots of calls to make, I often dial a phone number and realize too late that I don't remember whom I've called. We get lost, we lose things on our computers, we mess up a new recipe. These are all examples kids can relate to.

How we handle our frustration in these moments matters a lot to our kids. If we bang on the steering wheel when we make a wrong turn and curse under our breaths, we lose the chance to show that mistakes are part of learning. If we can laugh at ourselves, find the right way to go, and perhaps recall the story of the "long cut" we took in the car on vacation, the kids have the chance to see a real-life example of how we cope with our shortcomings and make up for them. Other times we will not catch ourselves and we will get angry and frustrated. We will not traumatize our kids if they see us tense and upset. Chances are they know what this feels like. But in the main, if we remember to let them know that we are not perfect, that we make mistakes and still manage to function pretty well, we might alleviate much of their anxiety and the pressure they feel to be on top all of the time.

Model Hard Work at Home

If we want to teach our children to persevere and work hard, they also have to see us model these behaviors. Stories of our difficult job in that big office building downtown might not suffice. Children need to see us in action to believe us. They will likely not comment on it, but kids appreciate when we are there to make meals for them and help tidy up the house. They can come to respect that we have work to do at home, like doing the laundry and paying the bills. If we stay up late to change an electrical outlet or fix a leaky faucet, they see we have personally invested our time and energy in maintaining our home. Saturday afternoon spent working in the yard or the garden gives children a sense of what sweat and grind are all about, especially if we ask them to help us out.

Not all of us are handy or enjoy working in the yard or cooking elaborate meals, and many of us can afford to hire people to help us with these chores. Given the stressed lives we lead, it is not surprising we need help, and I don't begrudge parents who look to outsource some of the jobs around the house. Yet it is worth thinking about the costs and benefits of these arrangements, beyond the money exchanged for services rendered. If our children only hear stories about our stressful days at work, but see that the main labor in their own homes is done by others, they may not get a sense that we truly value hard work in ourselves and in them. We may also be unwittingly teaching them that menial labor is beneath them, and that all they really need to focus on is their schoolwork and extracurricular activities and their playtime. We will look more carefully at the notion of chores for children in the next chapter, but it is worth considering here how they see our role and whether we indeed model the kind of effort we expect from them.

A Plug for Pluggers

Last chapter we talked about helping our children become independent and spend time on their own. If we were to try to sum up what we have been discussing in these last few pages, we would start by recognizing the value of helping our kids learn to cope with frustration. We also want to teach them to persevere and take risks, and to not be afraid to make mistakes. In short, we want to instill the value of plugging away, of keeping at it, stick-to-it-iveness, if you like.

Despite our dreams and hopes, not all of our kids will be fantastic athletes or brilliant students or accomplished musicians. Our child may not be the quick study who finds that everything comes easily. But if there is one thing most of us can attest to, we know that pluggers do well in life. Those children who are not deterred by challenges, who know how to remain focused on a goal and are willing to exert the effort to get there, and who have faith that their hard work will be rewarded in time are far more likely to become successful adults who can manage their own affairs. If we can begin to visualize this outcome for our kids and feel confident that we are teaching them the value of working hard through our actions and our words, we might rest assured that we are on the right track.

SIX

Fear of Taking Charge:
Cooperation

not long ago, my wife and I attended a large dinner party with our children. We had not met most of the guests before that night. It was a festive affair, with plentiful food and drink for the adults and games and snacks for the kids. The hosts for the evening were a gregarious and welcoming couple who did their best to make everyone feel relaxed and at home. I met some interesting people, and over dinner we had stimulating conversations about family life and the dilemmas of working parents.

All told, it should have added up to a pleasant evening, and in many ways it did. Yet when I caught my wife's eye about halfway through the night, I could see she was having the same feeling that I was. Most of the adults, comfortably ensconced in the dining and living rooms, seemed either oblivious to or unmoved by the fact that the children were running wild throughout the house. Some of the littlest kids were being picked on or ignored, and the older ones, the eight-, nine-, and ten-year-olds, were busy planning their next attack. They would run from room to room screaming and "capturing" the younger kids, who were then forced to hide from them again. Some of the preschoolers, including our youngest, had wandered off into another room, where they went through the available DVDs, most of which were inappropriate for their age level.

The kids' games were not my real concern, however. They were go-

ing a little too far, but many of them were having a good time and were
not really intending any harm. All they seemed to need were some reminders to play fairly and to stay more under control. But that was the
problem. None of the dozen or so adults gathered at the house seemed
to think this was necessary. They laughed off the interruptions as the
kids came barreling through the rooms without acknowledging the
grown-ups around them. There were a few inquiries into what was going on upstairs, but most of the parents seemed comfortable with a
laissez-faire approach and continued with their conversations. Pre-
dictably, as the night wore on the kids became more brazen and their
behavior continued to escalate.

After one little boy came into the house crying, Sheila, his mother,
went outside to check on the older kids, who were now having a water
gun fight. As she stepped out of the door she was sprayed in the face by
Will, the oldest boy present. She tried not to embarrass him in front of
his friends, but warned him firmly not to do that again. He replied
testily, "Try and make me stop." When she turned to another mother for
assistance, she looked away, saying, "Oh, that's just Will, Rita's son. He's
always like that." Sheila tried humor as a way to engage him, warning
him about the bucket of water she might toss in his direction, but Will
only became angrier and more provocative. Finally the other kids decided to abandon the game, seeing that things were getting a little out of
hand.

I mention this example not to point fingers at any of the parents
present that night. They were all nice people who clearly cared about
their kids. In many ways it was a pretty child-focused evening, with lots
of talk about coaching sports teams, helping with homework, and planning sleepovers. Yet for the most part, these folks were more comfortable talking about parenting then acting like the adults in charge.
There were anxious looks from Will's mother and a few others, but few
of the guests opted to check on their kids or expressed concern at their
play. At one point, my wife and I were teased for seeming overly restric-
tive and a little too concerned with supervising our kids. We laughed off
these comments and went ahead and looked in on them.

I wondered what prevented the other parents from intervening. Was it apathy? A wish to preserve grown-up time? I don't think either answer quite fits. The real hesitance for these and many other parents I meet comes from a fear of taking a strong stand. Nobody these days wants to be the bad guy, to be the one to ruin the kids' (and the adults') fun. Not that plenty of moms and dads don't *think* of doing something, like calling the kids on their behavior or cutting off their teasing. But few parents have the courage to stand up in a group and say, "Hold it!" or "Cut it out" or "Tone it down a little." Instead, it is more common for a kind of groupthink to descend on parents where we shrink back, accept the unpleasantness around us, and keep quiet about it.

The "Liberal" Dilemma

Like most of the dinner guests that evening, I like to think of myself as an open-minded and progressive thinker. I would guess that many of us present that night have similar thoughts about parenting. We want to encourage an open dialogue with our kids and teach them how to express themselves. For many this means doing things differently than their own parents did, and striving for a less punitive and more supportive, nonjudgmental home environment.[1] This style of parenting puts a value on creativity and curiosity over conformity and compliance. Children are meant to be heard and parents are attuned to listen to their opinions, wishes, and concerns.

Child-centered parenting is not, of course, a free ride of unmitigated bliss and engagement. Our kids will still squirt water and run a bit wild and gladly speak their minds but not always listen to us. Parents who adopt a more open family system are likely to feel more anxiety in these moments, to hesitate, or as we saw above, perhaps not act at all. The task is to balance the pendulum, to find meaningful ways to step in, to set limits, to be clear that when it comes down to it, the adults are in charge. It is this balancing act that causes the most stress in parents and inspires the most guilt and second-guessing.

As in many places in life, politics matter here. One dad came to me complaining that his eight-year-old son would not listen to him and was acting out in class. When I asked him to describe his parenting style and goals, he told me he wanted to teach his son to "question authority." Alas, the boy had learned too well for his father's tastes. Another dad described his daughter's attempts to stare down her kindergarten teacher. "She's a bit of a revolutionary, like me," he proudly intoned. After children had scribbled threatening messages about a custodian in one elementary school (including "Death to Stan"), one father stood up at a school meeting and offered, "I told my son it was a good example of self-expression; nobody likes Stan."

These may be extreme examples of liberal thinking gone wild, but many parents who view themselves as independent and rational thinkers subtly and sometimes more openly champion their children's rebelliousness. As a consequence, they are often ambivalent about asserting their own authority, fearing that if they do they will hinder their children's development and limit their ability to think for themselves. Some of these parents worry that if they are too strong with limits their children may become conformists and they may like their kids less. Not surprisingly, parents with these fears can find their way into sticky situations pretty quickly. As a colleague of mine once reminded me, "Idealists don't always make the best parents."

These child-rearing dilemmas have made their way into the parenting literature in the past twenty years, and we now hear frequent debates in the media between the liberal and conservative gurus. In *Raising America*, Ann Hulbert provides keen insight into the ways the two groups have emerged alongside and played off one another. On the left, we have the child-centered theorists, including Stanley Greenspan and T. Berry Brazelton, and on the right, the parent-centered group, led by James Dobson and John Rosemond. In their sound bites and quotations the two factions appear to have radically different visions of how to parent and especially how to discipline children. The backlash movement, led by Dobson and Rosemond, warns against all that warm and fuzzy floor time and nurturing and understanding, and their views on enforcing limits and spanking have gotten considerable airtime in the wake of the reports of children's increasing rudeness and disruptive behavior.[2]

A closer review of the actual texts reveals that the two groups are not always so far apart. Dr. Spock and his descendants do not advocate parenting without discipline, and the conservative thinkers are not against warmth and togetherness at home. But it is the more condensed and circumscribed versions of their views that have trickled down to parents, and we feel that we have to choose sides. I gave a talk to a group of preschool parents in New York a few years ago where I presented many of the ideas in this book. Afterward, a mother came up to me and said enthusiastically, "I really liked what you have to say. And I just heard another psychologist recently who has the same *right-wing* views that you have." I must have looked a little taken aback, as she caught herself and mumbled something about "respect and cooperation and all that."

At a meeting a month later, I gave a similar talk to nursery school teachers. At the end, an experienced, older teacher came up to me and said something that stuck with me: "The values you are talking about are in many ways foreign to our indulgent society; they run counter to our culture. I think we're really talking here about starting another *counterculture* with us teachers holding the flag." It was striking to me to see that the same ideas could elicit such opposite and politically laden reactions. I thought I was merely talking about the "Cornerstones of Child Development" (the actual title of both talks) and reasonable parenting styles. It has become clearer to me over time that how parents identify themselves ideologically has a lot to do with how they behave toward their children.

A quick caveat is warranted here: This is not another critique of liberals. My aim is not to tell parents to stop coddling and get tough with their kids. Most of the parents I meet genuinely try to connect with their children and treat them fairly, and I have no quarrel with their efforts. Instead, my intention is to look more carefully at how values that parents hold dear can, at times, lead to increased fear and anxiety that hamper their ability to act decisively. The goal is to find a bridge between the two poles of the advice industry, so parents do not have to feel hamstrung or worry that they are abandoning their principles if they wish to take charge and reassert their authority.

Wanted: A Rational Child

Some of our favorite cartoons and parodies depict children engaging in some form of outrageous behavior while their parents sit idly by, saying only, "Tell me how you feel." This caricature mocks a way of speaking to children in which overly sensitive parents are too concerned with their kids' emotional reactions and their ideas, and are unable to rein them in when they are misbehaving. I often hear this type of complaint from nursery and kindergarten teachers: "Joe rules the roost; he says and does whatever he wants" one pre-K teacher lamented recently. Such criticism assumes that parents could easily alter their behavior if they were worried less about their children's feelings and were more assertive with them. In my experience, the prescription for change is not nearly so clear.

Sometimes parents' inaction and anxiety stems from having a different temperament from their child. Quiet and unassuming parents who by their nature avoid conflict are more likely to struggle to set limits, and have a more difficult time with intense children of their own. Just as often, however, it is the way parents view their role that complicates matters. Many child-centered parents resort to words first, and calmly try to reason with their children when they act up. It's hard to argue with this position, though it can appear comical when a child is writhing on the sidewalk, and his mother or father leans down and says softly, "Just tell me what's wrong." We all know it's just not going to happen, not then anyway, and these parents would be better off waiting out their child's tantrum or scooping him up and carrying him away.

Looking back, many of us eagerly anticipated the time when our children could speak in full sentences and have a real conversation with us. We thought they would then understand our requests more fully, and perhaps even acknowledge the wisdom of our decision making! As it turned out, at ages two and three they weren't always the most reasonable debaters. At least there was kindergarten to look forward to, or maybe second grade and that seven-year-old "age of reason" we had read about. On it goes, and some of us are still waiting for our kids to get with the program. I do think young children have remarkable ways of using language and can have considerable insight into their own behavior. Yet insight, as some of us well know, is not always enough to bring about change.

Many parents get stuck here. They know that communicating openly is critical to forming relationships with their children and to instilling feelings of respect and dignity in the home. But if having a dialogue is the only option, they soon discover that their playbook is a limited one. On the sidewalk this can be painfully obvious, but many parents who adhere to this school of thought are at a loss when things go awry. I can suggest they speak firmly, cart their kids off to the car, or promptly end an activity if their children do not cooperate. But if this method feels like a radical shift in style, or if they worry about "hurting her feelings," parents are more likely to be filled with anxiety and guilt during moments of confrontation, and to waver in the heat of battle. And hesitating, as we have seen, can be the kiss of death. In these times we see young children's brilliance on display in their ability to read their parents and take control of a situation.

Fear of Anger

This anxiety is particularly acute for parents who try at all costs to avoid getting angry. If staying calm and measured is the essential feature of good parenting to them, then they risk all by stepping out of this role. Parents have been criticized repeatedly for giving in to or indulging their children, but most pundits miss the element of fear in their voices. Many mothers and fathers are concerned about the potential traumatic impact of showing anger in the house or on the street, and fear that taking a strong stand might squash their children's spirit. This is not just the idle worry of the overtherapied set. A generation of parents in this country now struggle to say no. Not long ago *Newsweek* featured a cover story on this topic, and offered advice about "How to Say No to Your Kids."[3]

Jill's dilemma illustrates this point. She came in to consult with me about her youngest son, Dylan, then three and a half. He was doing fine in preschool, but at home was another matter. Dylan refused to get dressed in the morning, wanted only pizza for breakfast, and would not keep his seatbelt buckled in the car. Jill worried that Dylan did not respect her, and was extremely concerned that he often called her "a stupid mommy" when he was frustrated. Jill assured me that she "always used a calm voice, and got down to their level" when talking to her children. This style had worked well for her older son and daughter, six and five, respectively, and they almost always responded to her requests right away. Before her struggles with Dylan, Jill had been suspicious of other parents who did not enjoy her success, and had assumed they "must not be talking to their kids the right way."

Jill was a dedicated and caring parent. I had seen her in action with all her children and she did, indeed, know how to talk to them; she *was* firm and warm at the same time. But Jill was now faced with a third child who had a much more challenging temperament and did not respond willingly to her reasonable requests. We discussed how she could start with firm instructions for Dylan ("You need to clean up *now*"; "We are leaving for school in five minutes"), but that she should anticipate that he would have difficulty with transitions and direct commands. I also suggested that it was okay if she got frustrated with her son from time to time. Jill eventually found some relief as she learned to tolerate his anger, as well as her own, and allowed his tantrums to play out without too much talking. Dylan was three years old, after all, and she came to realize that much of his behavior was age appropriate, if different from his siblings.

Buying Peace and Quiet

For Jill, talking rationally had always seemed to be the best method for avoiding angry confrontations. Other parents hope that if their children are comfortable and well cared for, there will be less need to place limits on them and deal with their frustration. All the talk of our indulgent age sometimes misses this point. It's not just that children are spoiled or that parents are seeking to buy their affection or to replace family time with material goods, or provide luxuries and experiences that were denied to them in their own families. Parents often give in to children's requests for more stuff because they don't want to fight with them or lose their patience. At the end of a long day or tense week, few of us want to be the naysayers. We just want to get along with our kids, to relax and have fun with them.

Parents don't always think twice about their children's requests or their implications. We can forget that kids are supposed to ask for toys and games and treats. That's more or less their job; it doesn't mean they are entitled. (I want everything in Toys "R" Us and Best Buy too!) But our job is to teach them to delay gratification, to wait their turn, and to know that in due course their time will come, even if we can afford to do things differently. "Uh-uh" comes the reply, "I want it now!" Many parents are disinclined to do battle in these moments and, whether begrudgingly or not, give in to their children's immediate demands more often than they would like. Sometimes they do so with a caveat ("Okay, you can have candy this one time; please don't ask me again"), but their kids know better than to take those words seriously.

We are, of course, not just talking about the old trinkets and toys, the dolls and trucks and action figures of our youth. Today's kids are on a fast track to having the best and most up-to-date accessories. Given the rapid pace of the last few years, who doubts that we'll see iPods and cell phones in nursery school backpacks sometime soon? There appear to be few limits to what we will agree to buy to stop the arguing with our kids and avoid a confrontation with them, especially in public. The Game Boys, the PSPs, the motor scooters, the American Girl dolls, the designer clothes—we could go on and on with a list of expensive and sophisticated consumer goods that kids have learned to crave and expect from a young age.

In the end it is not really about the stuff. My primary concern is the loss of connection to reality that plagues many families. If children know they can get what they want by whining and demanding, and that they can play this trump card when their parents are vulnerable, how do they learn to respect their parents' authority or pay them much mind at all for that matter ("But you promised I could get it *today!*")? If keeping things amicable means giving in, what purpose does all the family harmony and togetherness really serve? If we are primarily interested in avoiding bad feelings in our kids and ourselves, how do we teach them to cope with struggle and adversity and to deal with limits? These are not rhetorical questions, and we will return to them in detail later in this chapter.

Grades Over Manners

There is one other reason why parents do not always focus on teaching respect and avoid taking charge of their kids. In many homes, it has become a question of priorities, of first things first. We used to think of the early years as a time when children learned to be socialized. This meant not only learning to make friends, but becoming aware of the larger expectations for behavior in our culture. Some of this involves old-fashioned manners; saying please and thank you, not talking with your mouth full, not interrupting while others are talking, listening when being spoken to by adults. Today, with all the worry about children's academic standing and the push to develop a keen mind from an early age, these social skills sometimes take a backseat.

In my experience, few parents consciously deemphasize the more traditional values of early childhood, but many are not as tuned in to fostering respect and self-discipline as they are to encouraging their children's intelligence. When it comes to reading to our young kids, teaching them to be computer literate, practicing counting and forming letters, most parents are pretty well up to snuff. If children start to falter in any of these areas, they usually stay on top of the problem. I often hear anxious mothers and fathers talk about their children's academic delays and the impact these may have on their child's self-esteem.

It may take considerable prompting from me, however, to hear about their child's strengths: "Oh, yes, he is a nice kid, a good listener, I always hear he's a pleasure to have on a playdate." If the situation is reversed, if a child is sailing along academically but is behind the curve in learning how to get along with other children and cooperate with adults, parents tend to show less concern. They may believe that their child's advanced academic standing and "intellectual curiosity" are the reasons that he or she has difficulty listening to teachers or following rules, and they may feel little urgency to address these difficulties.

A Risky Business

Some fifteen years ago, the essay "All I Really Need to Know I Learned in Kindergarten" by Robert Fulghum drew quite a bit of attention.[4] With a whimsical style, Fulghum described how by the age of five he had learned to depend on others, to share, and to play fairly, and how these lessons had served him well for his entire life. Somehow, despite the popularity of these notions just a short time ago, it seems as if we have lost sight of his message. We now have the proverbial cart before the horse, and live in a society where early academic prowess and enrichment take precedence over the social skills described so playfully in this essay. This predicament has sounded alarms in the child development and academic communities, and most researchers argue that *social and emotional competence* are in fact the critical features of learning readiness for children entering kindergarten.[5]

Mental health professionals also worry about the diagnostic implications for "advanced" and indulged children who have learned to take control and to flout authority at a young age. Some of them will likely remain self-centered as they get older, and have difficulty accepting help from adults. Others are at risk for developing more serious narcissistic personality problems. They may have difficulty forming genuine relationships and learn to treat people as a means to an end. Narcissists tend to bristle at any criticism and act as if they are in complete control, although remaining vulnerable and insecure beneath their brash exterior. This is a particularly dangerous combination in adolescence.[6]

Those of us in clinical practice have seen a disturbing trend in elementary-age children who have not mastered certain social skills, especially kids who have little self-control and respect for rules. Many of them enter school with a disregard for its basic paradigm: that the teachers are there to teach and they are there to listen and learn. Despite the fact that schools do have a much more interactive curriculum than they did twenty or thirty years ago, most teachers still expect a reasonable amount of cooperation and respect from their students by the first grade.

I often hear from parents after what I call the "second grade crash." Suddenly, or so it seems, their son's or daughter's behavior that had once been viewed as "sassy" and "charming" is no longer cute. Now their child is viewed as rude or obnoxious, and as interfering with the learning going on in class. Instead of eliciting snickers from his friends and the occasional groan from the teacher, he is sent out of the room or to the principal's office.

Take the case of Charlie, a seven-year-old boy in private school. He had always been precocious and witty, and was always one step away from trouble in nursery school and kindergarten. Charlie loved to push the envelope with adults and demonstrate his cleverness. This time he had gone too far. Charlie had told his teacher she had "hairy armpits," much to her chagrin but to the delight of some of his classmates. When he came to my office, Charlie did not understand what all the fuss was about. He had apologized, and what was the big deal anyway, he had always teased his teachers and the other adults he knew. He meant no harm. It took some time for Charlie to understand that listening to adults and seeking their help and guidance did not make him any less smart. Treating them with respect was also far more likely to give him the positive attention he craved.

Fortunately for Charlie, his parents recognized that he no longer accepted their authority and the school's rules, and was in danger of becoming a more serious discipline problem. They began to expect him to treat people differently at home and in school, and were serious about following through. "Charlie, cut out the sassiness" became their mantra, and he knew this was a signal to curtail his wisecracks and listen to grown-ups.

With parents of younger children it is sometimes harder to make an impression. I had one pre-K teacher come to me in distress after a conference with a set of parents. She had just told them about their daughter Angie's escalating behavior, which culminated in her spitting and kicking the teacher the previous day. Angie's parents listened politely, and then her mother suggested to the teacher, "You and my daughter seem to have a personality conflict."

Four-year-old Jasmine was referred to me by her school after a series of bullying incidents and a number of threats of violence toward her teachers. After I evaluated her and reported to her parents that Jasmine was very angry and often felt out of control, they remained nonplussed. Yes, they were concerned and would take my recommendations into account, but they really thought that the upcoming kindergarten year would be good for her. She would finally be "challenged" by teachers who really "understood" her, and they suspected this would mitigate her negative behavior. I never heard back from Jasmine's parents. Things might have turned out fine for their daughter, but from my perspective they were taking a big risk.[7]

Future Shock

Jasmine's parents were more focused on the here and now and the short-term consequences of her behavior. In that sense, they are far from alone. In the hustle and bustle of working and raising young children, few parents find it easy to look ahead a few years to imagine what the future will hold for their children. When I sit down with nursery school parents, I often tell them stories about older children to try to help them visualize the next phase and to think beyond their children's academic prospects. I may mention twelve-year-old Tom, who had adopted his father's confrontational style and had in the process alienated most of his middle school teachers. There was Jack, another son of "question authority" parents, who in eighth grade had unleashed his anger at school and barely hid his contempt for his teachers.

Childhood is a progression. As parents, we have to deal with the immediate concerns and conflicts, while trying to keep one eye on the horizon. If we believe that gaining a reasonable measure of self-control and learning to cooperate in groups are pretty important social skills for kids as they grow into young adults, we may put more of our effort into encouraging these traits when they are young. If we recognize that unbridled anger and hostility toward authority figures are likely to bring serious consequences down the line, we should look for ways to teach our preschoolers and elementary-age children to be respectful as well as assertive.

There is another story I like to tell. A few years ago there was an extreme case of binge drinking at a high school dance in a local town. Nearly a third of the six hundred or so students present were reported to have been drinking heavily, and nearly two dozen students had to be taken to the hospital with cases of alcohol poisoning, including several ninth grade girls. Realizing things had gotten out of hand, the adult chaperones made plans to curtail the evening and to contact many of the students' parents.

A number of kids who were present told me versions of the story, and they all described one episode that was most telling. At one point the principal of the high school came onstage and informed the kids of his decision to end the dance, and spoke briefly about the outlandish behavior he had witnessed that evening. Each of the kids reported a similar version of what happened next: None of the teens present paid much attention to the principal, and continued on talking and joking and doing what they were doing. They were unmoved by his strong statements. To me, the students' blatant disregard for the ultimate authority at school, more than their drinking, was the saddest part of that evening.

A week later, the principal and the school superintendent lamented in the local paper about the failed attempts to get kids to see the seriousness of their behavior. Every year they had tried a different program to curb the binge drinking at their school, from model curriculums, to lectures from substance abuse counselors, to attempts to scare the kids straight with movies of accident victims, and stories of brain damage resulting from drug and alcohol use. Nothing, it seemed, had ever had much impact on the students. The school administrators were deeply troubled that the uproar from local parents had more to do with the suspensions levied on students and how this might look on their college applications than their excessive behavior that evening.

My response to this principal and message to the parents of nursery school children is fairly simple: Of course it hasn't worked. You cannot teach kids self-control and discipline and respect for authority at age fourteen or fifteen or sixteen. By then it is way too late. We can't expect the schools to take on a role that parents have not adopted, especially if the focus at home is on excelling in academics, not building character. This is no less true in the early years. Though teaching social skills and togetherness is part of the mission of most preschools and kindergartens, it is not solely the teachers' job to help children to listen and respect adults. If we do not start down this road by the time our kids are two or three or four, we risk courting disaster just a few years later.

A Voice from the Past

So what can we do to avoid that second grade crash and set the tone in the early years? Let's revisit the discipline methods of our parent's generation to see what is worth salvaging. First a word on spanking. Many parents come to me claiming that spanking is the only thing they can think of that might get their kids to listen. They remember it had an impact on them and they are tempted to go this route, but they are not sure it's really worth it. They feel guilty when they have gotten physical and worry about the psychological impact on their kids.

My advice: Don't make spanking a regular part of your discipline routine. There are three different reasons I am wary on this point. First, spanking is no longer generally accepted in our culture and our kids know that from a pretty young age. I have heard a number of stories of preschoolers threatening to report their parents to social services or arguing that hitting is "illegal," and this makes for a convoluted cycle of control and authority at home. Second, most of us are ambivalent about using force and feel bad when we strike our children, and our kids know that. We often end up apologizing to our kids, and their original behavior that led to the confrontation gets lost in the mix. Most importantly, we may feel that we are being judicious and restrained when we use physical punishment, but kids have heard over and over from their teachers (and in many cases, from their parents) that any hitting is a sign of being out of control. If we are trying to teach children to stay in control, we are on pretty shaky ground when we spank them. Recent research that links frequent spanking with increased aggressive behavior in children should also give us pause.[8]

Back now to the "good old days" for a moment. Much has been made about the false idol of nostalgia, and we have to be careful not to condone previous generations' use of fear and coercion to get kids to listen. But there were some generally accepted social mores that are worth revisiting. First, the basic assumption of school and of adult/child relations in general was more or less accepted by children. Like it or not they had to listen and respect the boundaries of the adult world, especially in the world outside the home.

Threatening an unfamiliar adult with a water gun or a snowball would have brought an angry response at one time. Many of us, in fact, purposely pushed these limits, knowing that if we hit a passing car with a well-timed snowball its occupant would stop and chase and scold us if we were apprehended. That was the whole point, and in many ways it reaffirmed that we kids were different from the adults.

This brings me to what I like to call the "Other People's Kids" dilemma. Not long ago, few adults would hesitate to reprimand neighborhood kids for obvious infractions. If you hurt somebody or purposely broke a toy or vandalized property, children expected to hear about it from nearby grown-ups, and the presence of any adults was often enough to dissuade us from going too far. Some of us still cringe at the words we heard when we were kids: "I'm going inside to call your parents." We knew what would be waiting on the other end of the phone. We might not have been happy, but we were not shocked when somebody else's parents or a neighbor stepped in to discipline us.

Today even simple admonishments to other people's kids can bring angst-ridden moments. Few parents feel they are on solid ground when they speak to their friends' children or their kids' classmates about excessive roughhousing or teasing. Many of the parents I know avoid the after-school playground or school yard games because they do not want to be in a position to speak out to another child. Too many times parents, and especially mothers, feel they are subject to angry stares themselves or rationalizations from parents—"He's tired," "Just a little cranky today, I guess"—that disavow the inappropriate behavior they have witnessed and their attempts to intervene. As a result, parents often feel handcuffed and anxious in public settings, and can come to feel that there are no longer universally accepted limits on behavior for young children.

I spoke in chapter 3 of the courage that it takes to be a parent. These are the moments when this virtue is given a pretty mighty test. To speak up, to risk drawing the ire of other mothers and fathers, takes a good deal of fortitude these days. There are ways to do this that make it more palatable. We don't want to be seen as protecting only our own child and scolding another. Often it is more appropriate to say something like this: "Hey, guys, that's a little too rough, why don't you all choose another game." Or, "Come on, kids, let's not leave anybody out." If we can remain firm but respectful to both the children and their parents, we have an opportunity to not only stop the immediate behavior but also serve as a model for other parents who may be struggling with the same issue.

Parents, Not Punishers

There is one other lesson from the near past that bears repeating. As one of the mothers I worked with for a long time finally concluded, "My first job is to be their parent not their friend." This seems like such an obvious and trivial statement of fact, but it sums up the main problem in many families. We want to be close to our kids, we want to be their buddies, but when it comes down to it, we need to be the adults in charge.

We have to be careful not to be lulled into the oversophistication trap with our soon-to-be rational children. Too much of a role in decision making (including deciding on their own punishments!) only tends to make kids more anxious. Despite their obvious displeasure at limits, most kids experience a sense of relief when their parents are clear, concise, and consistent in making decisions. A few choice words can sometimes be enough: "If you hit your brother, you will go to your room"; "If your don't clean up your toys, there will be no TV for the night."

Being an authority figure does not mean being authoritarian. Learning to be an effective parent is not an invitation to abuse our power or to act in an overly harsh manner. We do not have license to strike back at our kids when they are "nasty" or "mean" to us. I have heard more than a few parents who describe their kids in these terms, and report giving as good as they get. One mother who found no other way to reach her five-year-old son resorted to biting him on the foot in retaliation for a wound he had inflicted on his little brother. Others angrily report that their children are "lying and stealing" or "manipulative." These judgments are not only value laden and unduly critical when applied to young children, they also imply that our kids have a great deal of control over us. After all, somebody has to *be* manipulated for that label to stick.

Our kids need limits and to understand that there are a few rules they have to conform to. But if we implement discipline in a manner that is hostile and rejecting, we may meet our short-term goal of getting our children to listen, but at great cost to their ongoing relationship with us and their self-esteem. These are, however, not incompatible goals. Research shows, in fact, that children who live in homes with clearer rules and limits have *higher* self-esteem.[9] Our task, and it is a challenging one, is to find a way to be effective and clear without sacrificing the warmth and comfort of our home lives that we treasure.

Teaching Respect and Cooperation at Home

Use Clear and Direct Language

In chapter 3, we discussed the merits of confident parenting, of letting our children know that we are not afraid to assert our authority. Being comfortable adopting a "business" tone of voice is essential to this process, as is developing the capacity to deliver clear, dispassionate messages about the behavior we expect from our kids. Our children need to understand that certain things are not optional, nor are they up for discussion. Simple commands will often suffice: "It's time to go upstairs and brush your teeth"; "Put your shoes on, we're leaving in five minutes." The goal is not to be the constant taskmaster, but to provide a clear message of what is essential and what is not. Sometimes it means emphasizing "when" not "if," as in, "When you get dressed and have breakfast, you can play with your new action figures." Most of us could benefit from worrying less about how our kids will feel about these dictates, especially if we balance them with warm exchanges throughout the day.

Adopt a Signal That You Mean Business

For many mothers and fathers, especially those who find that switching to a business tone is a struggle, it is helpful to have a prearranged signal that informs their kids that they are serious. The "1-2-3 Magic" approach popularized in the book of the same title by Thomas Phelan is a good example, and its success lies in its underlying simplicity and easy-to-follow strategies.[10] Parents are instructed to start counting, without emotion or discussion, when they witness difficult behavior, having previously informed their child that there will be a consequence if they get to "3." I have seen countless parents who report that nothing else works, but when they start counting the kids seem to perk up and take notice. For the first time, many parents feel they have a real playbook, or at least the start of one. Success begets success, and many feel committed to sticking with the counting strategy as a way to jump-start their kids and keep them on task.

Follow Through on Requests

The problem with any parenting strategy, unfortunately, is that the kids figure things out pretty quickly. They may hustle upstairs to the bathroom on "2," but then what? In time they often learn to go through the motions of complying with our requests, without really acceding to our wishes so readily. We still have to follow after them and check to see that they did brush their teeth and wipe their faces. Homework will not suddenly be neatly and fully executed without some checking from parents. We're back again to consistency, follow-through, and endurance.

This can't be just one parent's job. If Mom has worked hard to get the kids fed and dressed for bed and settled and Dad comes home to play at eight; the best-laid plans and routines can quickly go south. If he is a little less focused on the business that has to happen at bedtime, the kids may learn to take those rules less seriously. (Sometimes it seems that in a generation mothers have gone from "Wait till Daddy comes home!" to "Oh, no, *Mr. Fun Guy* is here.") Kids need to see that both of their parents are committed to getting them to cooperate and do what they need to do.

The Power of Privileges

A joint effort, consistency, and reasonable signals to our kids are all important aspects of teaching kids to cooperate. These are not enough. To really be effective, we have to let the kids know that they have some "skin in the game." Pleasing their parents and feeling good about doing well are ways to entice our more cooperative sons and daughters. Most kids, however, need to know that there are a few other things at stake. To start with, we may have to reorient them, and point out that access to TV, video games, fancy toys, treats, playdates, and leisure activities are not entitlements! They are, lo and behold, *privileges*. And privileges are to be earned; they are not God-given rights. Before being allowed privileges, kids have to take care of their responsibilities.

A number of years ago a mother of five- and seven-year-old boys came to me with a list of complaints about her children, foremost being that "the TV seems to always be on in my house." I thought perhaps some genie had control of the clicker or that there must be some bizarre malfunction in her equipment, but alas, that turned out not to be the case! I could replay dozens of similar conversations that speak to this feeling of powerlessness over the things our children possess and the way they spend their time. Whether we worry about their fragile psyches, or if they will keep up with their peers, or what else they might do if they are not occupied, we seem reluctant to make their access to fun activities contingent upon their behavior.

Therein lies the rub. If our kids know that when it comes down to it, at the end of the day they are still going to do and get what they want, that they can play their computer games and watch television and go out with friends no matter what happens, why should they listen to us? If trips to the ice-cream shop are a regular Friday afternoon treat, no matter how they have behaved with us the previous few days, what message are we sending them? If we have plans for ice skating as a family on Saturday afternoon that we would not reconsider no matter if they fail to clean up their toys or are rude and disrespectful that morning, what motivation do they have to change their behavior?

Again, we have to be clear and straightforward with children, and use language that connects their privileges to taking care of business. Here are a few statements to try out with young kids: "Help me clean up your room; then we can go to the park"; "If you behave on our errands, you can have a lollipop at the dry cleaners"; "Come to the dinner table without a fuss, and we can play a game after dinner." These are all short and sweet, but convey a clear message: "I expect you to listen and cooperate with me, and if you do, you will have more options to have fun or earn a treat." I have no illusions that words are enough, of course. But we need to start somewhere, and practicing being clear and on point is the first step to getting our kids to do what we want.

Chores and Pitching In at Home

Kids should have fun playing with their toys and have the chance to go on outings with their parents and see their friends for playdates. These are all good things. We should not expect kids to work all the time, or to be little busy bees helping their parents do chores all day. That said, children can understand that they do have responsibilities, and we can expect them to be helpful and to chip in at home. From the age of two or three kids can learn to put their clothes in the hamper, to clean up their toys, to help bring in the food at mealtime, and to clear their plates from the table. Most of them learned to do all this and more in pre-school, and indeed three- and four-year-olds often fight over who is going to get what job there! School-age children should be finishing their homework before dinner without too much help from us. It is also not too far afield to expect young kids to help sweep or clean their rooms every week, or to help tend the garden or rake the yard.

In his review of trends in twentieth-century parenting, Peter Stearns reports that the amount of household chores performed by children declined significantly in the past few generations due to several factors. Concerns about children's welfare and vulnerability had a role in this reduction, as did the overall decrease in labor-intensive household tasks in the era of modern appliances and suburban living. Over time parents wanted children to focus more on schoolwork and less on chores, partly because it was "easier" for parents (still mothers, mostly) to do things themselves. Children were no longer thought to be capable of measuring up to the new standards of cleanliness and organization in the home. More subtly, menial tasks came to be devalued in many middle-class homes, and parents themselves looked for ways to be free of doing laundry, house cleaning, yard work, and other jobs that had previously been shared with children. As more household tasks were outsourced it was harder to argue that chores were essential for kids, or that making a contribution to the family's basic functioning served a real purpose for them.[11]

I mention this recent history because it speaks to our ambivalence over how involved our children should be in working at home. After all,

On Take Your Child to Work Day a few years back, my son, who was eight at the time, accompanied me to a nursery school where I was a consultant. We sat in on a class for three-year-olds where the teacher was handing out jobs. At one point he was trying hard to get my attention, though I told him we would have to wait until we left the room to discuss his observations. When we finally had a moment alone, he blurted out, "Dad, they have it all wrong! Don't they realize you're supposed to have two line leaders in the threes class?" He could see that I didn't understand his certainty on the issue. "Don't you remember when I was in the threes? We definitely had two line leaders." I was flabbergasted. After five years, my son could still name all the available jobs in his preschool class and which ones he preferred most. I like to recall this moment when parents ask me if all this hard work and "job business" in the early years really leaves an impression.

it is hard to ask them to do the things that we don't want to do ourselves. As they get older, they are much more likely to sniff out signs of hypocrisy. A mother of a sixteen-year-old boy once asked me to raise the issue of chores with him, specifically making his bed, which she felt he was resisting in an unreasonable way. When I mentioned it to him, he sat up and asked slyly, "Did you ask her if she made *her* bed today?" Younger kids are not likely to be so direct, but they will detect signs of weakness. They might point out the amount of schoolwork they have to do or the playdate they are dying to have to avoid taking care of their in-house business. Take six-year-old Mark, who was supposed to make his bed and clean up his toys on his days off. His parents were stymied when he refused to do his job on Columbus Day: "It's a Monday, not a weekend," he righteously replied.

My purpose here is not to make a strong case for chores per se, but for parents to consider a framework in which children have a commitment to the family as a whole. As a friend of mine likes to say, children can learn early on to be part of the solution, not just part of the problem. If we get stuck on their performing one specific task, say making their beds, we may lose sight of the larger picture, that children can (and often want to) be helpful and can learn to appreciate that they make a real contribution to the family. If we adopt a model of the family as a working unit, the idea of responsibilities and privileges will make much more sense to kids. When we are all in it together, each person has a role to fill and each one of us benefits from the support and hard work of the other members of the family.

Expect and Enforce Reasonable Behavior at Home and in Public

As I mentioned above, caring for their things, completing schoolwork in a timely manner, and helping in the kitchen are important duties for kids. So are helping out with the care of younger siblings and pitching in when someone in the family is ill. Perhaps the most significant way that children can earn their keep and their privileges is by acting in a reasonable manner. For starters this means being respectful to their parents and other adults. Pretty basic stuff, but the behavior I witness in the supermarket, at school, and in my waiting room suggests that many young children have not gotten this message.

Let's take the case of five-year-old Nathaniel, the son of recent European immigrants. Although he was doing pretty well in the latter half of his pre-K year in school, he was by all reports a holy terror at home. He refused to listen to his mother's directives, and would not get dressed in the morning or go to bed in the evening. Nathaniel spoke to his mother in a rude and angry voice most of the time, and would lash out at her if he was unhappy with her suggestions. At the time, his father was working two jobs and was not at home much, but when he was available, Nathaniel was no more responsive to him.

I gave Nathaniel's mother a few suggestions. First I recommended that she limit all access to television. He had grown accustomed to watching TV whenever he pleased, and he had recently received a small set for his room. Nathaniel was also getting into frequent skirmishes on the playground after school and refusing to leave when his mother called for him. I recommended that until further notice, they avoid the playground, and that they return only after Nathaniel made a genuine pledge to respond to his mother's time limits there. In this way, I hoped that Nathaniel would get the message that these two activities he enjoyed were privileges and that he could earn them back as he started to behave in a more age-appropriate way. His mother found this to be a pretty straightforward and concrete plan, and she made a commitment not to give in to him. We met periodically over the next few months, and though her son was still a handful, Nathaniel's mother began to feel like she had some control over him.

With smaller problems, situational interventions will often do nicely. Cathy complained that her three- and five-year-old were getting very hyped up before Christmas, and had lately been ignoring her and fighting with each other all the time. I asked her about their family traditions during this season, and she told me her kids loved to bake cookies with her and to tour the neighborhood to look at holiday lights in the evening. Fine, I said, "Make those the privileges that they can earn each day or two if they are good listeners." Amanda complained that each trip to town with her three-year-old ended in a tantrum on the street. I suggested she make plans for a quick outing together for hot chocolate at the end of their errands, but only if her daughter behaved pretty well in the other stores.

The point is not to discover hidden magical solutions to children's difficult behaviors. Often it is the simple pleasures, and time with their parents in particular, that we can hold out as rewards for a job well done or a day or two of relative harmony at home. "Relative" is a key word here. I expect that young children will whine and have tantrums, and I know they are prone to falling apart when they're tired and hungry. When targeting behaviors to change, we want to be realistic and specific, and not make blanket statements about their mood or willingness to comply. I often chalk the latter up to "attitude," and I am more willing to ignore their snarls and harrumphing if they eventually do follow through on what is expected (a reminder that bears repeating when they reach adolescence!).

Using Behavior Charts

Sometimes it is worth putting our expectations in writing, and a behavior chart can be a helpful way to jump-start a process of change. Listing three or four specific, positive behaviors that we would like to see (and putting a weekly chart on the fridge or on the kids' bedroom door) helps to orient children, and lets them know that we will be paying close attention at certain times of the day. Parents may choose to focus on getting dressed in the morning or brushing teeth and staying in bed at night. Coming to the dinner table without too much of a fight might be on the list, or cleaning up toys before beginning the nighttime routine.

We may speak about behavior in more global terms ("Speaking respectfully to Mom and Dad"; "Playing nicely with my brother"), but we need to be clear about what that means in action ("Not screaming and saying 'I hate you'"; "Not slugging him or pushing him down"). Again, perfection is not the goal, but we can expect kids to make a reasonable effort to change their ways. If they meet the criteria we have established, like getting checks for three or four good behaviors, they earn a sticker for that day that can be traded in for rewards immediately or at a later date. In my experience, charts can be effective for four to six weeks if everyone stays committed. After that, they tend to gradually lose their meaning, but by then parents can reasonably expect that their children's positive behaviors have become more internalized.

Logical Rewards and Consequences

The rewards for good behavior need to be clear. Sometimes it involves access to television or video games or other previous entitlements that have since been limited. It helps when the rewards have a logical connection to the behavior in question. When four-year-old Henry refused to clean up his favorite train set, I suggested to his mother that she put it in the attic for a while until he could demonstrate that he was able to keep his toys neat and respect time limits on playing with them. Six-year-old Emma was having a lot of difficulty on playdates, refusing to share and speaking disrespectfully to her sitter and other mothers. Despite her mother's reluctance, I encouraged her to inform her daughter that she would not be scheduling playdates for at least two weeks, and that Emma would have to demonstrate that she could speak respectfully to the adults at home before she could again visit another child's house.

Using rewards for good behavior can seem unduly harsh to parents, especially if they feel that their children now have to earn experiences that they want them to have. Playdates are a prime example of this, and many mothers and fathers who worry about their children's social skills do not want to put these in jeopardy. This despite the fact that their children are often motivated to see their friends and are more likely to respond to their parents' requests when playtimes lie in the balance. Participation in sports is another good example, as many parents do not want to hinder their children's athletic progress. I do not suggest that this be the carrot for a child who is hesitant to play and already ambivalent about his skills. But for the more gung-ho competitors, connecting playing time to their home behavior can make a marked difference in their level of cooperation and compliance.

I generally prefer that parents avoid holding out new trinkets or toys or money as rewards, as that can make everyone feel that good behavior is more of an economic transaction or, worse, bribery. I do, however, encourage parents to use dedicated time with their kids as incentives for good behavior. This can include going for ice cream with Mom, or going to the diner with Dad on Saturday mornings if they have had three or four Gold Star days. Children at ages three and four often benefit from more immediate privileges, say, earning an extra book in the evening or playing a special tickling game with Dad when he comes home. We cannot, of course, take them for ice cream or dispense these special treats at other points in the week, as that would defeat our purpose. The goal is to impress upon our kids that they can earn more fun times with us as they cooperate more, and that we will be willing to celebrate their efforts with a cup of hot chocolate or an extra trip to the park. These outings provide a concrete way to toast their progress and hard work, much like adults do when a friend receives a promotion or a spouse completes a large project at the office.

Help from Other Adults

We should feel free to leverage other important adults in this process, particularly our children's teachers. In my mind, getting dressed and making the bus is part of a child's school responsibilities, and it makes sense to ask teachers to help monitor our kids' progress in meeting these expectations. Sometimes a simple admonishment from a different trusted adult can hold sway when children will not listen to their parents, and most early elementary teachers I know are experts at embellishing: "I'm shocked, Amanda; you love school and I thought you were always here on time. Your mother told me you were working on getting dressed yourself."

These few words can cut right to the chase, and as we so often see, our children seem to behave better when compelled by the adults in school than by the folks at home. (Not, of course, that we would want it to be the other way around, would we?) Nathaniel's teacher was more than willing to ask him how his mornings had gone at home, and she worked hard to help his mother reclaim her authority with him. Religious figures, grandmothers, even police officers, can play a role in helping our children understand that we mean business. More than one mother has told me the story of how a quick drive by the local precinct house was enough to remind her preschooler to never again fight over buckling his seatbelt. After all, it's the law!

Do as I Say or Do as I Do?

I mentioned above that the goal of teaching discipline is ultimately not compliance, but to help children develop self-respect and self-control. Parental rules and limits provide the external structure that children can gradually imitate and internalize to gain more control over their more unruly impulses. This is a difficult task these days, especially for boys. Yet clear expectations, consistency, and rewards for good behavior do not guarantee that our kids will eventually get beyond a "law and order" sense of right and wrong. Too many children learn how to play the game, and how to feign compliance and deference without taking it seriously or paying these ideas much mind once the adults are out of the room.

The bottom line: If we really want our kids to be respectful we have to model this behavior for them. There is no substitute. Other adults are important in our children's lives as we have just seen, but first and foremost kids look to their mothers and fathers for examples and directions on how to behave. If we insist on being treated with respect, but do not return the favor to our children and our spouses, our kids will quickly discover that we do not mean what we say and we value respect and cooperation in name only. Our children are always watching us, listening to our tone, picking up hints of contempt. "My dad is always being facetious" said eight-year-old Matthew, not really understanding the words he was using but well aware of his father's sarcasm and penchant for criticism.

Over and over we hear that our children are more influenced by our actions than our words, but at times we seem oblivious to this idea. When a five-year-old tells me, "I can fire my babysitter any time I want" he may be overempowered, but he is probably also imitating his parents' limited commitment to his caretaker. When parents disrespect babysitters, nannies, and teachers they not only lose potential allies in the battle to gain control in their homes, but they also send the message that these other adults are not really to be taken seriously. If I hear this repeated by a young child, as in "My mom and I agree my teacher is way too strict," I know we have our hands full.

I remember a supervisor of mine telling me years ago, "Don't ever park in the handicapped space," as a way of illustrating the power of parental modeling. We can translate this pretty broadly for parents: Obey the rules, respect other authority figures, treat people the way you would like to be treated. Let your children know that these things matter to you. If there is one thing parents should take special care to root out at a young age, it is disrespect for other people, no matter what their

Children should respect their teachers and not feel they can criticize them at will. That said, it does not mean that parents and kids can't have legitimate issues with teachers and other adults. A particular adult may be too strict or not that nice. Parents have every right to validate the way their kids feel in these situations, but they have to be careful not to give them too much authority to complain or intervene. If things are too far out of line, the adults involved need to work to straighten things out. Children need reassurance that their views are being heard at home and that their parents will find an appropriate forum to express them. They also need to know that it is still their job to treat the adults involved with respect and kindness.

limitations. We might all learn from the example of Wellington Mara, the late owner of the New York Giants, who was widely admired by his peers and his employees. He once gave the following reply to a sportswriter who had criticized his background:

I'll tell you what you can expect from an Irishman named Wellington whose father was a bookmaker. You can expect that anything he says or writes may be repeated in your own home in front of your children. You can believe that he was taught to love and respect all mankind, but to fear no man.

It is perhaps easy to dismiss such words as part of the quaint eloquence of a bygone era, politely repeated in eulogies but without much relevance today. Yet for those of us who want to do things a little differently and reinvest in the notion of teaching respect for other people to our children, they may serve as a catalyst to measure our own capacity for decency and goodwill, and our willingness to put our virtues to the test.

seven

Fear of Slowing Down: Mindfulness

for many readers, the title of the last chapter probably made intuitive sense. Worries about how to get kids to listen and cooperate are pretty commonplace. We now have *Nanny 911* and a whole reality TV genre dedicated to teaching parents to take charge at home. But "fear of slowing down" sounds more puzzling. Why exactly would we want to slow down? Didn't we talk earlier of having endurance and keeping up with the pace of family life? Isn't a large part of our job to teach our kids to keep up, and get them to adapt to the hard-charging world where the most active, involved, and competitive succeed? Isn't that what we're really worried about?

I will try to answer these questions in this chapter and offer some insights into what it means to slow down and why it matters. I am not suggesting we stop doing everything and adopt a rustic, carefree, or slacker lifestyle. That's not reality for most of us, even if we wanted it to be. As parents we have financial and family demands that we cannot easily escape or ignore. I am, however, advocating that we find more balance in our lives. We could all benefit from feeling less pressure to do it all. Again and again I see the strain on parents of young kids who feel compelled to do more and wish to do less. I also believe that there is intrinsic value in teaching our kids to be calm and focused and mindful. Later in this section we will explore how children's reliance on electronic games and television affects their ability to slow down.

First let me relate a conversation that Linda, a colleague of mine, recently had with a close friend of hers I'll call Cassandra. A proud mother, Cassandra glowingly described how adept her teenage son was at multitasking. In one sitting he could write a paper, instant-message friends, check his e-mails, listen to music, and answer the occasional call to his cell phone. She could not imagine having absorbed and mastered all that technology when she was her son's age. What impressed Cassandra the most was his ability to nonchalantly integrate and process all this information at the same time.

Linda kept silent. But her thoughts drifted to the college students in her practice, tense and overstressed adolescents who are incapable of detaching themselves from their electronic accoutrements for more than a short time. Sometimes Linda gives them assignments to take a walk, to spend some time alone. One sophomore happily reported that she had done just that. When asked to tell the details she hesitated a bit. "Well, I was talking on my cell phone most of the time." That's progress; Linda knows it is slow going to get college kids to change their lifestyles and slow down their pace. Linda thought about this as she listened to Cassandra and wondered what lay in store for her son in the next few years.

The Technophile Generation

Most parents can relate to Cassandra's optimism. Realizing that information is coming at us at a fast and furious pace, we feel our kids need to keep ahead of the game, to adapt and manage all this data or be blitzkrieged by it. We try to give our children a leg up from an early age, to teach them how to use available technology to process and store information and shortcut and enhance the learning process. After all, BlackBerrys, cell phones, and computers have helped make many of us more productive and efficient, and allowed us to stay connected no matter where we are. Is it such a leap to try to train young children on their junior equivalents: Leapster, Brainy Baby videos, and Game Boy?

This reasoning has been up for serious debate of late. Psychologists argue over whether there is evidence to support learning through television and computer games. Reports of increased vocabulary, problem-solving skills, and counting in children exposed to certain educational programs and software have raised hope in families who are wired, and drawn fire from critics who feel that electronics are a poor substitute for traditional learning methods. Inevitably the discussion veers in other directions: How much television is too much? What is the right age to introduce children to the computer?

The electronics discussion can sound a little like the liberal/conservative debate on discipline. In this case, however, the experts on both sides of the political divide tend to weigh in against too much early exposure to media, while the spokespersons for the television and software industry point to emerging research that children have much to learn from electronic sources. A lot is at stake here, given the fact that kids under age six in the United States spend about two hours a day watching TV or videos, and that 36 percent of young kids have televisions in their bedrooms.[1]

Most parents of the little kids that I know do their best to sort out this conflicting advice. They try to limit television time or use it judiciously, like when Mom needs to take a shower or cook dinner, or everyone in the house is about to kill each other! Computer games are age appropriate and the emphasis in many homes is on educational games and videos that appear to teach something. I have heard many parents swear by Baby Einstein videos for teaching colors when nothing else seemed to work. Until research convincingly demonstrates otherwise, why not expose kids to these tools from a young age, to get them adept with the mouse and the controllers and let them know that we value learning in our homes?

Most of the discussions about children and media focus on this cost/benefit argument. Yet there is a fundamental problem with this line of reasoning, because the devil is not really in the details. We shouldn't only be thinking about what kids are or are not learning from computers and TV right now. As parents we need to step back, peer into the future, and ponder this question: Are we enhancing our children's brainpower with all this new media or are we preparing them to end up like Linda's college students, frantic and dependent on their electronic toys for entertainment and stimulation? It's hard to maintain this perspective for very long; we don't have a crystal ball, after all. We can, however, focus in on more pressing concerns: What lessons are we trying to teach our young kids and how do their experiences with media and technology enhance or interfere with those goals?

The Frenzy Folks

Before we go further, we have to look at the bigger picture. This interest in children and technology doesn't exist in a vacuum. Parents make decisions about what experiences are appropriate for their kids in large part by how they fit into the family and neighborhood lifestyle. We are a nation of multitaskers, on the go from early morning until late at night. With our cell phones and PDAs we are constantly available to our spouses, our children, and, of course, our employers. Leisure time is down, work and commuting hours seem to be ever expanding. In most families, free time is dominated by recreational activities, kids' sports, movies, and other entertainment and cultural outings. Few people, it seems, feel comfortable just hanging out. In this country that sounds like a synonym for *lazy*, and nobody wants that label applied to them.

Many parents approach child rearing with the same energy and intensity they bring to their jobs and other pursuits. In New York, we have Alpha Mom TV, a cable network designed to educate mothers on the finer points of doing everything the best way possible: how to plan the perfect birthday party, purchase the right learning tools, and gain admission to the best nursery schools.[2] The less ambitious among us still feel compelled to keep up-to-date on the latest trends in parenting and education. Few parents can escape from planning and chauffeuring their kids through a packed schedule of organized sports, dance, music and art classes, playdates, and birthday parties.

This all seems so normal that it qualifies as old news by now. The therapists who worry that adults keep busy and work too hard as a way of warding off anxiety sound a little too Freudian and out of touch with the real-life demands on successful professionals. Perhaps there is merit in these arguments, but in recent years we have seen a surge in stress-related illnesses and other evidence that suggests that the frenetic pace has its costs. There has also been a huge increase in reported rates of insomnia in adults. In the five-year period from 2000 to 2005, sleeping pill prescriptions were up 60 percent in this country. The majority of the prescriptions are for women (The advertising tie-ins for sleep medicines with shows like *Desperate Housewives* suggests the drug industry has a taste for perverse jokes).[3] Rates of depression, fatigue, and sheer overload have also kept pace, all occurring at higher rates in women.

Stress reduction classes have become big business, as many people have sought ways to soothe their nerves and learn to cope more efficiently with their day-to-day activities. The booming spa industry, with its promises of relaxation and tension relief, has been another beneficiary of these intense times. Many parents benefit from the techniques they learn in classes, and there is no doubt that massages and other spa therapies provide a soothing outlet and a temporary respite from stress. But even the lucky few who have access to these outlets are not likely to really slow down or make radical changes in their lifestyle.

Doing It All for the Kids

The reason for this, or at least the one I hear frequently, especially from mothers, goes something like this: "I'd like to do less, and not run around so much, but I do it for the kids. They're just so busy and I don't want them to miss out." Somehow word has gotten around that good parents do more and plan more for their kids. We all know that is not necessarily true, and can think of mothers and fathers who are connected to their children and less frantic about doing things. But a packed schedule remains the gold standard. We want our kids to keep up, to have the same lessons and social experiences that their peers have, and play on the same teams as them. We feel guilty if we want to take a weekend (or a month!) off.

We will look more closely at the pluses and minuses of organized activities for children in the next chapter. But for a moment, let's each ask ourselves this question: Is all this running around good for *my* child? Do our kids really need that many playdates, soccer, gymnastics, and art classes to be happy and successful? Do they need to start in earnest at age three or four? I don't mean to make light of these issues or to deny that children can benefit from early exposure to outside instruction (swimming comes immediately to mind). But many of our kids don't get it. Danielle complained to me that her five-year-old son, Alex, was not particularly interested in physical activities. "We're a sports family!" she concluded, as if that were the final word on his destiny.

Temperament differences like these often create maddening dilemmas in families. There are some young children who would rather stay at home in their pajamas on Saturday morning than go racing around town. Annie has a son like that. Four-year-old Will doesn't like to visit the park on his free days, although she can eventually coax him to go. She confessed, "It's very hard for me, I'm not like that." Annie is a planner and a doer and has lots of energy, and Will tries her patience. She worked hard to arrange a trip to the local science museum for Will and a buddy on a day off from preschool. She hadn't planned on the busloads of preteens who arrived there for a class trip, disturbing the calm day she had envisioned. Later Annie reported, "It was a good day, fun, but too much for Will. Really, it was too much for me also." Sometimes it takes an outing like this, where everyone feels stressed, to get parents to reconsider what benefits these activities bring and to weigh them against the costs, monetary and otherwise, of planning trips for children who would rather stay home.

I'm not suggesting we adapt ourselves completely to our kids' temperaments. Children who are shy or retiring or slow to warm up often need to be taken by the hand and led where they otherwise might not venture. But we also need to appreciate that most children below the age of seven or eight need to have plenty of quiet downtime. They also tire pretty easily, and need breaks to recoup and regroup. It's not surprising that our kids don't have much energy after school, especially if at age four or five they are attending class for six hours. Coming home and resting is often the best way to curb the meltdowns that occur so frequently in the early evening hours.

The Wired Bunch

Most parents more or less accept these limitations and make some accommodations for their younger children. Yet the prevailing ethos remains: Do as much as you can handle as soon as you are able. If the kids have to be home, why not get them busy with some educational games on the computer, so they can learn some prereading skills? If they want to relax, at least they can be watching *Sesame Street*, so they're picking up new vocabulary and learning to count and sing in rhyme. Hand-held devices, like Game Boy and the more sophisticated PSP, seem like reasonable choices to keep kids occupied, quiet, and technologically proficient at the same time. It's not surprising that many parents conclude that these electronic outlets fit in pretty well with their active and goal-oriented lifestyle.

So what is all the fuss about? As long as our kids don't watch television all the time and do a few things besides playing video games, why should parents worry? Brazelton and Greenspan and all the other experts who call for limiting screen time to a half hour or an hour a day seem so out of touch, and just a little too old-fashioned. Besides, haven't we seen some reports in the press that things are not so clear-cut? In fact didn't *Newsweek* proclaim on its cover not that long ago that "TV is Good for Kids" and give us words we were waiting to hear: "Parents have a little less reason to feel guilty" if their children are watching quality educational programs.[4]

The New York Times provided us more to be hopeful about when it gave front-page coverage to a study linking aggressive video games with improved visual attention skills in adolescents.[5] Steven Johnson has perhaps made the most persuasive argument. His book on the upside of pop culture, *Everything Bad Is Good for You*, has drawn considerable praise for arguing, among other things, that the more sophisticated video games require higher-order thinking, and that the current crop of reality shows and dramas on television require much more active participation and sophisticated cognition than their predecessors.[6]

We'll spend some time looking more closely at these arguments in a moment. But first let me offer a disclaimer. I'm not anti-TV, and I can appreciate the guilty pleasure of escaping from the daily grind by relaxing in front of sitcoms and ball games and the occasional nugget on the History Channel. I know that many kids welcome this time with their parents and that a lot of healthy families have routines that revolve around their favorite shows. I also have an appreciation for technology; I could not imagine life without e-mail or my computer. Technology is the new rock and roll for many of the older kids I know, and I am ceaselessly amazed at what they can configure and work out on their laptops. The computer also provides a creative outlet for many preteens and adolescents who struggle with learning problems, and gives them the opportunity to use their untapped reasoning capacity to feel as competent as their peers.

TV, Computers, and Lessons for Life

Let's get back to the eight and under set. Before we can decide what is helpful or not helpful, we have to determine what kids need to learn at an early age to be successful. When kindergarten teachers are asked to list their expectations for what children should be capable of before they enter their classrooms, a few things come up repeatedly. They want their kids to show some independence and initiative and not be afraid to try new things in class. Teachers place a premium on kids' respecting others and their ability to share and play cooperatively. Good listening skills and the ability to follow directions are also high on their list. They also prefer kids who can sit and focus and think quietly at times. No kindergarten teacher who has been around for a while expects all her kids to have mastered these tasks. But most do expect that their students have made some strides in these areas during preschool and that they come into "big school" *ready to learn*.

Now we return to our original question. Does time spent with the television, the computer, and video games interfere with these goals or help prepare our little kids? First let's take independence, a subject we tackled in some detail in chapter 4. You might remember my reservations with playing DVDs in the car, because they limit children's opportunities to be alone with their thoughts and ideas. When our kids are watching television and playing video games and exploring on the computer they may be doing some interesting things, but we would be hard-pressed to say they are acting independently. They are, after all, dependent on the content on the screen to keep them engaged.

The fact remains that most children in this country spend too much time in front of screens when they could be doing other things. This is a key point. It's not just a question of whether TV or computer time is bad or good. With limited downtime, many preschoolers and elementary-age children do not have much chance to play on their own, and the time they do have is getting considerably squeezed by the lure of television and electronic games.

How about initiative? Aren't the more wired kids inclined to be explorers, leaping to try the latest things in class? They might be by nature, but for lots of kindergarten kids I know, their gaming mind-set doesn't generalize too well. Translation: school is "boring!" It can't compete with the bells and whistles they're used to. In the classroom, things don't happen quite so fast, and the teacher doesn't instantly tally their point total and bump them up a level. As the work in kindergarten gets a little harder, with the introduction of counting sequences and letter forming, for instance, the kids get much less instant gratification. If they haven't learned to focus and slow down by then, they could be in for some trouble.

For some time, television has been criticized as requiring less mental effort than most schoolwork, learning to read in particular. If we apply Steven Johnson's argument to preschoolers, we might argue that the opposite is true for video games. The problem, though, is that three- and four-year-olds are not playing Zelda. They are not mastering intricate landscapes and anticipating changes on the fly. They are playing Mario Brothers and Donkey Kong. For the less agile among us, these games are not a breeze, but for the young boys who play them the most, they are not particularly difficult.

I have sat and watched five- and six-year-olds jump from level to level pretty easily. Most kids can master these game cartridges in a week or two. This is no accident, of course, because then they (or their parents) have to go out and buy more games. The gaming industry seems to put just enough challenge in their products so the kids don't get bored, but not so much that they have to experience any real frustration. The learning to be done in school, by contrast, requires children to practice repeatedly and to gradually experience and master more frustration. It's no surprise that some kids don't find school much fun.

We spent a lot of time talking about cooperation and respect in the last chapter, but let's look more specifically at media influences on young children. I mentioned above that in many families the routine of watching shows together can be a nice bonding experience. Be aware that content matters. It's one thing to watch *Survivor* and other reality shows with older kids, and to discuss the virtues of competition and the risks contestants take that their vulnerabilities may be exposed for all of us to see. But such subtleties are lost on young kids. It may be fun to watch *American Idol*, but it's hard to avoid the fact that the show relies on rejection and humiliation for a healthy dose of its appeal.

How do we explain this to our kids? I've listened to a mother tell me how she enjoyed *American Idol*, but was hard-pressed to explain to her sensitive seven-year-old son why it was so popular and not offensive to grown-ups. Even some of the seemingly innocuous sitcoms rely heavily on a constant game of insults and "gotcha" moments. They are also populated by hapless dads who act foolish and bewildered most of the time. These shows can give kids the impression that it is fine to speak their minds, and all the better if they do it in a sassy and provocative manner. If adults are indeed as clueless as they appear on screen, their own moms and dads will be none the wiser for these remarks.[7]

i see lots of cases of preadolescent boys who light up when talking about the intricacies and challenges of World of Warcraft, but can barely muster the energy to compare the intensity of that experience with the thought of sitting in math class. As many teachers will tell you, it's hard to compete with the multidimensional worlds that students experience on their computers and PlayStations. The pace, the energy, and the constant feedback loops of electronic games are not easy to replicate in real-life situations.

Video and computer games bring their own challenges to teaching respect, and not just because of the much publicized concern with their aggressive content. Unlike more traditional games like chess or checkers, children learn how to play electronic ones on their own or from peers, and their parents generally have little interest in playing alongside them. Gamers feel little need for adult assistance, and while this may be a step toward independence, it also deprives them of meaningful contact with their mothers and fathers. Parents lose out on the chance to tune in to their children's experience and teach them the rules of the game and how to take turns and respond to frustration. It is not a quantum leap to suggest that children who are avid gamers are more apt to come into school with less conviction that adults are there to be helpers, and with less faith that there is much to be gained by listening to their teachers. If kids cart their handheld devices wherever they go, they also get less experience making eye contact, saying hello, and generally interacting with people. This does not bode well for learning social skills and how to function in a group setting.

The Young and the Restless

When I speak with kindergarten and first and second grade teachers, they often talk at length about the bad behavior in their classrooms and the lack of respect from their students. Those who have been around for a while claim this has changed dramatically over the years. What's behind all this negative press kids have been getting?[8] Perhaps we expect too much of them at an early age, and the new emphasis on early academics is to blame? This is a popular theory these days, especially to explain the difficulty that boys are having in elementary school. If we probe deeper into the problem with teachers, it does appear that the requirement to sit and focus and listen to instruction is too taxing for many young kids. If the kindergarten curriculum presupposes a reasonable degree of sustained attention, this can create an impossible dilemma. Many of the kids will not keep up with the work and are more likely to act out and get into trouble.

This explanation is plausible, but a little too simplistic. Most of the kindergarteners who land in my office are among the *brighter* kids who have no difficulty managing classroom assignments. The more challenging work is often the only thing that grabs their attention. They struggle instead during downtimes when they have to sit and be quiet or listen to a story from the teacher. Despite all the concerns about less time to play and more work in kindergarten, these are expectations that haven't changed much over the years. So why is it so much harder these days for kids to slow down and be calm and wait their turn?

The easy, and maybe the most obvious, answer: It must be a biological thing. We've all read about the prevalence of attentional difficulties in kids, especially boys. Perhaps the increased classroom demands explain why these problems are emerging at a younger age. Maybe the key is to become more educated and better at diagnosing attention-deficit/hyperactivity disorder (ADHD), and providing early intervention for the children who need it. Researchers at the Centers for Disease Control report that the number of kids diagnosed with ADHD has increased in recent years, from 3 to 5 percent in the 1980s to as many as

8 percent of children (and 11 percent of boys) in 2003.[9] Many of these children will need behavior therapy and some will require medication to be able to function well in and out of the classroom.

Without venturing too far into the debate about ADHD and medication, there are reasons to take a long look at this hypothesis. In the first place, many of us forget that attention is not a fixed or easily assignable trait. In other words, we can't readily put all the inattentive kids in one corner and all the focused and perfectly calm children in the other. All the attributes being assessed when we talk about ADHD—activity level, impulsivity, attention, and organization—exist on a continuum. Picture the normal bell curve. A small number of kids are quite good at paying attention and will be at the far end, most are okay and will bunch up in the middle, and a few outliers will straggle behind the group. At some point we cut the curve and assign the label ADHD to the children who score below a certain threshold on behavior ratings of attention and disruptiveness. Despite the discrepancies in reported rates of ADHD, in all the large research studies the vast majority of young children do not meet these criteria (only 4 percent of four- to eight-year-olds in the CDC data).

Learning to Focus

All the hoopla and fierce commentary on ADHD in the media and the academic journals focus primarily on whether we are stigmatizing normal behavior and overdiagnosing children, or ignoring important avenues of treatment for kids who desperately need it. One not so small point is usually left out: We can, in fact, teach kids how to pay attention and focus for longer periods of time. These are not just biological givens that we can do nothing about. Learning to focus is a developing process that unfolds over the course of the first few years.

Ask any preschool teacher about this. They don't expect three-year-olds to sit in a circle in September for very long, maybe a few minutes at most. But come spring, after lots of coaxing and practice, most of their students will sing songs and listen to stories for ten or fifteen minutes. In the fours' class down the hall they use that as a starting point, and gradually expect the kids to sit for twenty to twenty-five minutes before they are ready to move on to kindergarten.

There are always one or two kids who will have more difficulty than the rest, who are more restless and impulsive by nature. They need extra attention from the teachers and usually benefit from specific strategies that help them remain focused. Take four-year-old Kevin, for instance. He had a reputation for mean behavior when I first observed him in preschool, mainly because he ran around willy-nilly and bumped into kids in the classroom and on the playground. As we talked, his teacher, Susan, admitted that Kevin was actually not such a bad kid, but she was concerned that he could not slow down for a minute. This was torture for everyone during circle time, and many of the kids had begun to complain to their parents about Kevin.

I suggested that Susan seat Kevin close by her during circle time, and put her arm around him to keep him calm. When I returned to her class the next week she told me that she had decided to go a step further. She had put Kevin in a big teacher's chair right next to her, while she occupied a kid's chair and the rest of the children sat on the rug. Kevin loved his "throne." He gripped its sides tightly and still wiggled during circle time, but he had stopped calling out as much and was no longer running around the room. The other kids showed little jealousy toward him. They were all happy that Susan could now get through a whole book, and anyone who tried to climb into his seat was quickly scolded by the rest of the group. "That's Kevin's chair," they would cry out.

Kevin was lucky. He had an understanding teacher and caring parents who were intent on helping him succeed and not be ostracized by the rest of the group. He also attended a nursery school that believed that encouraging children to slow down, listen, and play in an organized way were essential ingredients to later learning. His teachers were not interested in what label I could apply to Kevin—they knew full well that he struggled with attention problems and hyperactivity—but were interested in how to teach him to focus and stay calm during free play and group time. We charted his behaviors together, and helped to orient Kevin to the idea that he needed to "work on staying in control and taking turns with his friends."

Kevin was one of those kids who are outliers, well behind the curve to start. After a year or two he was still pretty active, but he was approaching the middle of the pack. With a lot of adult attention and practice he gradually learned how to stay calm and more attentive in class. There are many other kids who don't jump off the radar screen like Kevin, but still need to learn how to stay focused and play quietly. For some of them, this struggle is less directly tied in to their temperament or a marked biological inclination toward impulsivity and hyperactivity.

A lot of these kids have simply never *learned* to slow down. Many live in families where a hyper pace is the norm, and they have adapted to that lifestyle. They love being on the go and need to be constantly doing something active and engaging. If there's a lag in the schedule, they complain of being bored. A good number of these kids turn to their electronic devices in these moments, and their parents generally welcome the respite from their demands to be entertained. If they happen to gravitate toward something educational on the television and the computer, well, all the better. At the very least they are kept quiet and occupied and out of everyone's hair.

The Fast and the Furious

This cycle of high activity, dissatisfaction with downtime, and the search for electronic alternatives raises another question. Does the buzz kids get from their video games and computers and action shows further limits their ability to focus? Not so long ago, the answer seemed to be clear-cut. Marie Winn proclaimed in her influential book, first published three decades ago, that television was the "plug-in drug," good for lulling kids into a passive inactivity and a trancelike state and not much else.[10] Yale University psychologist Jerome Singer, who conducted some of the influential early studies on the impact of television on children's imagination and aggression, was similarly critical of the "mindless and unresponsive watching" that characterized most children's viewing habits. In their recent book, Stanley Greenspan and T. Berry Brazelton describe the "hypnotic state" they observe in preschoolers while they watch television, and the subsequent flattening of brain waves on their EEGs. They also speak warily of the post-TV-watching phenomena of irritability and frenzied behavior in young children.[11]

Daniel Anderson and other psychologists have taken issue with the passive-viewing argument. They have demonstrated that the more creative educational shows, *Dora the Explorer* and *Sesame Street* among them, require kids to more actively attend to the screen and distinguish between what has meaning and what does not, and are pretty good at improving problem solving and letter and color recognition.[12] Nearly all researchers agree that the more sophisticated shows, like *Mr. Rogers' Neighborhood*, allow children time to process and review the material they have watched through breaks in the flow (when Mr. Rogers doffs his cardigan or turns away from the viewer momentarily) and repetition of main ideas. Few studies have looked at the impact of video and computer games on children's attention, but some researchers point out that since they require more direct engagement from kids than most television shows, they are likely to elicit the same pattern of more active attending.

Parents are left to try to reconcile these two points of view, but if they look more closely at the experts' writings, they are not quite so divergent. Nobody really takes issue with watching Mr. Rogers or tuning in from time to time to *Sesame Street*. The real point of the new research is that *content matters*; it's the message, not just the medium, we should be studying and refining. If we take this at face value, that all TV shows (and presumably, all computer and video games) are not alike, we have to face a more sobering reality. Our kids are not going to be interested in *Dora* and *Sesame Street* forever. Boys in particular are likely to seek out more action and adventure shows with more stimulating and gripping images in both their cartoon and real-life formats.

These shows have been criticized for increasing levels of aggression in young viewers.[13] The impact on their attention spans gets less press.

But the intense stimulation that kids experience in watching these shows has for years drawn considerable fire from psychologists. Their critique is fairly straightforward. Children naturally respond to rapid shifts in images and sounds. Most children's shows manipulate kids' attention by maximizing these orienting features. In other words they use all sorts of bells and whistles to keep kids glued to the screen. The rapid, staccato pace of commercials follows the same design, but even more intensely. (It can be enlightening to play a game at home where the object is to count how many scene cuts are in each thirty-second commercial.)

The attention-grabbing features of most TV programs pale in comparison with the whir of most action and adventure games designed for computers and video gaming systems. The graduates of *Reader Rabbit* face similar options in the software market as *Sesame Street* viewers, and the poky educational games are soon replaced by more rapid-fire jumping, driving, and attack ones. Boys, who have enough trouble slowing down to begin with, are the ones usually drawn to these games. The study quoted in *The New York Times* may make a convincing case that playing aggressive video games increases older kids' reaction times, but this is essentially saying that if we practice focusing on a flashing screen and making rapid hand/eye movements, we are going to test well on measures of visual shifts and short, quick movements. It says little about kids' ability to sustain their attention in the absence of intense stimulation.

The Risk of Overstimulation

For many of us who grew up watching a fair amount of television and playing our share of arcade games, this can sound like a serious overreaction. Why can't we just relax and let the kids have their fun? After all, didn't we turn out okay? I'm not immune to these arguments, but I think we have to look more closely at the differences in content today.

I'll give you a personal example. A few years ago my wife and I wanted to rent a family movie, and we looked through the rack of old titles we had enjoyed as children. We came upon *Chitty Chitty Bang Bang* and both of us went instantly into nostalgia mode (a dangerous, trancelike state, according to our kids), fondly recalling the first time we had each watched it. We had an early dinner and then sat down to watch with our eight-year-old son and five-year-old daughter. After about an hour into the movie, and a couple of song-and-dance routines by Dick Van Dyke, my wife and I turned to each other, and admitted somewhat sheepishly, "This is a little boring."

To our surprise, our kids were transfixed, and they loved the slapstick and silliness. They were engrossed in the story, despite the fact that during that hour there were really only two scenes (one in their home/invention center and the other on the road rescuing the damsel in distress). It was getting late, so we turned off the movie, vowing to let them watch the end of it the following evening. We hustled them off to bed, and then came down to watch one of our favorite shows: *The Sopranos*. The contrast, to put it mildly, was shocking! It wasn't just the content differences and the violence and gruff language of the latter. The sheer pace from the opening credits was striking. The in-your-face dialogue, the rapid scene cuts, the loud music; together they were like being hit over the head after the slow, soothing rhythm of *Chitty Chitty Bang Bang*.

The funny thing was, neither of us had ever thought about *The Sopranos* in that way. It seemed so normal, until we compared it back-to-back with a very different viewing experience. It's a little like playing chess and then settling in for a car chase game like the Fast and Furious in the local arcade. My son and I happen to like both of these. It's amazing, the buzz you get from the latter, the sheer adrenaline rush from smashing into other vehicles and racing over hills and turbo-charging with the Nitro button again and again. In my experience, it takes a good amount of time to decompress postgame, and the thought of sitting and focusing on a game of chess or reading a book in the aftermath seems pretty far-fetched.

I'm not railing against *The Sopranos* or arcade games. In moderation, both have their place; at least in my life they do. The problem arises from the amount of time kids are exposed to these types of high-stimulation environments. I am particularly concerned with children who live in families where the TV and the computer are a constant backdrop, in the morning, during meals, and throughout the afternoon and evening. Without sounding too alarmist, we need to consider that we're talking about little kids whose brains are still actively developing. The real concern is that too much stimulation at an early age will alter their brain functioning in such a way that they will require constant multimedia feedback to stay tuned in.

The fact remains that there is not a formidable body of research to support a direct link between television watching and the ability to attend in quieter settings.[14] But there is also not much data to refute this thesis. Without resounding evidence to guide them, parents are left to make the difficult choice about how much television kids should watch and video games they should play. As we contemplate our options, we may want to ask ourselves a variant of the opening line of the Hippocratic Oath: Isn't our job to first do no harm? And don't we want to err on the more cautious side rather than risk that our kids will be exposed to information and stimulation overload? With this in mind, we should tread carefully when deciding whether to proceed with those Baby Einstein videos, Leapster computers, PlayStations, and television sets in our children's bedrooms.

Raising Mindful Children

To some extent, evaluating the relative merits of television and video games is like debating how much sugar we should have in our diets. At the end of the day most nutrition experts agree that a little taste of the real thing here and there is not going to kill us, as long as we don't overdo it. They caution us to be careful of the artificial substitutes and processed sweeteners that could do more lasting damage. Keeping track of our intake might be another suggestion, along with a warning to cut back if we notice that we are constantly craving sugar-filled snacks. To test our dependence, we might occasionally try a few days of a sugar-free

the American Academy of Pediatrics (AAP) recommends that children under the age of two not watch any television. For older children, AAP suggests that parents limit TV to one or two hours per day, and that children be allowed to watch only after they have completed their chores and their homework. They also suggest that parents restrict television viewing during dinnertime, and not allow children to have TVs in their bedrooms.

regimen and then adjust our behavior accordingly.

This is all reasonable, scientifically grounded advice. However, it addresses only one aspect of our physical well-being. If we reduce our sugar intake but don't exercise, keep smoking, and eat only fatty foods, we're in for trouble. The health experts assume that we have this knowledge, and that decisions concerning sugar are part of a larger concern with our physical wellness.

Advice about television and our children's mental health should follow the same logic. Reducing our kids' dependence on TV and video games is not an end in itself. It is part of a larger goal of helping children learn to slow down, to be calm, and to focus on one thing without any artificial incentives to do so. In chapter 3 we talked about mindful parenting and the ability to stay connected with our kids and to concentrate on the more meaningful aspect of interactions with them. In a sense, we are talking about helping our kids develop their own capacity for mindfulness. This includes learning how to become more aware of their own thoughts and ideas and feelings. Mindful children also recognize how to soothe themselves and how to block out distractions.

Sometimes I joke with parents that they should give up their children's other activities and enroll them in yoga! I mean this only half in jest, and have, in fact, come across a few excellent yoga teachers for young children. The methods of yoga—relaxation, meditation, physical stretching, and deep breathing—can do wonders for fast-paced kids who struggle to get more control of their bodies and their minds. In my experience, deep breathing in particular can be a quick remedy for when things are getting out of control, and can be more effectively applied if parents have learned these exercises with their children. "Let's all take a deep breath before we start" has become a mantra in many classrooms (and at the dinner table in our house).

The idea of mindfulness for kids is not just a New Age fad. Ultimately, learning to slow down may be more of an advantage than learning to multitask and rapidly process large amounts of information. If we take school, for instance, little credit is given for always being the first to respond to a teacher's questions. The children who can attend more evenly over time, and gradually shift from one topic to the next (learning the alphabet and then sound blending, counting to one hundred and then adding and subtracting), are likely to have the fundamentals in place and be better prepared to move on to more advanced reasoning skills.

Reading requires a good deal of mindfulness. Sounding out words, making sense of their use in context, and comprehending the larger meaning of sentences strung together are no small tasks for first and second graders. Performing these feats at the same time demands a degree of patience, quiet, and sustained attention, all while blocking out competing information (other kids talking, the sirens going by) and focusing on the task at hand.

There is tremendous variability in children's reading abilities, partly due to differences in aptitudes in processing and comprehension. But there is little debate that there is a connection between kids' ability to slow down and their readiness to read. Many of the children that I know who are active, on the go, and avid video game players don't like to read, even if they can get through a book pretty easily. It's just a little *too slow* for them.

Improved school performance is not the only rationale for teaching kids to be more mindful. As a culture, we appear to be gradually losing the ability to reflect on our experience, to cultivate what David Levy calls the "contemplative dimension of life." Levy has written extensively about the impact of technology and electronic communication on our quality of life. He has doubts as to whether the young multitaskers in our midst have the same "ability to focus on a single thing, the ability to be silent and still inside, basically the ability to be unplugged and content."[15]

I don't intend to be sounding any antitechnology alarms here. As I've mentioned, computers and the communication options they present have opened up worlds to our kids that many of us never dreamed of when we were young. No doubt about it, technology is here to stay; our kids need to become adept at managing multiple sources of information. By five or six, kids should become familiar with computers and learn to handle other technology.

What we all need is more balance. These days fast-paced, multifunctioning, and technologically sophisticated households are the norm. Most preschoolers can handle the mouse, and I know more than a few first and second graders who know their way around their parents' BlackBerrys. Some of these same kids are much less adept at cooling down or chilling out, at thinking quietly and steadily and just plain relaxing without much going on around them. I would argue that these skills are essential not only to learning, but also to de-stressing and decompressing after long and active days. I also firmly believe that we can do a much better job of teaching our kids how to slow down. To do this, we have to see the value in quiet time, solitary play, and reflective thinking, and recognize that these are skills that will serve them well throughout their lives.

Slowing Down at Home

This notion of cutting back and slowing down sounds good in theory, but in practice it often requires a significant shift in gears at home. Consider Andrea's dilemma. She was a bright professional woman who had stopped working to care for her three children a few years before she came to my office to talk about Sam, her oldest child. He was in first grade and lately he was having a lot of trouble in school. Sam was a bright kid, but he always rushed through his homework and his hand-writing was barely legible. He was having trouble sitting still and had re-cently been in trouble once or twice for not listening and calling out in class. Sam was beginning to loathe getting up on schooldays, and An-drea was growing concerned about his self-esteem.

On the face of it, Sam's story is not an unusual one, and there were certainly hints that he may have had a serious attention problem. As I spoke further with Andrea, she revealed some interesting trends in his home life. Sam was a very active kid in a hard-charging family. He was currently enrolled in four activities: swimming, karate, basketball, and soccer. Homework was wedged in between activities, and Sam often didn't get to it until after dinner. The rest of the week was filled with playdates, family outings, and dinners with neighbors. Andrea admitted that she was pretty worn out. Despite having been an excellent student when she was younger, she confessed that she had a very short attention span these days, and lamented, "Now I can barely read a book."

Andrea was aware things were moving too fast, and she had already tried to slow things down. After a previous meeting, she had cut out tele-vision during weekdays, and her kids no longer seemed to miss it. Now we talked about making more fundamental shifts. She agreed to talk to her husband about dropping one or two of Sam's activities, or rotating them on a seasonal basis. I suggested that Sam needed a set time to do his homework before dinner and needed a quiet space in the house where he would not be disturbed by his younger sisters. I thought it might also help if he had time to run outside and burn some of his stored-up energy before getting started on his work. We also looked at his sleep patterns, and Andrea made plans to get him to bed earlier dur-ing the week.

The next step was to more actively plan for times when Sam could be more reflective and have quiet play alone or with his siblings. We de-cided that Sam would have twenty to thirty minutes of alone time with-out any electronics each afternoon, when he would have to entertain himself with the toys in his room. I also urged Andrea to have more of a routine at dinnertime and to sit around the table with the kids for at least thirty minutes each night. Andrea loved reading to the children, but found she rarely had time to do so. We discussed how to incorporate this more regularly into their bedtime rituals. Andrea had also told me that her husband, Rob, liked to play board games with Sam and his four-year-old sister. I encouraged her to have him set time aside on Saturdays and Sundays to play Monopoly and checkers with them.

Andrea understood that this commitment might preclude their attending as many events outside the home, particularly on weekends. But she was committed to devoting time to help Sam learn to feel more in control and more calm. I let her know that she should also consider having the school psychologist observe Sam to see if she would recommend any adjustments in his classroom. Perhaps she would suggest that Sam sit closer to his teacher and help both of them develop a signal for when Sam needed to get back on track in class. When Andrea checked back a month later she was feeling much calmer, and she was pleased to report that Sam was much happier in school and enjoying his quiet family time at home.

Teaching Mindfulness at Home

Build in Alone Time

In chapter 4, we discussed the value of alone time in helping kids feel more independent. Quiet, solitary play also requires a good deal of attentiveness, and an ability to tune out other distractions in the house. Storytelling games with dolls, battles with action figures, and other imaginative games provide a means for young kids to lose themselves in play and make up their own worlds where they rule the roost. Sometimes kids need help getting started, but once they have the basic framework, four- and five-year-old children can often create elaborate scenarios that naturally pull for them to be more focused and creative. We'll talk more about imaginative games in the next chapter.

Encourage Reading

As we discussed, books demand a significant amount of concentration and calm on the part of the reader. Parents sometimes overlook these attributes when they think about reading to young children, but helping them to develop good listening skills is just as important as getting them to be more adept at letter recognition and decoding words. Dedicated time for reading at bedtime and at other points in the day can set the stage for quiet and reflective moments that further stimulate children's imagination. We should start these rituals when kids are toddlers, though we have to be aware that they might sit only for a few minutes at that age.

The books we choose should be fun and age appropriate. I don't have the space here to go into great detail about specific books, but the Dr. Seuss series deserves special mention. They are full of enchanting and colorful stories, and their singsong rhymes are appealing to preschoolers and continue to be popular with many kids well into grade school. Most six- and seven-year-old children who are starting to read on their own still value special time when they are read to by their parents, and we have to be careful not to make independent reading a complete substitute for the quiet time we have with them. Parents sometimes overlook that many older children (even up to age eleven or twelve) also like being read to, well after they are capable of reading chapter books on their own.

Schedule Special Time

In recent decades, child experts have come to focus on specific periods when parents and kids spend time together. Stanley Greenspan recommends that parents schedule "floor time" with their infants and toddlers. Others refer to "special time" or "hang-out time" when parents set aside other activities and give their kids their full attention. Critics sometimes argue that these methods sound a bit stilted, as if we have to schedule appointments to be with our kids. But if we look at the frenetic pace of most of our lives it's hard to argue with this idea. As I said earlier in the book, if we don't schedule it, it's not as likely to happen. The goal is not just to have 5:00 to 5:15 be special time, but to work in moments throughout the day when our kids feel we are connected to them and disconnected from everything else, including our phones, PDAs, and the television.

Play Board Games Together

As kids get older, we can join them in their imaginative games at their behest. Some kids want us to help them build elaborate structures out of Legos or blocks. Others like to play board games or cards. These games generally pull for more self-directed, thoughtful, and planned movements than their electronic counterparts. Think of the example of playing chess. To play reasonably well kids have to learn to anticipate their adversary's moves, to plan ahead two or three moves, and to think about the various outcomes of each decision.

For younger children, games like checkers, Memory, Othello, and Stratego mimic the strategy and planning of chess, and require a lot of concentration and quiet study of the board. If they're playing with their parents, kids also benefit from pausing midgame and reviewing their strategy. We're not there to make them grand masters, however, and the games should be fun and exciting, not overly competitive or rule-oriented.

Some parents are not very interested in playing board games with their kids. They may not see the appeal in these rule-based scenarios, or find the repetitive and random aspects of younger-age games, like Candy Land, a little boring. Here a little teamwork can help. One parent may be more attuned to their children's imaginative play or love reading to them, while the other may prefer to play games and sports with them. Sometimes, though not always, there's a clear split along gender lines, with dads preferring the latter and moms the former. If this is the case, the parents should go with their strengths, as long as they have an appreciation for what their spouse is doing with the kids. It's also helpful to switch roles from time to time, so parents don't get type-cast ("Dad only likes to play sports") in the eyes of the kids.

Games can teach impulse control, fairness, and a tolerance for frustration that comes from not winning every time. We don't sit down to play gin rummy or Uno with our kids and automatically think of building these skill sets. Nor should we. Game playing should first and foremost be a time for fun and relaxing. But teaching kids to play card and board games reminds me of the Jewish belief about the many levels of charity. It is fine to give someone money or offer other assistance, but the highest form of charity is to give someone a job so he can support himself. Similarly, if we teach our children games that they can then play with each other, we give them tools that they can use over and over to practice attending, slowing down, and thinking before acting, all critical to their success as they grow older.

Preserve Family Mealtime

Compared to a generation ago relatively few middle-class families in this country enjoy the luxury of having regular meals together. It may seem odd to use the word "luxury" here, but given parents' work schedules and the explosion of activities for kids, family meals have become a scarce commodity. Many mothers and fathers I meet regret this state of affairs, and wish they could re-create the kinds of evening meals they had in their own childhood. Their longings invoke a nostalgia for an easier time when family rituals held sway, and parents were not pulled in so many directions. Many of us are susceptible to these visions, but in my experience, parents can readily trade in these memories if they think there is more to be gained elsewhere (in the office or on the soccer field, for instance).

Mealtime is not only for eating. It is also a critical learning opportunity for kids, and eating together is perhaps the best time for parents to teach children how to slow down and be mindful. If we take the time to prepare meals together with our kids and allow them to serve the food and be active participants in conversation, we are modeling what it means to decompress and take time out from our busy lives. Dinner and other meals are also a time to show kids how to cooperate, to share and be helpful. It may sound trivial, but passing the potatoes, not eating until everyone is served, taking turns in conversation, and learning to sit still are all valuable lessons. Manners aren't the only thing to be learned

i n the past few years a series of more child-friendly cookbooks have come on the market that suggest meals that parents might actually want to eat. *The Kids' Cookbook*,[16] available at Williams-Sonoma, has proven to be a big hit in our house.

at the dinner table. We have the chance to teach children about controlling their movements, listening to conversation, waiting for others, and choosing moments to speak up.

Baking and preparing meals can be soothing and rhythmic rituals. Kneading bread, licking the chocolate off the spoon, stirring the soup, or getting covered in flour allows children to regress and relax. It's not only tasting the food, but it's the touching, the smelling, and the watching it all come together that are so satisfying to kids. It's amazing to see how even the most distracted children seem to respond to cooking projects in school, and the eating that follows. I don't want to overdo it here, and certainly don't want to place any guilt on working parents who have little time to prepare meals during the week. In many families, the weekend will offer the only extended periods of time for cooking. I know many parents who have made a commitment on Friday evenings or Sunday afternoons to have longer meals together and to get their children involved in preparing and serving the food for the family.

There is another reason parents sometimes avoid mealtime that is not due to conflicting schedules. Despite our romantic vision of the good old days, the thought of actually getting our little kids to sit still and act reasonably at the dinner table for even a short while can seem preposterous! I had one dad who was willing to consider many of my suggestions, but when it came to having meals together with his two young children he begged for mercy: "Please, anything but that!" Often parents are completely perplexed at how their own parents managed to get *them* to sit when they were little.

I have no illusions about mealtime. It takes trial and error and a serious commitment to make it work. Parents also need to firmly believe that dinnertime matters, and not only in a warm and fuzzy way. We have to remind ourselves of the "Pay now or pay later" adage I referred to earlier. We can't just let it go for a few years and then expect our six- and seven-year-olds to be proper ladies and gentlemen at the table. We have to start when they are two or three, with reasonable adjustments for their age. Our kids might come for ten minutes, fidget and fuss some. But if they see that we remain firm in our expectations ("I know it's a little hard, but we're going to sit together for a few more minutes") and we model speaking calmly, taking turns, and sitting still, they are likely to gradually get the idea. If they have older siblings who are a bit more socialized already, younger ones can adapt more quickly to our expectations.

How we define those expectations remains the key. In some families both parents argue that there is no way they could ever have meals all together during the week. I don't suggest that parents quit their jobs or completely abandon their busy lives. I do ask them to shoot for having at least three dinners a week together as a family. Some working mothers and fathers can also squeeze in other meals here and there. Breakfast is another good time to sit with young kids. We may be rushed in the morning, but our kids are often more responsive early in the day. If they see that we are committed to sitting and talking and relaxing with them, even for a short time, our children are likely to take our cue that this is an important way to prepare for the day.

From Fear of Slowing Down to a Plan of Action

I doubt that many parents will read the previous few pages and take issue with the idea of reading to their kids or playing games or having meals together as a family. We recognize that there is value in spending these times with our children. The problem lies in how we feel these ac-

alcolm Gladwell's *Blink*[17] is a fascinating book, but one that can easily be misinterpreted. If you review his examples of people who have learned to act decisively with limited information—the art historian, the car salesman, and the army commander—they have all learned to respond quickly and intuitively only after years of experience and training in their respective fields. They have honed the ability to "thin-slice" information after intensive immersion and concentrated study of their subject matter, not by training themselves to act quickly or think on their feet.

tivities fit with our overall goals. We may read to our kids to encourage learning and phonic awareness, but are we as enthusiastic about the way that reading offers children a chance to focus and unwind? Evening meals sound idyllic, but if the choice is between dinner together and swimming lessons, isn't the latter naturally more important? Isn't it better to be doing something?

This dilemma reminds me of the high school English classes where teachers warned us against the use of the passive voice. "Always go with the active verb if you have the choice" is the advice I recall. We are a nation of doers who believe that the key is to "get in the game." Slow down, be mindful, stay focused? These ideas fly in the face of conventional wisdom, and sound more than a tad passive at first glance. Don't we want to train young minds to be quick-witted and fast-reacting? Aren't these the keys to being an effective student and a successful athlete? Haven't we read about the hot new theory in psychology about making judgments in the blink of an eye?

The only way we can overcome our anxiety about slowing down is if we accept the notion that being thoughtful, in control, and focused are essential elements of an active and engaged mind. Giving our children time for quiet play and reflection now will help them down the road when they have to sustain their attention for longer periods and absorb, process, and synthesize more complex information. If we can honestly repeat this to ourselves, and to our spouses, we may rest a little easier. Parents who recognize the value in teaching kids to de-stress and re-main calm can also feel more comfortable with the choice to give them these opportunities, and to limit their screen time and unpack their schedules. We have to remember that slowing down does not mean idling in neutral or going with the flow. If we embrace mindfulness in our families, we can have confidence that we are teaching our kids to think, a gift that ultimately means more than just about anything else.

eight

Fear of Unstructured Time: Exploration

Sometimes the world seems upside down, at least when it comes to defining what a "normal" childhood is these days. That was a constant struggle for Sharon, a working mom in her midthirties. Sharon had consulted with me a few times over the previous two years, and now she came in with a new dilemma. Her six-year-old son, Will, was a rambunctious and spirited boy who loved to play outdoors. He especially loved to bike ride with the older boys in the neighborhood, and to build forts in the woods behind his house. Sharon was concerned about this. Shouldn't Will be involved in more activities? Where would all this exploring lead him? Did it make sense to give him more opportunities for "enrichment"?

Sharon noticed my puzzled look. I couldn't help it. Here was a caring, relaxed mother who was giving her active first grader the free time to roam and discover and socialize on his own, and she was beating herself up about it! Sharon had already cut way back on TV time in her house because she wanted her two kids to be doing other things. Now they were, and deep down Sharon was proud of that, but she couldn't shake that nagging feeling that everybody else was doing something more productive. "No, Sharon," I assured her, "you are not a negligent mother."

I meet parents like Sharon pretty regularly. Susan was frustrated that her five-year-old daughter, Maggie, didn't want to join the local kickball league. Tina and Robert were surprised their first grader, Grant, was more interested in imaginative play and action figures than organized baseball. Mark felt compelled to find challenging academic classes for his gifted four-year-old son, Stuart, lest he waste some of his early potential. Contrary to popular stereotypes, none of these parents were the supercompetitive, hard-charging types. If you met them socially you might describe them as laid-back and relaxed. But when it came to their kids, they were right there in the mix, caught up in the maelstrom of fear and anxiety at finding the right set of enrichment activities for them.

Then and Now

When Sharon and I began to explore her worries about Will, it became clearer to her that the outdoor time he cherished was not so different from how she had enjoyed spending her free time as a child. She could recall many days spent running through her yard and into the neighboring fields, or riding around town on her bike with friends. This is not unusual. Many parents who come to me with concerns about their kids' use of time end up relating nostalgic images of their own childhoods: wandering the neighborhood, gathering in the backyard or on the street with friends, retreating to the attic or the barn to make up stories and plays.

They are wistful remembrances, and often reflect a longing for childhood experiences that seem out of step with their current family lives. With weekends and many weekdays spent shuttling between soccer and baseball practice, swim lessons, dance classes, and birthday parties, many parents complain that their own children have little time for solitary thoughts, imaginative play, or kid-directed games. Yet they say this with a certain resignation in their voices. It may be nice to take a brief respite to consider the good old days, but in the end we have to get down to business and get our kids "involved."

It has become so common for all of us to rush around on our kids' behalf that changing the situation doesn't seem to be an option. "It is what it is," we have to adapt or they'll be left behind, goes the current thinking. The fact that this state of affairs directly conflicts with some of our fondest memories as children, and that we are driving ourselves more than a bit crazy in the process of shuttling to and fro, should give us pause. More often than not it does not. Somehow parents have lost control of the concept of what's good for children. Indifferent to our own desires and the distant voices of the experts who beg to differ about hyperscheduling children at a young age, we plunge forward when our children are preschoolers and sign them up for all the "usual" activities.

Bad Things Happen to Nice Kids

Liz and I were discussing how to get her kids to watch a little less television, and ways to give her active and energetic second grader more time to run around. Her boys loved to shoot hoops in the driveway and would stay out there for an hour or more when they had the chance, but this created a dilemma for Liz. She only felt comfortable letting five-year-old Harry and seven-year-old Mark play outside if she was there to watch them, and she had lots to do inside. "How long do you feel comfortable leaving them alone?" I asked her gently. "Maybe a few minutes, I guess," Liz admitted wearily. "We live on kind of a busy street and I just can't help think what might happen if I was inside and something happened to the boys."

We all know that Liz is far from alone. The fear of child predators and other strangers lurking in our midst can make most of us pretty frantic, even if we know the statistics reveal that our kids are twelve times more likely to get hit by lightning than to be abducted. Even the minuscule chance of something terrible occurring while we were off our watch is enough to cause nightmares for many parents. In a world where so little seems to be within our control, at least we can protect our kids from any unforeseen harm.

It's hard to argue with this logic. I know firsthand because I often try to play the devil's advocate with parents. I want kids to learn to be independent, to practice making mistakes and handling frustration, and to take risks. I believe kids need a chance to handle increasing levels of responsibility as they grow older if they are to be prepared for the freedom they will have in adolescence. If we cut off outdoor exploration and are afraid to leave our kids alone outside, we make it much tougher for them to accomplish these tasks. Playing basketball and making up games in the driveway and the backyard are pretty good ways for kids to assert themselves and try to master new challenges. Somehow the basement playroom does not afford them quite the same opportunities.

We'll come back to outdoor time later in this section, but first it's important to appreciate how radically things have changed in the past two decades. In recent years parents have been besieged with dramatic stories of bad things happening to little kids. The media outlets stick with a tragic story for as long as they can, and the repetitive cycling of old news further heightens our suspicion that lots of terrible people, perhaps not just strangers, are ready to pounce at any place and at any time. Into the fray have stepped a new wave of technology promoters, who claim they can ensure our children's safety with Nanny Cams, Spyware, and even personal GPS tracking systems. Ironically, the same generation of parents who now depend on these devices would have protested loudly against a lack of trust and any invasion on their privacy and personal space when they were adolescents.

Somehow the virtues we used to depend on—trusting our neighbors, looking out for other people's children, and giving our children a longer leash as they proved worthy of more independence—no longer seem relevant. I realize that certain realities have changed, including the increase in working mothers and the absence of kids hanging out on the block or in the neighbors' backyards. But this is not the whole story. One of the primary reasons kids are not out on the street is parents' reluctance to let them wander far, and belief that they are safer in organized activities under adult supervision.

At workshops, I often relate my memories of walking the neighborhood on my own when I was five or six years old. I could go to a few friends' houses and cross streets by myself, although my eight-year-old brother was often nearby. These stories can sound apocryphal, and sometimes I question the accuracy of my remembrances, so I hesitate before telling them. Inevitably, more than a few parents in the audience raise their hands and tell the group that they were allowed the same freedoms at that age. We often share a laugh when we talk about telling our kids these stories. They look a little puzzled and doubtful, as if we had just told another tall tale of walking to school a mile in the snow in our bare feet, back in the age of dinosaurs.

A "Safe" Alternative?

The experience of kids today is radically different, but they are no less inclined to be explorers. With limited options for outdoor discovery, they turn to other avenues. They might become experts at wielding the television clicker and ticking off the names of their favorite characters and shows. Often they are drawn to the computer, and particularly to the wonders of the Internet. I have preschoolers who talk to me about their favorite Web sites where they like to play games or buy "cool stuff." Their parents usually limit the sites they can access and have some forms of parental controls in place, and rest assured that no harm can come their way on the Disney or Nickelodeon sites.

Yet some of this exploring does not always stay so innocent. I hear plenty of stories of second and third graders who have found their way to pornography Web sites (which populate much of the Internet), of kids who become obsessed with eBay at a young age, and others who receive e-mail solicitations from carmakers, toy dealers, and music companies. If you asked most law enforcement officials what poses the greatest danger to our children, many of them would speak out strongly about the perils of surfing the Web, including the Westchester, New York, District Attorney:

> Children using the Internet can communicate with strangers and access material that is inappropriate for them. The dangers that threaten our children, i.e., pedophiles, scam artists, hate groups, and pornographers, all exist over the Internet. The difference is that cyberspace provides anonymity to people intent on harming children.[1]

Many law enforcement agencies warn against the dangers of blogs and online profiles that have become a regular part of the middle and high school social scene.

We have to be careful not to go overboard here, and I do not want parents to exchange one big fear for another. But even if we have the best intentions about keeping our children safe and indoors, we have to be aware that the time they spend on the computer is not a totally risk-free alternative to outdoor play. Just as with television and video games, kids do not stay loyal to age-appropriate sites forever, and as their minds wander their keystrokes can take them to places we do not want them to go. The e-mails or instant messages to grade school friends can be friendly and cute, but the majority of cases of harassment and bullying and threats of violence involving older children are from online communications. To some extent parents can control these risky behaviors by keeping the family computer in a public place (like the kitchen or family room) and letting their kids know that they will occasionally be looking over their shoulder when they are online. These safeguards are not foolproof, however, and when our children are still young, we have to think carefully about where we want them to do their exploring and compare the risks of their physical surroundings to those in cyberspace.

Busy Bees or Idlers

The fear of letting children roam too far is only half the story when it comes to explaining the preponderance of scheduled activities for kids. Perhaps just as deeply, parents fear another bogeyman, one who sings the siren song of idleness and lack of direction. We feel that our kids, from an early age, should be doing something "productive"—learn an instrument, try a foreign language, take gymnastics or karate, swim, play soccer, dance in the local ballet. There is this nagging worry that if we don't start soon, the train's going to leave the station, and our kids will never catch up to it. We've heard about early brain development and "critical periods." Wasn't Mozart writing symphonies at age four?

It is easy to poke fun at other parents who get so crazed. But who among us is immune to feeling these pressures? A few years back I came home and announced to my wife that I thought we should sign up our seven-year-old son for a cartooning class and karate lessons. Not that he had ever shown the least bit of interest or inclination toward either one. It just seemed like a good idea to me. She looked at me as if I had two heads, and asked me (without much empathy, I might add), "Have you lost your mind?"

Temporarily, I think I had. My son was happy playing baseball, his only organized activity at the time, but I couldn't help but feel that he had so much more *potential*. In a world of shrinking opportunities, many of us believe it is our job to make sure our children hone their talents at an early age. We have all heard the success stories. Didn't Tiger Woods's dad have him on the golf course at age three? What about those tennis stars who lifted up a racket shortly after reaching for their spoons? The fact that we logically know these are one-in-a-million stories does little to deter many parents who picture their sons playing center field for the Red Sox or scoring the winning goal in the World Cup qualifier.

Most of these fantasies are harmless ones that may reflect our own childhood dreams or mesh with our kids' desires. If we feel these stirrings at the weekly T-Ball game for our first graders and revel in their first hit, we are not guilty of being sports-crazed parents. The problem starts when the scale gets tipped too far in one direction. I don't deny the value of one or two activities for kindergarteners, but when I hear about the four during the week and the three on the weekends my antennae go way up. Sometimes things start out slowly, then quickly morph into a completely different experience.

Take girls and dancing. A neighborhood ballet class or an Irish step dancing instruction at the local community center sounds like fun and requires no great commitment. But for some of these programs the next steps involve a rapid ramping up of practice time, competitions, and family travel. In two years or less that little hobby can become a child's obsession, or better yet, her second job. For many children, the fun and playfulness can get lost in this transition, and they can feel increasing pressure to perform at a high level or risk disappointing their parents and teachers.

Certain activities are more likely to pull for a big commitment at an early age. In addition to dance, gymnastics, competitive swimming, and travel soccer and hockey all require a great deal of time and energy from their participants, some as young as six or seven. These are all worthwhile pursuits, and I can personally think of no greater pleasure than a spirited game of ice hockey. In another time and place, however, some of us were fortunate enough to learn these sports and activities on our own, and had the luxury of time and freedom to skate as long as we wanted on the local pond.

Those days may be behind us, and I know there is not always wisdom in waxing nostalgic, but we have to consider very carefully how many organized events our children should have each week. Is it okay for an eight-year-old to dance four nights a week? Should a six-year-old in the local theater production practice three nights a week for two months? Does a five-year-old need to play lacrosse, basketball, and tennis on Saturday? These questions can sound absurd to our own parents, many of whom think we have lost all perspective. But in this era of extreme sports demands, piles of grade school homework, and the constant chatter about travel teams and getting an early leg up on college admissions, stepping back and getting perspective is no easy task.

In many families parents disagree over how much is too much. Usually I find it is the mothers who are more willing to put on the breaks, while the fathers tend to keep the burners up high. Many of these dads enjoyed playing sports as children and many continue to be active, and they want their sons and daughters to have the same experiences. Although they realize they may not have joined a team until age nine or ten, they lend little credence to this fact, and typically argue that, "It's just not like that anymore." So they sign their kids up for baseball, soccer, and basketball at age four or five, well before the rules of those games are understood by the kids and a few years before they can muster a reasonable facsimile of a real ball game.

Some parents will point out that their plans include a reasonable assessment of scheduling and logistics. As Rick, the father of five- and seven-year-old girls put it, "Yes they're pretty busy, but they have two activities Saturday morning, and then a two-hour break before the afternoon tennis lesson. I made sure to build that in." Given Rick's busy life as an active family man and an advertising executive who manages multiple clients, this seems pretty manageable. The problem is that young children cannot readily handle the demands of an adultlike schedule. It was no surprise that Rick's daughters were starting to balk at the prospect of their free day being chopped up into hourly segments.

Proceed with Caution

There are plenty of young children who don't understand their parents' enthusiasm for organized activities. They are happy making up stories, playing in the mud, or climbing trees. They may be dreamers who love to get lost in their own thoughts and imagination. Parents sometimes misinterpret these temperamental differences and look upon these kids as uninvolved or worse, "lazy." I often spend time reassuring parents that just because their son or daughter is not so interested in kickball or soccer or gymnastics at age four or five, it doesn't mean that they will never try anything new.

Often the best course is to wait a year or two, or to pick one activity that a parent and child can do together, such as swimming. The biggest hurdle in parents' accepting this advice is their concern that they are giving into sedentary or mindless pursuits when their children could be so much more productive. As we shall see shortly, those same activities that seem to lack purpose or direction can be the most important endeavors in the life of a young child.

The trend in organized activities starting at younger age forces parents to make decisions and commitments before they have established family routines and rituals. Let's imagine a family that includes a preschooler, a toddler, and an infant. We know that life can be pretty chaotic when kids are this young, with lack of sleep and exhaustion a frequent companion for the parents. Setting dinner- and bedtimes can be a challenge, and organizing outings to the park can seem like a Herculean effort. These parents would be doing pretty well if they could get their older two children to preschool and arrange a playdate or two during the week.

Throw one or two or three scheduled activities into this mix and the normal chaos can become a whirlwind where both parents, and Mom in particular, are likely to feel lucky if they survive from week to week. The situation becomes that much trickier to manage for mothers who organize the family schedule and also hold down a full- or part-time job. Parents may say they are going with the flow in the community by choosing this route, but many feel that in fact they have very little in the way of choice. They also have less time to step back and consider how much is too much, especially if their four-year-old daughter begs to do all the activities that her friends are doing, and their two-year-old son enjoys his twice weekly playgroup across town.

Not that long ago, families enjoyed a much longer nesting period. Many activities didn't begin until the kids were in the later years of elementary school. Parents had more time to get their kids into a routine, and the rhythm of mealtimes, baths, and winding down from the day took precedent. Siblings close in age were expected to play with and amuse each other, and were not carted off to separate enrichment activities. In most cases, parents felt less inclined to adhere to a schedule, except for visits with grandparents and other family obligations.

These then-and-now comparisons are problematic, and we have to recognize that many families today like being more active and on the go than the previous generation. Many parents struggle to find the right mix, and to identify which rituals matter most to them. Sometimes the decisions get postponed, intentionally or by default. Yet it is not easy to turn around a few years down the road and declare, "We need to have dinner together regularly and we need more family time, too." If we have not set up quiet periods and alone time for our kids when they are preschoolers, it's not a simple matter to put on the brakes and get them to slow down when they are eight or nine.

The onslaught of appealing classes and lessons for our little ones, and the pressure we feel to get them going at an early age, make it that much more critical that parents take time out to look at the big picture. Early in the game (before we should be expected to have *perspective*), we need to step back, draw a deep breath, and decide which activities really matter and which our kids can sample at another time. This notion that everything doesn't need to happen right away, that time *is* on our side, can be the most difficult thought to muster and maintain, especially with the flurry of activities all around us.

The Sporting Life

That advice about waiting a few years sounds reasonable enough, if we're talking about signing our kids up for chess or drawing or piano lessons. But when it comes to sports, it sure feels like the time is now. The explosion of soccer leagues and T-Ball games and basketball clinics for children as young as four or five must be rooted in some theory of early physical development, is it not? Aren't the games kids play a good way to teach them about working hard and handling frustration, two of the recurrent themes in this book?

I am a big believer in physical fitness and of getting kids active from an early age. And it's true that sports are a great way to teach lessons about persistence and trying our best. The question of when to start is another story. Child development experts argue that kids cannot fully understand the rules of games and social interaction required until they are seven or eight. Kathy Hirsh-Pasek and Roberta Golinkoff make this point about soccer in their book *Einstein Never Used Flash Cards*:

> When are kids developmentally ready to cope with the idea of team and rules? In these complex games, the key is understanding not only what you are supposed to do, but also what the person next to you is doing and might do next. You must be able to anticipate what the person on the other team might do next. So as a child, you might learn that you should kick the ball forward, but if that is all you do, you are not really playing the game of soccer. In

*fact anyone who watches four- or five-year-olds on the soccer field
will attest to the fact that when the ball moves into the field, you
find a clump of children from both teams all trying to kick it at
once. What's most fun is when young children kick the ball into
their own goal—so much for rules![2]*

This doesn't mean that getting out on the field on Saturday mornings in
the fall can't be enjoyable for little kids. It can also be a great place for
families to hang out and socialize for an hour or two, but we have to
keep in mind that we are not likely to put our kids' soccer career in jeopardy if they miss a few weeks or if they'd rather wait another year or
more to join a team.

Most adults who work with little kids understand this and try not to
push them too hard at too early an age. Inevitably, however, we hear
the stories of coaches who ramp up the competition, and drop not-so-
subtle hints that the third-grade travel squad will be determined by who
performs the best in the first- and second-grade leagues. Parents can
easily succumb to the fear that it may all be in good fun now, but the
going gets tough just around the corner. These pressures eventually
trickle down to the kids, most of whom just want to have a good time
and not worry about the next game or the upcoming seasons.

The other experts, those who have been involved in a high level of
athletic competition as players or coaches, find this a particularly disturbing trend. Bob Bigelow, the former professional basketball player
and frequent lecturer to parents, argues that all the positives in playing
sports—having fun, exercising, and naturally developing skills—have
been offset by the surge in competition and the pressure on coaches to
provide a good "product." Bigelow points to his own experience as a
gangly ten-year-old who was no more coordinated than his neighborhood friends. Like most children, he would have been ill prepared for
the rigor of "select" teams where the priority is to identify and mold
young talent. Bigelow argues against organizing travel teams before the
seventh grade.[3]

Jeff Van Gundy, the coach of the Houston Rockets, was dismayed by

t o give an indication of just how far out of whack things can get in organized sports, here are a few lines drawn verbatim from a flyer for a third-grade baseball team: "Travel team baseball is highly competitive and even the best players are often frustrated by the level of competition they face. Travel team baseball requires an enormous commitment of time and energy. There are usually three games as well as mandatory practice and batting cage sessions every week. You will have to devote your summer to baseball. Vacations, camps, weekends away, and even sleepovers are definitely not encouraged by the coaches. It puts a team at a severe disadvantage when players are away for any length of time. Travel team baseball is for kids whose first priority is to play baseball above all other summer activities."

So much for the lazy days of summer!

the behavior he witnessed in coaches and parents in local gyms during his year off from coaching. He was shocked by the high expectations and the pressure put on young children. His recommendations for change: "If I coached kids, it would be for each kid to improve by the end of the season and to love the sport. You can't be results-oriented with kids, and you can't treat a seven-year-old girl like a thirty-year-old man." Van Gundy is wary of the amount of time children spend in organized basketball and other sports, and he believes the best way for kids to improve and have fun is to play by themselves, where "the only adult present . . . is the one who comes with the key to open the gym."[4]

Others see the danger in kids specializing too early in one sport and of the gradual transformation of seasonal sports into year-round activities for kids as young as seven or eight. There may be lots of child-friendly instructors, but the specialized camps that advertise to parents often emphasize drills and skill building rather than the fun of playing the games. Sports can start to feel like a chore after a few years, and there are plenty of stories of third graders who can't take how serious the leagues have become, and drop out of organized sports altogether.

"Am I Good Enough to Play?"

Talk about the costs and benefits of an activity. If our kids learn early on that games should be more like work and that the aim is to defeat the other team at all costs, we should probably take a serious look at our priorities. But we should also be concerned by a more subtle message that some kids take away from organized sports. Valerie had wanted her five-year-old, Danny, to be in the local leagues with his friends, and she had signed him up for soccer and T-Ball. Danny was still a little clumsy, though he was a good swimmer and a fast runner. In both team sports he felt he lagged behind the other boys, and after many games he would be on the verge of crying. "I'm not very good at this," he would often tearfully tell his mother. Despite her reassurances that he was a pretty good little player, Danny always felt he was letting someone down. His father was not quite as sympathetic, and urged him to toughen up and get back in there.

This idea that our kids need to be very good at age five or six or seven is absurd, but we can sometimes be hard-pressed to convince them otherwise. If they miss the net frequently or can't hit the ball straight when they are young, it does not mean that they will not progress as they grow older. But if they are in a team situation where these failings are measured and recorded, or at least seem to be, how do we expect them to maintain perspective? After all, many adults struggle to keep a clear head about their children's future prospects.

The oft-heard lessons from the past bear repeating. We know that Michael Jordan was not considered good enough to make his high school team when he first tried out. We hear lots of stories of athletes who came of age relatively late and only began to specialize in one sport in college. I attended a banquet recently where the New York Giants

i f we thought there was such a thing as a clear path to a career in professional sports, the actual statistics provide a good reality check. According to a recent study, only about one in sixteen thousand boys who play fourth-grade basketball will spend any time in the NBA. And though it might appear to be pretty reasonable to aim for that college scholarship, less than 1 percent of boys playing in elementary school will go on to play at the college level. As for tennis, the same guide reports that of the three million ten- to eighteen-year-olds who play tennis competitively, only about 175 will earn any money professionally playing the game. That's about a one-in-seventeen-thousand chance. If we think our children are likely to turn pro in their favorite sport, we might also want to consider playing the lottery on a regular basis. The odds are no worse.[5]

kicker Jay Feely spoke to a group of grade-schoolers. There was a moment of stunned silence when, in response to a question from one of the kids, he informed the audience that he didn't play organized football until *ninth grade*. He became a kicker only because his team didn't have one, and he volunteered because he had played soccer for the past few years. So much for a carefully drawn up plan to a career in professional sports!

Games for Kids

Organized sports for kids have a long history in this country. Little League baseball began in 1939. Not long after came the first complaints that things were getting too structured. In *Summer of '49*, David Halberstam's stirring account of the Yankees/Red Sox rivalry that season, he describes a conversation between two of the Yankee sluggers. They both agreed that youth baseball had become too regimented for good hitters like themselves, who could easily get "fifty hits in one day" in local sandlot games. Even back then many youngsters were loath to give up their independence and hand their games over to adults for the sake of wearing team uniforms.[6]

This is the real sticking point. As much as parents and coaches maintain that they have the best of intentions and that they do it for the kids, league games frequently turn into adultlike competitions and evaluations. The second graders who would rather fool around than sit on the bench get labeled "troublemakers," and those who are less adept at fielding and hitting quickly get designated for the B league. Many coaches remain committed to fairness and equal playing time for little kids, but they sometimes do so under the watchful eye of parents who wish their children were in a more challenging division against tougher competition. Fun and games and other kid stuff get pushed a little lower down the totem pole in the process.

We talked earlier of some of the lessons children can learn from sports, and I believe there are many. Organizing games, making up teams, playing fairly, practicing with their peers, supporting each other, and most importantly, learning to have fun and revel in their freedom, are all part of playing games together. The key is allowing children to proceed at their own pace and to set their own rules for the games, even if they bear little resemblance to the real sports that they will compete in later. If they can figure out how to develop and play spirited games and resolve their own disputes without the help of adults, they will be much further along than most of their peers.

That may sound far-fetched; how do five- and six- and seven-year-olds make up their own games? If we give them the chance, and don't get caught up in strictly adhering to the rules, we are likely to be pleasantly surprised. Kids can draw up base paths and put together makeshift goals, and most little children can arrange a kickball game when given the opportunity. These fledgling games are often treasured and re-

One of the frequent complaints I hear from my own children and the kids I work with is the tendency for school-yard sports to deteriorate into squabbles and fights that end up ruining the games. Even with simple sports like kickball, it is hard for many children to agree on the rules and play fairly without an adult to supervise them. Many kids who love sports avoid these games because the conflicts grow so tiresome.

counted by kids and allow them to feel that they, and not the adults around them, are in control of their own sporting life.

We don't have to provide them much equipment, either. Backyard soccer and whiffle ball games are pretty easy to set up. Adjustable hoops for basketball allow little and not so little kids to test their mettle, and nets for street hockey games or lacrosse require only a driveway or a little open space in a school yard. The Nerf equivalent of all these sports allows kids to play indoors as well without risking serious damage to a playroom or basement. Our job as parents is to supervise lightly or to assist with the initial divvying up of teams, and to help the kids agree on a few simple-to-follow rules.

The biggest contribution we can make is not investing money in equipment or serving as referees. What we can do is to provide a context for our children to play games on their own without the pressure of team sports. This involves two key elements. Setting aside time when the kids can play outside and organize games on their own is one. The second is more difficult but is based on simple math: Our kids need other kids to play with, especially if they don't have siblings close in age. We can solve this problem by doing our best to round up a neighborhood gang, by inviting groups of kids over, and by working to establish a community where the adults support children playing on their own. We will talk more about this in chapter 11, but suffice to say that our kids will greatly appreciate our efforts to give them what they want most: a time and place to play without interference or interruption.

A Cure for the Bored:
Explore the Outdoors

In many ways, kids' experience of nature has run a parallel course to their time spent playing sports. Much of the exposure children have to the outdoors is carefully scrutinized and supervised by their parents, teachers, and other adults. They may spend time in the local playgrounds, but they are usually safe and sanitized and often free of much green space. Backyards allow for more wandering, but many parents prefer that their kids spend dedicated time on their swing sets or in their playhouses where the risk of injury or infection is minimal. Many suburban neighborhoods were built without sidewalks, and modern planned communities are built primarily for cars, not for casual walks along the side of the road. Despite the recent influx of wildlife into residential neighborhoods, most of us are far removed from rural or wilderness areas, as the suburbs extend far beyond the edges of the cities that first sprouted them.

The debate about the relative merits of the trends in suburban living fills the pages of the academic journals of sociologists and urban planners, but few parents worry about how changes in the natural environment have come to affect their young children. As long as they are safe and get some fresh air and exercise, why would we give it much thought? In fact, in many ways, our kids' experience of nature has become an *afterthought*, well below concerns about our kids' emerging intelligence, social skills, technological prowess, and performance in sports. In his illuminating book on this subject, *Last Child in the Woods*, Richard Louv describes how we have come to minimize the benefits of the natural world, and to marginalize it as a place for killing time, and not much else.[7]

This may sound a little extreme. Surely most parents want their children to learn to love and respect nature. In my experience, it is not a question of the ideals we cherish but how these translate into our children's day-to-day lives. I hear parents tell stories, sometimes fondly, of children who like to climb trees and collect rocks and look at bugs, followed quickly by a wish that they would buckle down and do something more productive. Six-year-old Bobby loved to roll in the mud and make forts with the branches and sticks he gathered. His parents were worried he didn't want to spend more time with friends. Twin second graders Emma and Annette were forever stymieing their parents' attempts to enroll them in activities, much to their chagrin, because they preferred to fool around in the backyard and explore all its little nooks and crannies.

In order to condone and encourage our little explorers we have to have faith that they are up to some good out there. If we're going to make the choice to give them more free time to wander rather than sign them up for another activity, well, frankly, we have to explain ourselves to our friends and neighbors who may not see the same value in leisurely outdoor time. Here goes. I'll try to make the case that the great outdoors is a wondrous place for our kids to roam and make the most of their unstructured time.

First let's look at the potential benefits of nature for our children's mental and physical health. We know that there has been a huge surge in obesity in children in recent years. There are a number of factors at work here, including meals on the run and other less than ideal eating habits in families, but I believe the largest impact has come from the sedentary lifestyle that has become a more accepted part of family life. Many parents feel that their kids work so hard in school and in their sports and activities, they need downtime. So they allow a little TV and computer time after school and on the weekends, and this trend starts out innocently enough. But electronic games and the television have a hypnotic pull for many kids, and it often becomes a huge battle to get them to unplug for a while. Other activities, including going outside and being physically active, can easily lose their luster.

Despite the surge in organized sports, our kids are in worse shape

i n the Kaiser Foundation report on television viewing habits (October, 2003), four- to six-year-olds who
watched more than two hours of TV or videos every day
spent an average of thirty minutes less per day playing outside. This may seem like an obvious connection, but it
bears repeating that kids who watch more television tend
to get less fresh air and exercise.

than ever. This may not actually be so contradictory, because much of
the instruction kids get requires a lot of listening and standing about
rather than actively running and playing the game, and children who
participate in sports do not always get enough exercise from them. In
addition, the more organized sports resemble work, the less interested
kids may be in playing those games on their own. If they've punched the
clock already, and completed their physical tasks for the day, why go out
and run around anymore? They may look for another way to unwind
and de-stress, and the electronic media at their fingertips can appear to
be the perfect solution.

Rigorously running and playing in the yard is usually a much better
way to relieve stress and ensure that our children are getting enough exercise. It also allows them to feel that being outdoors and being physically active are fun and a natural part of their lives, not just a
programmed experience designed by the adults in charge. All children
benefit from this experience, but none more than kids who are energetic and highly active. Free time to run around after school is the best
cure for these stir-crazy kids, who need to burn off their excess energy
before they can focus and slow down later in the day. Loosely organized
sports and games in after-school programs can serve the same purpose,
though again, the rules and structure, however minimal, may be more
than some of these children can handle after a long day cooped up indoors.

The restorative and stress-reducing power of the outdoors is not only beneficial to more active children. Taking a long walk in the woods, climbing an oak tree, sitting in the sun in springtime, and listening to the roar of the ocean can offer soothing relief and improve the mood of most people. Many therapists have started to recognize the healing powers of the outdoors for children who have suffered loss and other serious trauma, and have tried to incorporate outdoor spaces into their work.[8] No matter what the issue, I almost always suggest that parents who consult with me build in more outdoor time with their children, even if it means just lounging with them in the hammock. Having been raised in New England, I suggest that kids be nudged to play outside whenever the temperature is between thirty and ninety degrees!

Observation and Imagination

Giving children the chance to relax and rejuvenate are some of the benefits of outdoor play, but they don't stop there. Roaming in the woods and the backyard gives our kids the chance to be little scientists, observing, exploring, and collecting as they wander. Right outside their doors they can see butterflies resting on flowers, squirrels chewing on nuts, ants busying themselves around their hills, and weeds sprouting up here and there.

Questions abound during these times. What happens when we follow animal tracks? Why do flowers and plants lean toward the sun? What happens when water mixes with dirt? These are all hypotheses that young kids can test out for themselves. Their trial and error experiments lead them to a different level of understanding of the physical world, and give them the chance to separate out and categorize different types of flora and fauna. This is a type of learning that is not easily replicated in the classroom.

In his updated list of multiple intellectual abilities, Harvard University psychologist Howard Gardner points to these skills as part of a "naturalist intelligence." The developing naturalist shows an interest in recognizing and distinguishing types of plants and animals and how these species interact with one another. Gardner describes how some of the great natural scientists, including Charles Darwin and Stephen Jay Gould, displayed an early fascination with plants and animals and their surroundings. He contends that the ability to recognize and categorize different patterns in nature is not only important for biologists and mathematicians, but is also crucial to the work of artists, poets, and social scientists. Gardner cites research that indicates that children's early language learning and classification systems are based upon "natural forms of categorization rather than those forms that have evolved to deal with manufactured objects."[9]

Little explorers have a chance to take risks and stretch their imagination. Think back to Will and the tree house he built with his friends. No prefab kit can re-create the thrill of hammering away or placing makeshift boards in uneven ways between two sturdy branches. Our kids may not live like *The Swiss Family Robinson*, but that doesn't mean they can't have adventures in the nearby woods. I use "woods" loosely. I remember being six or seven and creeping my way up the street with friends to the "scary woods." Looking back, this was just a few trees and overgrown bushes that encompassed no more than a single family lot (which, of course, is what it has become today), but we had hours of adventures there building forts and hiding places and planning ways to sneak up on each other. If you don't quite have this space in your backyard or on your street, you can find suitable terrain in most city parks or preserved lands, or on the edge of your school playgrounds.

Nature presents endless possibilities for play. A little open space and an explorers' mind-set are all our kids need to develop fantasies of pirates, of pilgrims and Native Americans, of trailblazing pioneers or wild game hunters in the deepest and darkest jungles. Richard Louv cites a number of recent studies in this country and abroad that show that green spaces encourage more fantasy and open-ended play than traditional playgrounds. This is true for both boys and girls, and natural surroundings seem to allow for more egalitarian play where creativity and dramatic skills are more valued than physical competence. I have witnessed this spirit of adventure and collaboration on numerous occasions in our own neighborhood, among young and older children alike. There is something about being outdoors in a free-flowing way that allows children to feel less encumbered by the usual social hierarchies and to open up their minds to a world beyond the here and now.

A Place for Dreamers

Creative play sounds like fun, and most of us have some memories of our own outdoor and indoor adventures with our siblings and friends, but for better or worse, we tend to be more goal-directed than our own parents, and many of us can't help but ask what purpose this imaginative play serves. Sure, we have heard preschool teachers explain that children "learn through play," but I often see parents' eyes glaze over at just these moments on back-to-school nights. Despite all the enchanting stories of the imaginative games of the likes of Albert Einstein or Benjamin Franklin as youths, we cannot quite connect their adult achievements with their childhood fantasies.

Parents are also aware that academic expectations in elementary school have been significantly increased in the past two decades. The No Child Left Behind legislation has been translated into a new set of standards and testing from the early grades on up. I have heard a former kindergarten teacher comment, "Kindergarten is what second grade was like twenty-five years ago." It's not surprising that many parents feel an urgency to get formal learning started as early as possible. Many choose more academic pre-K programs and look for ways to help their children learn their letters, colors, and numbers as soon as possible.

I meet lots of parents who proudly report that their children are starting to read at age five (or four or three!), but I rarely hear about kids who are fantastic at playing and using their imagination. Sandy brought up concerns that her four-year-old daughter, Meagan, was always using puzzle pieces for other purposes. They were bridges in castles or parts of elaborate buildings, but rarely were they ever just puzzle pieces. I explained that puzzles have their place, but Meagan's use of these pieces in dramatic fashion was a terrific example of a child experimenting and playing with meaning. In adult terms, we would call this "thinking out-side the box." We know that many successful people have what Meagan already possesses—a well-developed capacity to go beyond ordinary so-lutions and frameworks.

Young children's dramatic play is a precursor to thinking abstractly, reasoning, and problem solving. In the words of Kathy Hirsh-Pasek and Roberta Golinkoff, *Play is to early childhood what gas is to a car. It is the very fuel of every intellectual activity our children engage in.*" Though it may sound counterintuitive, play is the best preparation for school. More sophisticated uses of language and reading comprehen-sion are based on an understanding that symbols (i.e., words) have meaning beyond what is actually written on the page. Play requires ma-nipulating symbols, and understanding that one thing can stand in for something else.

Unlike most of their experiences, imaginative play allows children to feel that they have power to control their fate and to develop mastery over their immediate environment in a way that organized activities can never match. They have the chance to test out theories, create their own narratives, and act out who they want to be. In studies, imaginative play is linked to increased patience and impulse control, and height-ened resilience and coping skills. Some of the social benefits linked to play are easy to understand; it is fun, interactive, and allows for children to build upon each other's ideas. But imaginative play, and role-playing games in particular, also train children to take other perspectives, to re-ally feel what it's like to be a teacher, a captured prisoner, or a brave knight. This perspective taking sets the foundation for developing em-pathy and an appreciation of other people's experiences.[10]

Playtime

The real beauty of play lies in its simplicity. Given the chance, most kids figure out how to do it. If we give children a box of dress-up clothes, a few cars or action figures, dinosaurs, a dollhouse, and some blocks, chances are they will get right down to business. The problem is rarely having the right stuff. What most of our kids do not have is enough *time to play*. Here's where the debate over structured activities really heats up. If we look upon play as of equal or greater value than the organized sports and lessons our kids have on the schedule, it is only natural to ask if we give it equal billing and equal time. In other words, do we build in time to play every day?

The answer, according to recent data, is no. In *Huck's Raft*, Steven Mintz reports that children's unstructured playtime fell by 40 percent in the 1980s and 1990s.[11] It's not hard to make the connection between this decrease and the explosion of sports and activities and enrichment programs for children during the same time period. Something had to give, and mealtime (down by a third) and playtime suffered the most. These statistics are distressing to many parents but few have ready solutions for their own families. It just seems so natural that everyone is so busy, and the organized learning and socializing opportunities they have committed to seem to be ideal for enriching their children's minds and bodies.

It is striking how out of step we are with conventional child development wisdom. This may sound a little funny coming from me. After all, one of the purposes of this book is to help parents make their own way, and not feel obliged to always follow the "experts." When it comes to play, however, there is no denying the facts. Fifty years of research has demonstrated that play is the essential ingredient for social, emotional, and intellectual development in young children. Unlike the debates over sleeping or toilet training or spanking, no child psychologist or pediatrician in the last fifty years, from Dr. Spock on down, has challenged the primacy of play. Every savvy early childhood educator I know stresses the value of play in the classroom. All the parenting magazines do the same thing. I suppose we are not always inclined to follow the lead of basic science in this country, but it is remarkable to see how far we have drifted from these core beliefs about play.

Threats to Play

The time factor is not the only reason for the reduction in children's imaginative play. In the last chapter we discussed the pressure on parents to keep their children up to date on the latest technology and learning devices. The problem with many of these "smart toys" is that they offer limited options for kids to use their imagination. Devices that seek to promote color or word recognition are often adept at training children in rote memorization, not at encouraging them to be active problem solvers. Though they are touted for their interactive experience, video and computer games usually provide their own ready-made story lines, and the kids who play them are responding to specific situations rather than constructing their own narratives.

More basic toys like blocks and dolls and animals force kids to actively brainstorm and engage with their toys, and there are few limits on what stories and characters they can create with them. Yet if children are used to being led in one direction by their electronic games and reacting to a predetermined set of choices, they may have a much harder time switching gears and making up their own pretend scenes. As much as we encourage them, they may find that using their imagination feels like hard work in comparison to the more passive experience of sitting in front of a screen.

We all know how kids tend to respond in this situation: "I'm bored!" I hear this all the time from parents. Jill told me how she would come home from nursery school with her youngest child at lunchtime. "What do we do now, Mommy?" Timmy would always ask. When she would instruct him to play by himself for a while or make up a game, he would hesitate and complain that "it's no fun, there's nobody to play with." After a few more minutes of this, Jill would usually turn on the television for "just one show." Over time, one show became two, and then three.

For many parents like Jill, holding their ground becomes a daunting task. We all tend to lose our patience when there's too much whining in the house. It's easier to give in and let them watch TV or play computer games for respite. In the future maybe we'll schedule classes or playdates for kids like Timmy. Though the travel time and logistics take their toll, it sometimes seems to be a small price to pay for eliminating the constant complaining that our kids are bored and have nothing to do. If our kids do not seem so interested in playing on their own or creating imaginary stories with their siblings, it can feel like it's no great sacrifice for them if we let their playtime slide. As long as they're busy and social and active, what harm can be done?

Playing for Keeps: Encouraging Young Explorers

Don't Fear Boredom

Most of us can relate to Jill's struggle with Timmy. At some point we have to determine if we can wait out our kids and not give in to their demands to be entertained or relieved of feeling bored. Again, we're back to endurance, and mustering the strength and fortitude necessary to hold the line against their onslaught ("I'm sure you can think of *something* to do"). This becomes slightly easier if we can see real value in boredom. That may sound weird; after all, don't children get into all sorts of mischief when they are bored?

Indeed they do. Having "nothing to do" forces children to think for themselves. Creative play often emerges from these downtimes, as kids get a chance to make up their own stories and their own games. Some of the most creative scientists and artists recall long days without much doing in their homes. They were forced to use their own devices to create games and invent imaginary worlds. It is no surprise that Einstein got his start imagining himself riding on light beams in the sky!

Join in the Fun

Some children are more naturally prone to imaginative play, and they take these gaps in the day in stride. They can easily fill them with art projects and pretend worlds with action heroes and dragons and princesses. Others, who tend to complain a bit more about the lack of available amusement, may have a hard time getting started. It's fine to give them a little help setting off by suggesting how they might play with their animals or dinosaurs or dolls, for instance ("Let's imagine we live in the jungle"), and by jumping into the action with them ("I'll be a knight; do we have any volunteers for princess?"). We have to be careful not to take over or construct our own stories, but if our children see that we are really interested in playing (and do our best to enjoy it!), they are more likely to keep going and lend their own twist to the tales. Even simple good guy/bad guy scenarios can provide rich amusement and fantasy, and kids can revel in their parents playing Captain Hook or another evil villain. Most kids who need help getting started can eventually assume these roles on their own.

Set the Stage for Play

In addition to setting aside time for play, we should also provide material and space for our kids to let themselves go. This does not mean that we have to have a fancy and well-stocked art room. A few paints and crayons and paper will usually suffice. Unstructured toys like blocks, dress-up clothes, and Legos that allow for multiple meanings and promote divergent thinking are generally the best props for stimulating play. For some children, especially boys, who are less drawn to creative play, action figures, army men, and plastic forts or castles often help get them into a stirring battle scene. We have to be careful not to overwhelm children with too many toys. In our house, empty cardboard boxes, an old blanket, and a few plastic swords have been more than enough to keep our three kids occupied in the basement on rainy days, and they have dreamed up many adventures in far-off kingdoms.

Tell Stories

Making up stories with our children of dashing adventurers, of witches in the deep, dark forest, or brave pioneers plowing through the wilderness, stimulates their imagination and allows them to envision other times and other places. These may emerge out of familiar fairy tales and other stories, but it is often more fun and more challenging to make up our own narratives and have the kids join in to add their own details or endings. They need not be superfancy or dramatic; little kids usually appreciate just about any of our storytelling attempts. Every year on Halloween the kids in our neighborhood look forward to my wife's ghost stories. She entertains three- to twelve-year-olds, and both the younger and the older kids in the crowd relish the suspense and humorous turns in her tall tales. The few dads present make do providing sound effects in the background!

Be a Model of Playfulness

What children love most is seeing their parents letting go and having fun. Tickling games, silly stories, dancing, singing, and just goofing around all bring shrieks of laughter from young children. Life can seem so serious for us and for our kids; they need to see that we have not forgotten how to have fun and have a sense of humor ("Dad was acting so crazy"). Fantasy games, stories, and creativity carry more weight in a family that relishes the value of being playful, and kids are more likely to be drawn to them if they see we value having a freewheeling good time ("Did you see Mom dance that goofy dance?"). Most of us adults could benefit from this reminder: We feel better when we smile, when we laugh and have fun, and are more likely to feel up to handling our everyday stresses. Our kids are really no different.

Choose Organized Activities Wisely

For children under age seven or eight, one or two activities a week are usually more than enough. We want to make sure to leave enough time for play and be aware that too many lessons or classes or games can make our kids stressed. It can also be difficult for them to feel connected to all their instructors and to each activity. Maybe they can try an instrument, or take swimming lessons, or sit in on a karate class, but limit the total ("You can each choose one activity this winter").

Remember, they don't have to do everything at once. There is time. When choosing sports, we should be careful to find leagues that are not too competitive and emphasize having fun, learning sportsmanship, understanding the rules, and developing a few basic skills of the game.

Nature Is Calling

While children are little give them time to enjoy being outdoors and in the "wild." No other setting can provide quite the same experience. In nature, they can learn to relax, to observe their surroundings, to think creatively, and to run and play without boundaries or structure. Think of the memories that we cherish from childhood. Many of us fondly recall searching for frogs at the pond, catching fireflies, learning to jump rope, building snow forts, and climbing enormous trees. Our children have their whole lives to join teams and go to lessons and be supervised by adults, but they will never have the chance to enjoy the outdoors in quite the same way again.

nine

Fear of Falling Behind:
Compassion

for the past few years I have noticed a pattern in my initial meetings with parents. Usually they come to talk about one of their children and they begin with a list of current concerns. Schoolwork might be an issue, or the problem could be following rules at home. Sometimes parents worry about their child's ability to share and play nicely with their friends or siblings. They may wonder what to do if their child seems uninterested in getting involved in activities or sports. A fair number of the young children I hear about are already struggling with anxiety or have intense personalities that lead to disturbances at home. After hearing about the presenting problem, I take a family history, review any medical concerns, and ask more specific questions about the child's developmental milestones.

Next I turn to the parents and ask them if there is anything else they would like to add. Here's where things get interesting. In these waning moments of the hour, I often hear about a completely different child.

Dan and Maggie were worried about their eight-year-old son Colin's ability to finish his work in class and maintain friendships. He disliked school and had not yet found a real niche for himself. Colin was often sullen and irritable at home. When I asked Dan and Maggie this final question they painted a very different portrait. It turned out that Colin was a thoughtful, sensitive kid who related well to adults and to younger children, especially his cousins. Beneath his brash exterior, Colin was a sweet boy who wanted to be liked and to not feel so out of sorts.

Had my meeting with Colin's parents ended a few minutes earlier, I would have been more than a little confused when I first sat down with their son. When we met a few days later, Colin's warm and friendly side emerged right away. Compared to a lot of children his age he was open and engaging, and genuinely tried to share his feelings about school and his home life. Colin told me he was feeling a lot of pressure from his parents about his academic performance and lack of interest in team sports. He knew he was a smart kid, and he, too, was puzzled that it took him so long to finish his homework. It was easy to see that Colin's tough guy persona was a way to protect himself from the teasing he received from other kids, who had a hard time understanding his independent streak and quiet, contemplative style.

My experience with Colin and his parents is not unusual. Most of the children I see have real strengths, and many are kindhearted and sensitive like him, but this is rarely what I hear about first. To some extent, this makes perfect sense. Parents do not come to me to extol the virtues of their children. They come with problems and are often feeling pretty desperate by the time they walk through my door. Their initial descriptions naturally reflect this urgency, but the list of concerns sometimes feels too limited. We almost always have to cover certain bases first: How are things going academically? Socially? On the athletic fields and in their kids' extracurricular activities?

I may hear more details about a child's personality, but there tends to be an emphasis on the traits that get them into trouble. Irritability, moodiness, low frustration tolerance—parents know that all of these are worth mentioning. And of course they are. We need to discuss how children's temperament affects their ability to interact with other people and to feel good about themselves. More intense and active children can wreak havoc in a family, and I need to hear about the particular situations where things get heated.

Even when kids are difficult at home and have frequent outbursts, I know this is not the whole story. Given the chance, most parents are more than happy to fill in the gaps about their sons and daughters, and they almost always have a few ready examples of their good listening, compassion, and bubbling enthusiasm. Sometimes with a little prodding they conclude in simple fashion: "He really is a good kid"; "She does have a big heart." These moments are a relief to me and the parents. I know that if a child has solid core values and a generous spirit she is likely to end up in a good place, and I readily share my optimism with her parents.

Be the Best You Can Be

I find it striking that talking about children's basic decency and goodness is often an afterthought for parents. I know that some mothers and fathers take these traits for granted. They expect good behavior from their children and don't feel much of a need to comment on it. Few parents would deny that they want their children to be polite, kind, and helpful, but these values are not always the first things we think about when we talk of raising successful children.

In this age of intense competition, parents usually focus more on the tangibles. They look for the clear yardsticks of their children's achievements and assess their own efforts in helping them reach these goals. These days, we can boil them down to the three S's: School, Sports, and Socializing. We are concerned that our children, from a young age, stay ahead of the curve academically. We help them learn their letters and numbers as soon as possible, and hope to have them reading by the time they enter kindergarten, even if we know that these are not reasonable expectations for them. They are out on the soccer field at age four or five, and the backyard game of catch feels all the more critical if we think the Little League teams will be divided into A and B squads by second grade. Playdates often begin in earnest in preschool, and we hope that our children are in with the right mix of kids and are beginning to show early signs of leadership ability.

Nowadays parents have a lot to worry about. Even friendly diversions and games and get-togethers can be fraught with tension over whose son is performing well and whose daughter is being left behind. The rising expectations have fueled a new culture of enhancement and enrichment programs for young kids. We now have private basketball coaches for kindergarteners, extra learning centers for preschoolers, and social planners who promise the ultimate birthday party experience for first graders. A small portion of the specialists who work with young children— occupational therapists, physical therapists, language therapists—are employed by parents who want their children to improve their coordination, muscle tone, and speaking abilities, although their current functioning is within the norm for their age group.

It may be easy to poke fun at all this anxiety, and to say that these are the pastimes of an overindulged segment of our society, but I believe that they are part of a continuum of worry that threatens most middle- and upper-middle-class families in this country. Many parents feel a great sense of urgency to get their children on the fast track and to keep them there. When it comes down to it, these goals usually take precedence, and teaching kids about moral development and integrity slides a little farther down the to-do list.

Raising a Real Go-Getter

Most parents I meet have solid values. They care about their children and look to help out their neighbors when they have a chance. In many cases their children do not seem as well intentioned—and it's not just when they're tired or cranky or hungry. They may lack manners or have problems with respect and cooperation, but it is often more subtle. Sometimes their behavior reflects a sense of entitlement. Lots of kids feel they have the right to make decisions by themselves and to do what they want to do in a given moment. Their parents, who appear to hold themselves to high standards, can often be heard explaining away the behavior they witness: "He's just strong willed"; "She's a real firecracker"; "He'll have no trouble getting his needs met."

How do we reconcile these conflicting images? Why do parents who are kind and generous not always expect the same behavior from their kids? There are no simple answers to these questions, but I believe that many parents are torn between making sure their children do the right thing and encouraging them to stay ahead of the pack. If we push our kids to compete and to get their share it is not always easy to convince them to be fair and inclusive. We have to remember that we are talking about preschool and elementary school children, who don't yet have a sophisticated sense of moral development. We can't expect four-year-olds to win with honor or kindergarteners to show graciousness to their opponents. If we set up competitions with clear victors, and groups divided into the front-runners (the advanced reading group, the A softball team) and all the rest, it is unrealistic to expect kids to avoid pointing out these differences or to forgo bragging about their achievements.

For young children, examples abound of a world divided into winners and losers: on their sports teams, in the competition to be the first reader or to have the most playdates, in the TV shows they see or hear about at home (like *American Idol, Survivor,* and *The Apprentice*). Despite the pull of "family values" in this country, parents are often confronted with another competing ideal to worry about. The people who "make it," who are financially successful and attain high status in their professions, appear to be those who are out for themselves and pursue their own interests above all others.

Parents may not be looking that far ahead, but they may well feel that in a world of shrinking economic opportunities, only the strong and self-involved will survive. As much as we want our children to be good, decent, caring people, we sometimes feel compelled (in ways that are not always conscious) to give them free reign, to teach them to "go for it" at a young age. Although it can be a bit awkward to watch some of their antics, there is often a hidden and guilty pleasure in seeing them get their fair share, jump to the front of the line, or perform better than their peers.

I am not suggesting that parents should never push their kids to excel or that children need to avoid competition altogether. Part of life, and indeed a recurring theme in this book, is teaching children to work hard and to bear down in the face of challenges. As we have seen, this can range from learning to tie their own shoes or to bounce back from mistakes or to practice their music lessons until they master a piece they are playing. We should feel a sense of pride in what our kids accomplish and help them enjoy the fruits of their labor.

The task for parents is to encourage perseverance while helping kids learn to be humble in their efforts and not lord their accomplishments over other children. Simple words of praise ("I am proud you worked hard and can now tie your own shoes"; "Boy, you really practiced to make those shots") let kids know that we appreciate their efforts without making comparisons with other children. The fewer group lessons and organized activities they have, the easier it is to talk to our kids only in relation to their own earlier attempts at mastery, and not what the norm is on their team or in their classroom. This way we can impress upon our kids that learning to work hard and to try their best are important values, not because they will always outshine others, but because they will respect themselves and feel good about their own efforts.

The Genius Trap

Ethan was a real pistol. I could tell that the minute he walked into my office. He spoke a mile a minute on a range of topics—geography, chess, history—you name it and he could spout off lots of facts and figures and intricate details. Not bad, I thought, for a rather diminutive seven-year-old boy. When I commented on this: "Hey, you're a pretty smart guy," Ethan was hardly surprised. I was not the first adult to have this reaction in his presence. "Actually," he began confidently, "I am a genius! My doctor told me so."

I was a bit stunned by Ethan's candor. I have met lots of precociously intelligent kids and many who are self-assured, but nobody has put such a fine point on it as Ethan had. I later learned from his parents, much to their chagrin, that he was telling the truth. After a long conversation, his pediatrician had announced that Ethan was, in fact, a genius, right in front of him!

I took a long breath when I heard that. I knew it explained a lot about Ethan. In our initial meeting his parents had informed me that he was having an extremely difficult time with his classmates, and was often teased and bullied by them. They knew that he was partly responsible for this treatment. Ethan was always claiming to know all the answers, and had to constantly prove to the other children that he was the smartest person in the room.

Ethan's early intellectual prowess was impressive, but it would turn out to complicate his emotional adjustment in two significant ways. First, like most young kids, Ethan had a hard time keeping his abilities in perspective. According to him, he was the brightest kid around, and he had no trouble letting other second graders know how he felt. Not surprisingly, the other children did not take so kindly to Ethan ranking them as second fiddles. They would often gang up on him after he acted dismissively toward them, although Ethan would later claim that he was "only telling the truth" or "answering the question."

Ethan also felt constant pressure to be the best at whatever he did. He was indeed a whiz in most academic subjects, in chess, and in cards, but he was outraged if someone beat him at any of these. Although he sounded as if he was full of pride, Ethan was, in fact, quite vulnerable, and could easily feel wounded or diminished if he was not in first place. There was little upside for him in being smart, as he expected to do well and took little joy from his good grades. Ethan was careful to steer clear of games in which he would not be among the best, and he usually avoided sports and other physical activities. He knew that given his size and his average motor coordination he would not stand out, and would likely be in the bottom half of his age group. Ethan chose not to play rather than suffer these indignities.

Few parents can contain their joy and satisfaction at seeing their children master more complex material or begin to display a keen mind. Usually there is little harm in letting our children know how we feel: "We are so proud of you"; "Boy, you're a real smart kid." The real risk comes not in these moments but in tipping the scale too much and too frequently in one direction. In other words, if our children begin to hear that they are "gifted" or need more challenging work than their peers, they are inevitably going to start making those same comparisons. They can easily begin to believe that they have talents that far surpass their classmates, and like Ethan, feel compelled to do everything they can to stay on top. They soon learn, however, that this is not an easy assignment. In the Lake Wobegon communities where many of us live, every child is "above average," and more than a few parents are committed to raising their own intellectual prodigy.

For many bright kids the challenge is not just to keep ahead of their peers. They often compare themselves favorably to grown-ups and want to enter the adult world as near equals. Eliza was a bright and sensitive first grader, and her mother was convinced she needed more schoolwork. Her teacher did not want to push her too hard, and outside of a few extra reading assignments, she rarely gave Eliza extra class work. When I met her in my office, Eliza bemoaned her teacher's stubbornness. "Mom and I both agree that she's a bit difficult," she calmly reported to me. Five-year-old David's grandmother was always telling him that he was "so wise" and sometimes sought his counsel when she needed help with a problem. When she babysat for him, David explained that he was "the boss of the house." Later that night when his grandmother set a limit that he felt was unwarranted, David called 911 to complain.

In retrospect these stories have a humorous side, and I admit that it is partly why I share them. But in the moment, they can be quite serious. Calling the police to tell on an adult in the house is no joke, and David's mother promptly called my office after this incident. This may not be a typical occurrence, but when young children start to feel that they are on the same footing with adults and can treat them like equals, many situations can easily get out of hand. If a six-year-old boy thinks he is smarter that his teacher, why should he listen to her? If a kindergartener believes the hype about him and his "wisdom," who can blame him for acting the sage and dismissing adult attempts to keep him in control? When the boundaries between young children and adults begin to blur, it should come as no surprise that they lose respect for their elders and scoff at the notion that they still have a lot to learn from them. If in their own minds they are experts already, they may see little value in patiently waiting their turn to enjoy grown-up privileges.

The Risks of Indulgence

I take for granted that most parents love their kids and want what's best for them. We're all at least somewhat prone to indulging them, even when it's against our better judgment. Just as with praising our kids for being smart, there is usually little harm done in giving a little extra to our kids or in telling them that they're special. But it is all a matter of degree and how far we take our praise. I expect parents to come in and tell me that their child is smart and talented in certain ways, but I sometimes get an uneasy feeling when I hear about their unmitigated delight in their offspring. On her daughter's preschool questionnaire one mother answered the question "Is there anything else you would like us to know?" the following way: "She's sweet and smart and realizes just how terrific she is!" I read this reply shortly before I met with her to discuss her daughter's misbehavior in the classroom and difficulty following the rules at home. I had a hunch (and it later proved to be pretty accurate) that this little girl may have taken this message to heart and did not feel beholden to any adult authority figures.

As we all know, overabundant praise is only one of the ways that we indulge our kids. Most middle- and upper-middle-class families in this country have access to far more disposable income than the previous generation, and parents often choose to spend much of it on their children. Hot new toys, designer clothes, and the latest technological wares and electronics top a long list of "essential" items in many homes. It's not just the kids who revel in them. Many of us share their fascination with computers, digital cameras, flat screen TVs, and MP3 players, and we have other grown-up toys at our disposal, including BlackBerrys, cell phones, and luxury automobiles. What used to pass for ordinary and modest family get-togethers can now inspire sticker shock, as fancy birthday parties, costly outings to town, and expensive vacations have become de rigueur in many communities.

It is not hard to wag a finger at all this spending and indict the current generation for being too materialistic. This is not really my intention here. Our focus on fancy goods and services *is* a problem, and we have to think very carefully about what message we are sending to our children. But the real challenge, I believe, is how to help our kids maintain perspective in a culture that seems more prone than ever to measure people's worth by the size of their house and their bank account. I thought about this when five-year-old Griffen regaled me with stories of his summer vacation in Europe, and announced casually (and without irony of course), "My favorite place was Provence." I chuckled to myself when I heard this, but I was also concerned that Griffen was putting too much stock in the uniqueness of his travel experiences, which far exceeded the more modest vacations of his less affluent friends.

For little kids, as well as some of their parents, "unique" sometimes translates readily into "better." Few of us would tell young children that they are special and different because they went to Europe, but this may well be their take-away message. Sometimes the travel brochures can do the math for them. Seven-year-old Allie came back from spring break and announced that she had just visited the "number-one tennis resort in America." As adults we usually know enough not to take such claims too seriously, but kids are much more vulnerable to these PR missives. It's not just the best trips they hear about. Whether it's the hottest clothes, fastest computers, fanciest cars, or the biggest houses, kids are aware of the relative worth of all these goods by the time they are in first or second grade, if not earlier.

I am not suggesting we abandon all of our worldly goods or our desire to lead a more comfortable life. But we have to be aware that kids can begin to measure their own worth and the worth of others by their possessions. After our first few meetings, Griffen started to complain that all the toys in my office were "no good," and he couldn't understand why I didn't go out and get better ones right away. He showed little respect for my play materials, tearing up sheets of paper and occasionally breaking toys that he thought could be readily replaced.

A mother related a story of how one of her eight-year-old daughter's

t he long arm of the media ensures that all kids in this country hear about what's cool, whether or not their families have the resources to acquire these goods. Having the best stuff has become a national obsession, and it is a value that is often shared by rich and poor and by working- and middle-class kids alike. Companies like Abercrombie & Fitch play off these desires, and seek to extend their appeal to both relatively disadvantaged and more affluent communities. In my experience, children across the economic spectrum are susceptible to these sales pitches, and can easily feel that the right clothes or the right electronics provide them a certain cachet with their peers. Like almost everything else, this trend has been pushed downward, and Baby Gap and other retailers are well aware that young kids and their parents want to get on board with fashion trends as early as possible.

friends reluctantly came to their home on the "bad" side of town and announced to her mom in a surprised voice, "Wow, this *is* actually a nice house." She offered a high five to the birthday girl when she saw her, casually commenting, "Nice TV."

It's not hard to imagine how this girl might grow up. I have known a number of children like her who seem to value things over people, and act with a brazen disregard for the feelings of others. For these kids, learning to act in a reasonable and decent manner will be difficult, and developing empathy will be a huge challenge. The reasons for this are pretty clear. If children learn early on that what really matters is what you have and that "good friends" are the kids who own the right stuff, they are likely to strive to be among the in-crowd and to do everything they can to protect their status.

In some communities, these desires can turn into obsessions and distort the values of children who are taught very different things at home. When I told Samantha, a devoted and thoughtful mother, that her seven-year-old daughter, Hannah, had attempted to take two fancy, hard-to-find markers from my office, she was horrified but not entirely shocked: "She wants so much to fit in and to have the coolest stuff. We don't buy everything for her, but she desperately wants to have the things her friends have." Samantha knew full well that she had her work cut out for her, but she was determined not to give in to her daughter's wish for more cool toys and hip clothes. She realized that these material possessions already had an undue influence on how Hannah felt about herself, and she was convinced that left unchecked, this zeal to acquire more stuff would never be fully sated.

Rough Boys, Mean Girls

In many ways, Hannah was lucky. She had concerned parents who were aware that she was too invested in things, and they sought advice about how to help her be more sensitive to other people's feelings. There are many children who are intent on jockeying for position with their friends and having the coolest wares who never get this kind of guidance at home. Sometimes it's because there are no clear red flags being raised. When a girl or, as is more often the case, a boy, knocks another child down in the playground in school, parents usually hear about it, and they know they had better intervene to stop the behavior. After all, nobody wants to get that call twice. Obvious verbal aggression is also easily recognizable. One mother of a preschooler reported how disturbed she was by her son's "greatness complex." He was always telling his friends that he was smarter or faster or better in whatever they did together. She knew she had to rein him in or he'd soon have no more friends.

Competition in the social pecking order is usually more subtle, especially among girls. Having the right clothes and accessories and other popular items are only one of the ways that girls look to strengthen their position among their peers. We have all heard of the wanton behavior of the "queen bees" in middle school and the "mean girls" in high school, but early versions of these popularity contests are visible in many preschool and kindergarten classrooms. Who sits with whom at snack time, who is allowed to play tag in the playground, and who has the most playdates are all part of the social currency for many groups of four-, five-, and six-year-old girls.

These tallies are meant to determine who fits in with the more exclusive group, and who will be included in the next round of social invitations. Five-year-old Amanda wielded tremendous power in her pre-K class. She was hosting the end of the year pool party at her house, and each time another boy or girl did something to displease her, she would threaten to withdraw an invite to the party. This social engagement became a tool to bully other children, and to get them to include her in all their games and conversations. Despite several warnings from her teacher, Amanda could not refrain from threatening the other kids. Eventually the party had to be canceled.

In Amanda's case the infractions were pretty clear, but much of the time this behavior flies under the radar screen. Unless someone is visibly upset by being left out or teased, teachers may not be aware that groups are forming around them. Parents may know that their child prefers certain kids and has a group of friends, but until something sours these relationships, they may not get any sense that there is intense competition among the girls. When things do go wrong, parents are often appalled by the revelations that are uncovered. Five-year-old Jessica started crying uncontrollably after getting gum caught in her hair. She did not so much fear being reprimanded by her parents, but she knew her mother would have to cut off several inches of her hair. She was feeling desperate and afraid to go back to school because she feared that the other girls in her kindergarten class would make fun of her, and she would no longer be allowed to be in the ponytail club with them.

Parents and teachers can mitigate much of the damage in these moments if they step in and give all the children a strong warning that this type of exclusion is not acceptable. This may seem obvious as you read this: "Just tell the kids to cut it out" would be the reply from many parents. I find that things are usually not so simple. Parents and teachers worry about hurting children's feelings or proceeding with any disciplinary action before they gather enough evidence of an infraction. Often the direct evidence is a little thin. For this reason, many kids feel that they can actively participate in social jockeying without much fear that they will be caught or punished.

Parents are also reluctant to criticize behavior that hits too close to home. In many towns, relative social standing is not just a concern among children and adolescents. Plenty of mothers and fathers have their own worries about where they fit in and whether they will be accepted by the right groups of people. If we spend too much time wondering what dinner party invitations will come our way and which lunch dates have priority, we are not likely to be in a good position to advise our kids how to handle similar friendship dilemmas. None of us are immune to these feelings, of course, but we have to remember that our kids are paying close attention. If they see that we view socializing as a competitive sport with clear winners and losers, they are likely to follow right in our footsteps.

A Clear Bottom Line

Regardless of how we feel about the pursuit of social status, children need a clear message from us about what behaviors we find unacceptable. They need to understand when they are crossing the line, even if their intentions are not malicious. In many nursery schools, teachers have outlawed talk about playdates, after too many kids have had their feelings hurt because they are not included in the after-school get-togethers. This may sound extreme and too PC, but think of the adult equivalent. None of us, no matter what age, would want to be in a roomful of colleagues or friends talking about their lunch plans if we were left out of the equation. By age five, children should have some sense of discretion and understand that their playdates and invitations to parties should not be waved in front of their friends or their classmates.

Parents also need to send a strong message about inclusion. Not every child will be our son's or daughter's best friend, but no young child should feel like she is always excluded from the group. In school, teachers usually pay close attention to this and know to nip in the bud any conversations about who is sitting with whom or who has the coolest stuff, but they often feel powerless about what to do with out-of-school problems. When I consult to schools I recommend that teachers not hesitate to use their leverage there as well:

> When Dana, an experienced pre-K teacher stopped me in the hall-way of St. Bart's, she looked much less chipper than usual. She explained that she had heard from a few mothers that a birthday party for one of her students had gone poorly over the weekend. Marshall, one of her more awkward students, was rejected by several girls and boys at the party, and left crying after nobody would allow him to sit by their side during lunch and no adult intervened on his behalf. Dana was at a loss, and wondered if she should role-play with her kids so they could learn how to handle these situations. I had another idea. I suggested we discuss in very direct and clear terms with her entire class the meaning of friendship and playing nicely with each other, in and out of school.
>
> Dana agreed, but she preferred that I lead the discussion. We sat all her students on the rug and I began asking questions about how they treated each other in the classroom. Almost all the hands shot up, and the kids had wonderful examples of playing with each other in the blocks corner and dress-up area and out on the playground. Then I asked them about what they did if they saw their friends outside of school, in the park, in a restaurant, or at a party. Again they were eager to speak, and all of Dana's kids, including Marshall, had no trouble talking about the right kind of behavior: playing nicely, saying hello, letting friends take turns, and "sit next to you."
>
> I applauded their comments, but then I changed my tone for a few moments: "You all have great ideas, but I want to be sure that

you understand what this means. Your teachers and I will be hear-
ing about what happens out of school, and we want you to prac-
tice what you just talked about. Words are not enough. We do not
want to hear about teasing or mean comments or children being
left out."

The kids were attentive and had stopped talking among them-
selves, and they assured me that they would be "good friends" in
the future. Dana chimed in that "Dr. Paul will be back in to
check on us in a couple of weeks, and I hope I can give him a nice
report."

My goal was not to scare these children, but to let them know in no
uncertain terms that there are reasonable standards of behavior and that
there are grown-ups who will hold them accountable. Adults usually
shy away from being this firm, and I would not be surprised if some
readers think, "Who is this guy to talk to these kids this way?" Given our
tendency to reason with young kids or to role-play situations with them,
it seems strange that we can actually tell them what not to do. We forget
that morality in young children is based on law and order, not a well-
defined conscience or a sophisticated sense of fairness and justice. Part
of teaching children self-discipline is expecting them to be part of a
community, and to care about other people. That means respecting
people's physical space and their feelings, and their rights to have access
to the privileges the other group members enjoy, like sitting down to
lunch at a birthday party.

I am not naïve enough to think that one conversation with a classroom full of children is enough to ensure that all of them will be good
citizens. Unless kids receive a consistent message from their parents
about how to treat their friends and neighbors and classmates, they are
not likely to restrain themselves from being self-aggrandizing or learn to
be more open about including others. In my mind, there are almost no
bad young kids, but there are plenty who have not received enough direction. Enthusiastically going on about playdates is not a major crime,
nor is saving seats for friends at a birthday party. Kids just need to hear

that it is not so nice, that it may hurt other kids' feelings, and most importantly, that we are not going to permit them to do it again. When it comes down to it, kids need to know that adults do have eyes in the back of their heads, and have a clear idea of what behavior those eyes want to be observing.

Cheers for the Good Kids?

All of the kids in Dana's class were happy and excited to tell me about their good deeds. There was nothing extraordinary about my presence in their classroom, but somehow they were buoyed by having a spotlight shine on their everyday kindness and friendliness. This was not a big surprise to me. I know that kids like to feel good and want to be helpful. I see how they scramble to do jobs in nursery school and kindergarten and help out their teachers in first and second grade. Given the chance, most kids would prefer to get recognized for what they are doing right, not reprimanded for what they are doing wrong.

Here's where things sometimes break down. Most parents know that they don't want to give too much attention to negative behaviors like whining or hitting, because their kids can come to find their parent's strong reactions enticing and be tempted to continue acting up. When parents see the opposite behavior, they sometimes don't want to upset the applecart, and they may be reluctant to comment in these moments as well. If two brothers are notorious fighters, we can understand why parents tread lightly when they are playing a game quietly together or sharing their toys. As much as I appreciate their hesitance, I encourage parents to look on these as opportunities to recognize good behavior, and to give the kids a pat on the back for treating each other well ("You guys played so nicely this afternoon"). If Mom lets Dad know about these positive interactions when he comes home, there is another opportunity to celebrate nice times in the family rather than focus on the mischief and anger that can come between siblings.

There is a more subtle and prevalent reason that praising good behavior has taken a backseat in many families. Most of us parents are pretty good at telling our kids "good job," after seeing them play a game of baseball, or bring home a good test score, paint a nice picture, or demonstrate their technological prowess. In the process, we can gradually become more focused on their performance and visible standards of achievement, rather than who they are as people. Young kids are quick to take in this message, and realize that to get their parents' attention they have to perform well in some easy-to-measure way. For a kindergartener, this may mean learning his letters or running hard on the soccer field. A second grader may know his parents will look through his school papers every night and want to see a solid effort on his homework.

In many parts of this country we have raised the academic bar so high and have begun extra classes and competitions so early that young children and their parents naturally come to believe that measuring up is what really matters. I often joke that if we had letter jackets for good kids, and travel teams made up of the nice boys and girls from each town, we might take our children's moral development more seriously. If kids knew that their parents took just as much pride in the way they shared with their friends and acted around adults as they did in their grades and their sports accomplishments, they would put as much energy into the former as the latter.

Goodness and Self-Esteem

Being nice and everybody getting along isn't the only point here. One of the hallmarks of self-esteem in children is their ability to identify and describe positive attributes about themselves. Being smart or a good ball player matters, but just as important are the values and personality traits that kids assign themselves. Are they "friendly," "fun to be with," "a good person," "helpful"? As the psychologists Robert Brooks and Sam Goldstein point out, teaching responsibility and compassion for others is critical to promoting resilience in children. The more they feel they are contributing to the greater good, the more kids are likely to feel confident and worthwhile members of a community. Helpful and giving children tend to feel more in control and more independent, and have a sense of satisfaction that comes from having a positive impact on the people around them.[1]

From a very young age children feel a tug between caring for others and gratifying themselves. Early on, the latter urges usually win out, as kids look to satisfy their own desires and express anger and frustration (think of those fierce two-year-olds' tantrums) when their needs are not immediately met. One of the first tasks for parents is to help children find more balance between their needs and the needs of others, and to learn to delay gratification of their wishes. Kids who have not received this guidance can appear out of control and enraged whenever they have to wait for what they want. If this pattern continues and these children do not learn to control their urges, they are more likely to become defiant in the face of limits and disrespectful and uncooperative toward adults.

Just as important as the way they behave is the way these kids view themselves. I have had many four- and five- and six-year-old children in my office describe themselves as "bad" or "mean" or "angry." Sometimes they have had this label applied to them by their parents or other children. Even if there is not a direct link, many young kids know how people feel about them. If their teachers or other adults think they're uncaring or selfish or mean-spirited, they are likely to internalize these negative associations. Once they do, it can be difficult to reverse the process, as these labels become a self-fulfilling prophecy. Mean kids tend to act in not nice ways, and the bad guys are more likely to slug their friends on the playground. This behavior reinforces a vicious, negative cycle in which the adults harden their opinions ("See, I told you he wasn't so nice") and children make similar claims: "I really am bad"; "I hate those kids."

The only way we can counteract these feelings is to give young children opportunities to demonstrate that they can behave differently. Kids have to do good in order to feel good. It doesn't simply come from telling them they are special or nice. This is essential for all kids, not just those who struggle with self-control. Every little boy and girl has

early in my career I worked with a group of severely traumatized young children in a therapeutic nursery school. Many of them had been labeled "bad" and then some, and most had been asked to leave other nursery schools. The staff members made a huge effort to help these children find ways to feel good about themselves, and we had a long list of jobs they could choose at the beginning of each week. My job was to get coffee for the teachers and my cotherapist from the school kitchen, as we needed to be well fortified for our work with the kids. I often had an incorrigible four-year-old boy named Joseph accompany me, mainly to give the other staff members a break from his frequent outbursts in the classroom. After several months, I turned to Joseph on one of our outings and asked him what he wanted to be when he grew up. Joseph, whose behavior had calmed considerably during the year, did not hesitate: "I want to be a coffee helper when I grow up!"

bad feelings; they get angry at their parents, jealous of their siblings, or envious of their friends. Our job as parents is to make sure that they know that their good intentions outweigh their more nefarious thoughts. By teaching them to take turns with their friends, to share their toys, to be polite to adults, to clean up after themselves, and to do little jobs at home and in school, we are showing them in concrete ways that they can be decent, caring people.

Over time we hope that these behaviors will take hold and kids can behave kindly toward others without constant reminders. The more they believe that they generally act in a friendly and gracious manner, the more apt kids are to define themselves in a positive way. These early self-statements, rooted in good behavior, can form the basis for a more complex sense of self that kids develop as they grow into older children and adolescents. In other words, "nice" might come to mean "honest and trustworthy"; "friendly" can morph into "caring and compassionate." As long as they continue to have the chance to display kindness and test these virtues in real-life situations, kids are likely to maintain a positive feedback loop that allows them to feel good about themselves.

Parents may find it helpful to remember that these are not short-term goals. If we study the lives of men and women of character and integrity, we can almost always trace a clear path to their childhood experiences and the influences of the adults near to them. We would all be proud to someday hear that we have raised children of character, and can imagine a few other descriptions of them that we would welcome hearing: a "stand-up guy," a "woman of conscience," or perhaps most simply, a "real mensch!"

Ways for Parents to Foster Compassion

Recognize and Value Moments of Caring

If we want to encourage our kids to be more giving, we need to catch them in the act. Praising children for small deeds of kindness and generosity lets them know that we value these behaviors and that we have clear evidence of their good works. These can include small, easily overlooked moments—sharing a toy with a friend, cleaning up after their little brother, helping to clear the dinner plates. A simple comment can make the point ("Nice sharing with Sam today"; "You did a great job cleaning up the basement"). More generous behavior, like choosing to attend the birthday party of an unpopular classmate, deserve that much more attention, particularly if it is the child's decision and not a family obligation.

Unlike more achievement-oriented pursuits, there are no clear yardsticks like grades or goals scored for compassionate behavior, and parents have to be the ones to apply their stamp of approval. This may include gold stars for being a good kid, but our main job is to let our kids know that we are proud of the moments when they think of other people and temporarily put their own desires on hold. We should not expect the balance to tip too far in this direction. Young kids are not inclined to forget their own needs for long, nor should they be expected to be unselfish all the time. Yet if our kids begin to show real signs of pausing to think of what a friend would want to do or what they can do to be helpful at home, we don't want to lose the chance to give them credit for their thoughtfulness. The more we affirm their basic decency and charitable instincts, the more likely we are to see these behaviors repeated.

Don't Fall into the Moralizing Trap

I have a general rule of thumb when I'm speaking to parents. I try to catch them every time they say something negative about their child, and ask them to explain what they mean. When I hear parents describe their kids as "manipulative," "entitled," or "spoiled," I ask for more information, and usually I hear something like this: "Well, he really tries to play us and get us to give him what he wants." Without getting too persnickety, I try to point out that it sounds like their son is testing them and is pretty demanding, but I'm not sure that it qualifies as *manipulative*. After all, it takes two to tango, and for "manipulative" to apply, the parents have to be controlled and forced to do what they don't want to do. That's a lot of power to ascribe to a small child.

Young children pay close attention to our words and our tone. If they sense that we view them in negative terms it is more than likely that they are going to pick up on our demeanor. As we discussed in chapter 6, parents often need to correct their children if they are being rude or acting in an overly demanding manner. Our best bet is to focus on the lapses in their behavior, not on the faults in their character. If a five-year-old slips an action figure toy into his pocket at a friend's house, he needs to be reminded to not take what is not his, but it does not help to repeat in or out of his earshot that "he tends to steal things." A four-year-old might tell pretend stories and vouch for their truthfulness over and over, but that doesn't make her a "liar" if there are a few omissions in her version of events.

We all slip into this shorthand from time to time, especially if we have a more demanding or intense child who is prone to testing limits. But we have to watch what we say and remember that our kids tend to internalize negative comments. I am more direct with parents like Bob and Amanda, who were pulling their hair out over their five-year-old son, and always talking about "the good John and the bad John." I understood their frustration, but John told me in private that he couldn't control "the bad guy" and feared that everyone in his family disliked him. John did have a lot of work to do, but it was helpful for him to hear that he was a "good kid who got very frustrated sometimes," and needed help controlling his anger. With children like John, our best bet is to point out his mistakes and reassure him that we will help him do better next time around.

Give Children Opportunities to Be Helpful at Home

A family is a two-way street, and parents shouldn't feel that they are the only givers. We are much more likely to be resentful if we are doing it all and our kids are not contributing much. As we discussed in chapter 6, young children can be given responsibilities at home—picking up their clothes and tossing them in the laundry, setting the table, cleaning up their toys, placing candy wrappers in the garbage. As they get a little older, they can help to cook dinner, take out the recycling, wash the car, or work in the yard. This is not just meant to be grunt work. Most kids, young and old, don't jump at their chores, but they do like to feel that they are pitching in and doing their fair share.

The goal is not only teaching young children to work hard, but also helping them to understand that they are beholden to other members of their family and their community. It does not make sense to expect less of our kids at home than what is asked of them at school and other places. By nursery school, children are expected to clean up their toys, put their mess in the garbage and help their teachers whenever they are asked. Most are more than happy to be of service.

If children are working with balsa wood or other messy materials in my office, I expect them to spend a few minutes cleaning, and I usually have them take a turn with the Dustbuster. At first some kids look puzzled that I would make this request, but when they see I am serious they usually comply. After a few seconds, these same kids are often reveling in the power of this little machine, and they beam proudly when I explain to Mom or Dad in the waiting room that they were "great clean-up helpers."

Have Clear Rules about How to Treat Others

We can't assume that our kids always know what we expect of them, even if they've heard it all before. Young children need constant reminders and frequently need to be steered in the right direction. If we allow them to speak to us rudely or make unreasonable demands and don't call them on this behavior, then we can't really blame them if they behave that way again. It takes patience and energy to ask them over and over, "Can you say that in a nice voice" or "What's the magic word?" (*please!*), but there is no real substitute for teaching them manners and respect. If we catch our kids talking back to adults or using a too-familiar tone with grown-ups and don't correct them, they are likely to take this as tacit approval for their behavior and see no reason to change. This is another one of those "pay now or pay later" dilemmas. If children don't hear a clear message about how to treat others when they are four or five or six, they are not suddenly going to become polite and well mannered at age eight or nine or ten.

Little kids are not always perfect gentlemen and ladies and we should have no illusions that they will be, especially with their siblings and friends. Arguing over who goes first or who won the game or who gets to pick the movie that night are pretty common, and not cause for alarm. Still, these are teachable moments, and kids often need our help to find fair and reasonable resolutions to their conflicts. Taking turns and sharing are the earliest ways that children can demonstrate compassion and goodwill, and we should insist that four- and five-year-olds play fairly. It is not too much to expect that by the age of six or seven kids can learn to win without rubbing it in, and to be modest when competing against less adept players in board games or sports or word games. By eight or nine children should have developed some compassion for those less fortunate than themselves, and parents should put an emphasis on showing kindness to the less accomplished athletes ("John sure tries hard"), the kids who struggle in school ("Reading is a little hard for Rachel"), and boys or girls who have been left out of the popular groups.

Become a Model of Compassion

None of us are perfect. We have plenty of stress and lots of worries and don't always think about how we should treat other people. In our lesser moments, we may be rude or curt or dismissive to other adults. Maybe it's a sour look or a muttered curse or a complaint about service when we're frustrated. As parents, we have to remember one thing: Our kids are always watching. Even preschoolers take special notice when their parents get out of joint, and recognize a tone or a look that says more than parents may think it does. I have heard lots of kids repeat things that would make their parents cringe: "Mommy was angry with my teachers"; "Daddy yelled at the man in the red car."

If we are to expect our children to be respectful and decent to others, they first have to see this behavior from us. The goal is not perfection (that car example could have come from one of my own kids), but it helps to remember these two adages: "Let the small stuff go" and "Be polite to see polite." We need to hold these in mind wherever we go with our kids: at the grocery store, in the bank, on the sidewalk, or in the park. Doing our best to let little frustrations roll off our backs can make a huge impression on kids, whether it's waiting in a long line patiently, not scolding a businessperson who makes a mistake, or not rolling our eyes at another parent whose son just knocked our little boy over. Behaving well is easier said than done, I know. But if we aim for holding it together 80 percent of the time, that's a pretty good example for our children.

Acting in a kind manner is even more important than containing our frustration. Children look to their parents at every turn to see how they speak to each other and behave toward other people, especially important adults in their lives. It's worth asking ourselves how we treat our children's teachers, their babysitters, and their grandparents. Do we do our best to be respectful and considerate and to recognize the important role they play in our children's lives? Whatever mixed feelings we might have in these situations, children need to see that we are respectful and polite to other grown-ups and are appreciative of the people who care for them.

Find Ways to Contribute to the Community

Parents with young children can find it hard just to get through the day and to manage the needs of all the members of the family. Asking them to do more than this can seem pretty outlandish, yet if we want to teach our kids to have a broader perspective and to appreciate what they do have, we have to find a way for them to help people who are less fortunate. Most elementary schools do a nice job of this, and even kindergarteners have had the opportunity to raise money for victims of recent hurricanes, tsunamis, famine, and war. Seasonal giving to local families in need is also popular, and many churches, synagogues, and schools organize food and clothing drives and gift-giving campaigns at the holidays.

The challenge for parents is how to make children's giving more personal and relevant to their day-to-day lives. To really teach the value of service, children need to have some hands-on experience with helping people in a direct way. Many families have these opportunities nearby. Making cards for an ailing relative, visiting elderly friends and neighbors, or delivering food to a family after a death or other trauma, are all noteworthy and have a tremendous impact on young children.

The most touching story I have heard in some time involved a group of twelve-year-old boys whose close friend was diagnosed with cancer. On their own, they decided to shave their heads in solidarity with their classmate, who had lost his hair as a result of his chemotherapy treatments. In a community where academic and athletic achievements usually receive the most notice, their sacrifice and ongoing demonstration of their loyalty and devotion was an inspiration to many parents, forcing more than a few to rethink their child-rearing priorities.

Some families find value in more structured and regular helping activities. They may join with a local nonprofit or religious group to provide Meals on Wheels to the elderly or to "adopt" a homeless family and help provide for their day-to-day needs. Others make their homes a welcome place for disabled children needing respite care or disadvantaged children who could benefit from a Fresh Air vacation. Although these activities may involve some expense, what they primarily require is a commitment of time and a belief that compassion means service to people in the community who do not have the same advantages. I know many adults who can recall with great precision the times their family was actively involved with one or more of these projects, and recount what it meant to confront real-life problems as a child, and to do something about alleviating other people's struggles.

Teach Kids to Conserve Natural and Man-Made Resources

Most middle-class families in this country enjoy an unprecedented bounty of goods and services that were unavailable to previous generations of Americans. Many of the everyday conveniences we take for granted are still rare commodities in much of the world. Given all their stresses and preoccupations, the majority of parents do not spend a lot of time musing over these inequities and our relative good fortune. Little kids, of course, are no different, and most of them have no real concept of the abundant resources they enjoy and the shortages that are endemic elsewhere.

The goal for parents is not to cast a pall over young children or to induce any major guilt trips. In modest ways we can make kids aware that they do have advantages and bear a responsibility to conserve natural resources and man-made goods. Running the water more slowly in the bathroom, using both sides of a sheet of paper for drawing, and recycling newspapers and plastic bottles are all practical applications that young kids can easily grasp and adopt in their homes. We can expect children over age three or four to take reasonable care of their clothes, to not waste too much food at the dinner table, and to understand that broken toys or electronic games will not be instantly replaced.

These family rules teach self-discipline and self-care, but they also provide a lesson that we do not have access to a bottomless well of raw materials. This can be a revelation to many children in middle- and upper-middle-class homes. Beyond that, parents have an opportunity to show that we all have a responsibility to care for the planet. In some families, that translates into strict prohibitions against littering and clear directions about cleaning up after ourselves in parks, on beaches, and at other public spaces. Other parents go the next step and have their children participate in neighborhood clean-up days or local programs to preserve wetlands or forests. When these activities are presented in a kid-friendly, fun, and educational way most children, in my experience, are more than willing participants. Young kids also understand that caring for the environment is another way we care for each other, and that using only our fair share of resources means leaving enough for everyone else.

Say Yes to Tolerance and No to Bigotry

Despite the widespread push toward diversity in this country, a healthy proportion of children live in places where there is not a lot of mixing of ethnic, racial, and socioeconomic groups. People of color and those who speak a different language can seem very different to young children who do not live in well-integrated communities. As we have seen, "different" can sometimes be interpreted as "not as good," and kids are liable to take notice and perhaps poke fun at people who do not look or sound the same as they do. We can, however, teach young children to be tolerant by sending a clear and firm message that differences are to be celebrated, not avoided. Most nursery and elementary schools include this message in their curriculum and look for ways the children can compare and contrast their ancestries and ethnic heritage.

School programs are a good start, but children form many of their notions about ethnic and racial differences by watching and listening to their parents. If they hear their parents make sly jokes about different people they come in contact with or detect a negative tone in discussions about integration or immigration, they are likely to develop their own skepticism about the benefits of living in a diverse society. In my experience, most parents are fairly careful about not impugning any racial groups or making gross generalizations. Yet some are less vigilant when it comes to class differences, and I hear many young children making not so subtle references to economic status when talking about babysitters, house cleaners, laborers, or waitstaff. In the end, it is up to parents to treat everyone who comes into their home with respect and dignity, and to show their kids that we cannot determine someone's character by their money or possessions.

Parents have a responsibility to teach their children to be open-minded and accepting of people. Being free of prejudice means not prejudging, and kids need to hear over and over that they need to meet and get to know people before they draw any conclusions about them. Kids will learn that they may have to stand up for what they believe, or at least refrain from any of the teasing and name-calling that they may hear from classmates or acquaintances in the playground.

Parents can show that they care about these issues by raising them at the dinner table and by sharing their own stories about the different people they knew growing up. By giving our children more exposure to different types of people, we are preparing them for the reality of living in a diverse, multiethnic, and multiracial culture. If we lead by example we are also giving them a solid foundation of inclusion based on experience, and a message that they should have compassion for other people no matter where they live or what they look like.

Giving Thanks

I am one of the parents whose children have more opportunities than I did growing up. I was by no means impoverished as a kid, and had no real sense that I lacked for privileges. But now I can't help but mention to my own kids how lucky they are after a nice vacation, and I often feel that they live a life of relative ease compared to the childhoods of their

a friend of mine related a story about his son's Little League baseball team. Although the team is integrated, most of the players are from relatively affluent families. Recently they traveled to a neighboring community and were beaten in a tight game by a team with a number of players from working-class Latino families. Rather than toast the hard-fought success of the winners, one of the other dads on the losing team, a respected professional, offered this consolation to my friend: "That's okay, this is all they have to live for. Their lives get worse from here; for our kids it only gets better." My friend was shocked and speechless for a moment, but then offered this retort: "Accept it, they beat us fair and square and they outworked us. They all seem like nice kids." All of this was within earshot of their sons and the other players on the team.

parents and grandparents. Like many of my friends and colleagues, I sometimes long to take them back to the old neighborhood, as if by osmosis they could get a real feel for what it was like to grow up with less material wealth and fewer options or amusements.

As you might guess, my children roll their eyes at these moments and wait for Dad's wistful remembrances to pass. To be fair, I can't blame them. My brothers and sisters and I had lots of fun and much less schoolwork and stress than they do. They've heard these stories, too. Still, I struggle to find ways to get them to understand that we have advantages that many families do not enjoy. I realize this is a lot to ask. Kids and most adults, for that matter, live day to day, and stepping back and appreciating what we have, the old stopping and smelling the roses, is no easy task.

Perhaps there is a better tack to take than lecturing kids about their luck. We might do better to focus less on the trappings of success and more on what really matters, namely our relationships with other people. Expecting kids to be thankful not for the things they have but for their family members and the other people who love them (yes, even their brothers and sisters!) is not too much to ask. Parents may feel less of the need for nostalgia trips if they can help their kids to cherish the time they have together and appreciate that playing and fooling around and telling stories and singing are more important than nice things or fancy vacations or big houses. If we not only teach our kids to be grateful for the joys they have but also impart the message that they have a responsibility to give back and share their gifts with others, we might someday deem our job a success.

part three

Finding Our Way

ten

Living Without Fear at Home:
Family Time and Family Rituals

helen came to me to talk about her two boys. She was in her early forties, a soft-spoken and thoughtful woman who had lots of questions about how to help foster a better relationship between her sons. At one point she turned to me and said wistfully, "You know, we're really not so nuclear anymore." I was a little puzzled. Somehow I didn't think she was referring to the Cold War. Helen saw my confusion and continued, "I mean, we don't spend nearly as much time together as a family as we used to, do we?"

I was struck by Helen's words, and since that time I often find myself thinking about the concept of the nuclear family. What does it really mean in today's culture? How do we reconcile all the demands on the individuals in a family, both kids and parents, with the notion of being part of a group? These are not just rhetorical questions or fodder for sociologists and family therapists. At some point, every mother and father will make decisions that determine the relative place of their family life in the larger social world that is dominated by work, school, children's activities, and social obligations. These are not all-or-nothing choices, of course. Every family will have some balance of private time and outside activities. The real issue is figuring how far the pendulum should swing in either direction and how much control we can have over its arc.

Let's take an example. Kate and I were talking about the demands on her son Jonathan. At eight years old, he was balancing travel soccer, baseball, and religious school in the spring. Each met twice a week or more. Not surprisingly, the weekends were becoming a blur of traveling between multiple games, meals on the run, and a couple of playdates squeezed in between. Jonathan's schedule was a constant source of tension between Kate and her husband, David, who coached the baseball team and assisted on the soccer field.

In two weeks there was to be a celebration of Kate's father's eightieth birthday, and the extended family was coming in to celebrate with him. That Sunday afternoon, Jonathan was scheduled to play in a highly competitive soccer tournament, one of the biggest of the season. David wanted Jonathan to play in the games and come late to the party. Kate was unsure, but the more she sat and thought about it, the more outraged she became. "How could a third-grade soccer game be more important than my father's birthday?" she fumed. Kate became more adamant and decided that her son would be at the birthday dinner no matter what.

When he first heard about the conflict, Jonathan told me he wanted to compete in the tournament, but he was torn because he loved his grandfather. Ultimately he went to the party, and when he and I spoke later he was happy his mother had made him attend. He was relieved that he did not have to make the decision. David also came around, and his support for the party helped alleviate Jonathan's guilt at letting his teammates down.

Dilemmas like this one play out thousands of times every week in living rooms around the country. Parents everywhere struggle to juggle their children's commitments to sports and other activities and find room for downtime and family obligations. These are not just logistical questions. Each decision not only sends a message to kids about the relative merits of each activity (if you chose soccer practice over Sunday school, for instance), but also gives them more subtle clues as to what has value in the family. An invitation for the family to attend a ball game with a work acquaintance of Dad may make for a promising evening. But if it replaces the plan to have pizza at home, cuddle on the couch, and watch a video the one night the whole family is home together, the kids may feel that private family time is less important to their parents than being with their grown-up friends.

We have to be careful not to overreach here. I love going to ball games with my kids and our friends, and we like hanging out with other families in the neighborhood, but let's get back to the question of balance for a moment. In many ways, it's a numbers game. If a family can have meals together two or three times a week and half of those are spent in the company of others, the kids are not likely to have a sense that family meals are an important ritual in their house. If we do not establish a pattern of family time when our children are young, they are also more apt to choose to be with their friends or take part in activities when the rare chance to be home together does come along.

Contrast that with my friend Catherine. In her eulogy for her father, she spoke fondly of the Saturday night card games that were a fixture in her kitchen during most of her childhood, and how she learned about life from her dad by sitting across from him at the card table. Catherine would be the first to admit that this didn't happen *every* Saturday, but the games took place with enough frequency to feel like an institution and helped establish the rhythm of her early years. In her mind those evenings spent playing games represented a sense of togetherness and joy, and captured what it meant to be a child in her family.

Rituals and Values

Why are these rituals—meals, game nights, celebrations—so important in a family? Isn't variety the spice of life? Isn't it good to mix things up a little? I remember thinking just that when our kids were toddlers. They would ask for the same books over and over at night, and frankly I was a little bored with *Goodnight Moon* and *Goodnight, Gorilla*. Like most children, our kids loved hearing the same stories again and again, just like they love to hear the stories of their early years and the "famous family foibles" from my own and my wife's childhoods. Years later these books continue to resonate for my kids, and *Goodnight, Gorilla* in particular has gone on to have a remarkably successful second run in our house.

For kids and adults, repetition is central to understanding and to making connections. A onetime experience may be exhilarating and memorable, but only with multiple exposures do we develop a sense of time and place and relationships. Think of how you feel visiting your favorite beach. The smell of the salt air as you get closer, the first glimpse over the dunes at the ocean, the feel of the sand in your toes, all evoke a feeling of pleasure and comfort that comes from the expectation of reconnecting with previous experiences at that particular spot. In the best of these moments we may have a feeling of timelessness, of being in the past and the present simultaneously. Visualizing this scene can be a soothing and powerful balm for our everyday worries.

Family rituals aren't always so soothing. Some can be downright stressful, like getting the kids to come to dinner. However, if we repeatedly make the effort to establish our own traditions—like Friday night or Sunday afternoon dinners, a weekly "Dad's home early" night, or Saturday morning in the park—we have a greater chance of establishing a *family identity*. We can give our kids a feeling that they belong to something bigger, that we have a shared sensibility, that the family stands for something. This doesn't mean there won't be plenty of individual differences between siblings, or between parents, for that matter. It does mean that our kids are more likely to understand and grasp the values that we are trying to teach them.

Think of what Catherine learned from those card games with her dad. She understood that he valued family time above other things, that he wanted her and her brothers to learn to take turns and be part of a group. He also wanted them to be able to think for themselves, to make their own decision in the game, and to live with the consequences of those choices. Her dad was definitely not one to coddle them if they faltered or to be too effusive if they defeated the other kids and the grown-ups. Catherine knew intuitively, however, that her dad was proud of their efforts to hang tough and to persevere. He was never one to tire easily, and his endless string of little projects in the house and in the garden taught Catherine and her brothers how to work hard and to be resourceful.

As I mentioned earlier, parents often come to me with memories of a simpler time when they were growing up (some fueled by nostalgic quests and revisionist history, of course), and wonder how to give their children the same freedom they had as kids. When they talk of their own family lives things are generally more complicated. Many adults have ambivalent feelings, about their parents and their family life, especially if they grew up in homes filled with a lot of conflict and anger. Even when they have mixed feelings however, most parents also have strong memories that their parents stood for something, and they often have a desire to leave their kids with the same strong impressions. Most of us can come up with a shorthand way of describing the key values that were modeled in our own homes. I learned from both of my parents that family loyalty came first, that there was no substitute for working hard, and that no matter how much success you have, you should be careful not to take yourself too seriously.

Identifying these values and which ones we want to emulate is not so hard. Figuring out how to put them into practice is another story. Driving our kids through the streets of Brooklyn or the south side of Chicago or any other old neighborhood doesn't quite cut it. They can't breathe in the life and spirit of a place without experiencing it firsthand, and the stories of the good old days, when things were that much tougher, fly in and out of their ears as soon as we tell them. We have no other choice; we have to practice what we preach and find the medium to transmit our core values to them.

Group Traditions

Families that follow established religious and ethnic traditions have a built-in mechanism for communicating many of their beliefs and customs. The major religions provide a spiritual and theological understanding of the meaning of life in this world and prophecies about what comes next, many of which spark controversies between and within faiths. At heart, the Christian, Jewish, and Muslim religions offer a similar set of guidelines for how we should lead our lives in the here and now, with prescribed lessons for children. Treat others the way you would like to be treated, don't rob or hurt people, and have compassion for those who are less fortunate. All these teachings are easy for young children to comprehend.

Following these guidelines is another story, and behind the simple messages lies an implicit challenge to do the right thing even when confronted with temptation or when outnumbered by others who are making a not-so-wise choice. Being part of a congregation can help children and parents feel that even in these moments they are not alone, and remind them of what principles they and their family hold dear. Children quickly realize, however, that membership in a church or synagogue does not guarantee piety, and that good intentions and prayers do not automatically make someone a good person. Unless we discuss and act on the values they hear about in service and in religious school, these lessons will ring hollow to our kids, and they are likely to develop a more skeptical attitude about adults well before they can spell the word "hypocrisy."

Reconciling the lessons in this book with those of the dominant religions is not a difficult task. Thinking and acting independently, learning to persevere, cooperating with others, and being mindful and compassionate, can be translated into other sets of teachings, albeit with more of a moral persuasion than I have intended in these pages. We might argue that teaching a child to become an explorer is not as well fitted to the more rigid doctrinal traditions, but helping kids be creative and do their own thing implies a willingness to go your own way, with or without the blessing of the crowd.

Ethnic traditions may seem more frivolous and they are easy to romanticize and satirize, but they offer children and adults a cultural identity that often carries significant meaning for them. The public displays of cultural pride during holidays or feast days provide a forum for expressing the enduring power of family heritage in this country. But it is in the quieter, more private family times when the shared values of a people resonate more deeply with children.

For an Italian (or Jewish or Chinese or Indian) family that enjoys cooking and eating together, preparing and sharing a family meal is about more than just food. It can evoke a feeling of warmth and sensuousness and being cared for that children may not find anywhere else in our fast-food, hit-the-ground-running society. The lengthy buildup and the spacing out of courses can encourage kids to slow down and to learn to appreciate that good things take time and work. Kids in these families get to experience firsthand that breaking bread is a communal occasion, and that fine food and drink are meant to be savored and enjoyed with others. In some traditions, like the Friday night meal celebrated in many Jewish homes, blessings and songs are interspersed with the meal. They encourage those present to pause and give thanks, and for the family to reflect on spiritual questions that are typically absent from dinner conversation the rest of the week.

Cultural traditions often dictate the form of life-and-death celebrations, and children usually join with adults to mark these events. Attending christenings, bar and bat mitzvahs, weddings, and other rituals can teach young kids how to be respectful and attentive toward others, and to appreciate that they in time will have their turn to join the adult world and be recognized more fully. Kids get to have cake and dance and enjoy the party, of course (or get tired and whine and ask to leave!), but parents can also use these occasions to reinforce the lessons they are teaching at home—working hard toward a goal, caring for others, being mindful of our blessings. Though parents sometimes choose not to take young children to rituals marking death (funerals, wakes, sitting shiva, and so on), these ceremonies and gatherings can help parents make the same point. The recollections and stories about family members at memorial services or annual gatherings can also be invaluable for children, and give them an early sense of what it means to lead a happy and fulfilling life.

Establishing Family Rituals
of Our Own

We've heard about some of the ways families can establish their own traditions. Meals, game nights, birthday and holiday celebrations, all provide opportunities for parents to have fun with their kids and to teach them a thing or two along the way. This is not a real dichotomy. We don't take time out from Monopoly to say "Now, kids, we're going to learn about turn taking and cooperation." In the best of traditions, the lessons are built in and seamlessly integrated with the experience. A family cleanup day may start with everyone pitching in to clean their rooms or rake the yard, but we don't have to hit our kids over the head that they are learning about hard work and perseverance. After we finish, we may go to the local pool or playground; practicing this kind of delayed gratification and earning of privileges is much more important to kids than talking about them.

Family time doesn't always mean capital R rituals. The regular meals and game nights are just as important in the long run as the big holidays, birthdays, and life celebrations. At first glance, it may not look like much of a tradition, but if every Saturday a father takes his son with him to pick up the dry cleaning and bagels, and they have an hour or so to talk and hang out, that counts! Any repetitive, focused activity in which parents are spending relatively uninterrupted time with their kids becomes a time to connect and to share what's important in the family.

Bedtime rituals are a perfect example. Slowing down, cuddling, reading together, being peaceful, cooperating when it's time to stop and say good night, are essential lessons and ones we get to repeat literally a couple of hundred times a year or more. All the more reason we have to work hard when our children are young to establish a routine about going to bed and staying there. If parents and kids are anxious about what's going to come after the fifteen to twenty minutes of bedtime stories, the value of that time will probably be significantly diminished. We can feel

g race before meals is one time that we *can* take a moment out of our busy routine to reflect on our good fortune. Pausing to give thanks or to think about others is, by its nature, a separate experience. But an opening blessing should help set the tone for the meal and not be something to rush through before we get down to the real business of eating.

the tension when things aren't going well, and we all know that when we're stressed, it is much harder for us to focus on teaching and for our kids to absorb any lessons.

Sometimes in the attempt to establish good routines, parents can feel like they have become prisoners to them. In the process, the joy and the spontaneity can be drained out of the interaction. Reading at bedtime is one example, and I know many parents who also struggle to maintain special time with each of their kids. Child development professionals (including this author) often suggest that parents do what they can to set aside time for each of their kids, but too frequently they fail to offer reasonable guidelines for what this means. Should it be two hours with Dad on Sunday afternoon? Do we have to do a special crafts project each time?

In my experience, special time has become something of a bugaboo for parents, and many well-intentioned moms and dads feel that they are coming up short on this score. Here are my suggestions:

- When planning special time, *frequency* is more important than duration. In other words, twenty to thirty minutes three or four times a week is more important than waiting for a two-hour block of time on Saturday.
- Try to find a time for each child that makes sense, but don't feel wedded to one time slot. If you have a four-year-old girl

who doesn't nap and a two-year-old boy who does, plan something for your daughter while her brother is sleeping.

- Try to find an activity that is unique, one that you really do only during those special times with that particular child. Age can again help distinguish between siblings. A seven-year-old might want to play checkers, a four-year-old might choose Candy Land.

- It can be helpful to refer back to the game or activity, to recall what you did during special time with your child ("That was a great game of Uno"). This helps to reinforce the routine, and to give the kids a sense that they each have a certain niche in the family.

- Give the child the choice if he wants to stick with the usual game or activity or try something different that day. If another child is particularly demanding of attention at the scheduled time, give the special-time child the choice about whether to include her siblings or wait to have private time at another point.

Like other rituals, special time is supposed to be fun and to reinforce a connection between parents and kids. These goals take precedence, but that doesn't mean we can't have another agenda. We know that games can be helpful in teaching frustration tolerance, and that construction projects help kids learn to slow down and plan their work. If our kids choose to play with these things, we can look for ways to encourage them to persevere, be mindful, and cooperate with us. Part of parenting (and good child psychotherapy, for that matter) is being able to shift back and forth, to stay in the moment with our kids while also taking time out to consider what meaning we are making with them.

Rivalry and Revelry

Many parents justifiably worry that reinforcing the concept of special time can create bad feelings between siblings, and set up battles for attention from Mom and Dad. This can be particularly troubling in families where the kids are busy with activities much of the week and brothers and sisters have little unstructured time together. The real risk is that things will become too skewed in one direction and that the family will be more like a collection of individuals, each trying hard to get his and her needs met. Inevitably, one child will be more demanding and get labeled as the difficult one, and the other kids will resent him or her and grasp for their own share of the limelight.

This pattern of sibling rivalry is a well-worn tale, an accepted part of the canon of modern parenting. We now tend to underestimate the potential for closeness among brothers and sisters and assume that conflict between the kids will be the norm. To minimize the arguments and keep the peace, parents may encourage kids to play their own video games or watch their own shows on TV, and simply warn them to "leave each other alone!" We have all been there, and giving siblings a break from each other at times makes perfect sense. But we also need to find ways that brothers and sisters can learn to tolerate each other, and enjoy being together.

Many of the lessons we have discussed in this book—teaching kids to become independent, to cooperate, and to explore, for instance—can be more easily learned in the company of other kids. Young kids are more likely to spend time away from their parents if they see an older brother or sister playing in the yard or the basement playroom. Older children usually like to teach their brothers and sisters how to play imaginative games (perhaps because the young ones are generally willing to accept the less-than-desirable roles). Parents will be more comfortable with the idea of kids exploring the outdoors if they are doing it together, even if it just means roaming in the backyard.

Choosing sides in games, playing board games, or building towers and mud piles together can help kids learn to cooperate without the constant supervision of adults. This doesn't mean that we don't have to jump in if a seven-year-old slugs his little sister, and we shouldn't be shocked if these communal games go awry. But if we're willing to let the kids keep at it and lightly monitor them, chances are they will, over time, learn to share and take turns and complete a sand castle on their own, and quite possibly, have fun together.

We can also give children joint tasks to do, and reward the efforts of the group. Amy, the mother of girls ages five and three, learned that trick. She would have them pick up their toys and their clothes. If they helped each other and did not bicker too much, they could then go to the park. She would not agree until *both* girls did their jobs. In this way we can help kids feel a sense of duty to each other, that they have some collective stake in the game, and that helpfulness and cooperation are the best options.

Acts of kindness and compassion toward siblings, like comforting a two-year-old who has lost her blanky or agreeing to share a recent windfall of candy with an older sister, offer real-life, at-home moments for kids to act on their family's values.

The critical element here is time. If six- and eight-year-old brothers see each other on the school bus or in the car pool and almost nowhere else, they are not likely to develop much of a sense of kinship or connection to each other. In many families, the real victim of the frantic scheduling game is quiet sibling time, the chance to hang out with each other without much to do. Many brothers and sisters no longer have to fill the void of long afternoons without any planned entertainment. Carting the kids to each other's sporting events or activities also increases the likelihood that they will be resentful of each other, and the little time they do have together is more apt to be spent fighting or bickering.

The thrust of this book is to help us to fight against our fears and to focus on what really matters in the lives of our kids. Reasserting control as parents also means using the teaching methods we have at our disposal. In families with more than one child, getting the kids to work things out, to play nicely, and to respect and care for each other can be the ideal way of giving them experience and offering guidance. Siblings can also learn that life is not always perfectly fair, and that sometimes they have to make do with fewer privileges than their brothers or sisters. No mistaking it, this is hard work. Kids aren't typically happy and serene and in love with their siblings. But if we make a concerted effort, and set a goal of encouraging revelry and not avoiding rivalry among brothers and sisters, we can give them the opportunity to practice getting along and to learn about being part of a group, right in our own homes.

Calling All Dads

The mention of time and priorities leads us to an obvious question, namely, "What is Dad's role in all of this?" We have to be careful not to generalize, and I know a number of families where the fathers are the primary caretakers and others where both parents work and the dads are full-fledged partners in child rearing. But the work commitments and time squeeze on fathers in middle- and upper-middle-class families in this country has left many of their wives and their children feeling like they are living in single-parent families during the week. I have heard from many divorced women who argue that the separation from their husbands has had little impact on the children, who see their dads no less than usual after the split. The notion of family dinners on week-nights sounds quaint and far-fetched in many families, and my attempts to have fathers come to my office in the early evening are often met with incredulous stares by mothers. "Oh, he's never home before ten"; I hear these words delivered in a casual and resigned tone on a regular basis.

In workshops with teachers who work in preschool and the early grades, I am often asked why kids are so disrespectful these days and why now, more than ever, they seem to rule the roost. My response may be a little simplistic, but I like to say that if the rooster doesn't really live there anymore, someone has to step into the void. Many of our young kids have no male role models outside the home to counterbalance their limited time with their fathers. There are few male nursery school teachers, and in elementary school the kids may run into a man in the principal's office or the gym but usually not anywhere else. Local sports teams are typically an exception, and part of the drive to get young kids, particularly boys, involved in organized sports at a young age is to give them more time with men who can act as role models.

Individual men and women have different strengths. It's not that men need to be home to take charge of their kids or to teach them discipline, though that is the way things get divided in some families. In well-functioning couples, husbands and wives tend to complement each other. They function as a unit and formulate goals together for their kids, and both parents spend some time thinking about their respective roles and their relative strong points. To join in this process, men have to be on board with sharing parenting duties, and not leave the lion's share of decision making, special time, and rule enforcement to their wives.

In my house, it goes something like this: My wife is more patient and is much better at teaching our kids to slow down and be mindful. She has also been more attuned to their acts of compassion and has built in some regular ways for them to help each other out. I am the one who is more likely to push our kids to try new things and work hard, and am probably a bit stronger when it comes to reining them in or getting them to cooperate with us. I also tend to play more games and plan outings for the family. This doesn't mean that we wake up in the morning and divide our child-rearing efforts like we split up the chores in the house (if we did, my wife might argue that she does 80 percent of *both*), or that we never help each other drive a point home. We do have a general sense of where we like to focus, and take some comfort knowing that the other adult at home will pick up the slack when need be.

The bottom line is fairly simple. The job of parenting is too big for one person. It is a tag team event, where one of the partners is inevitably going to need rest and refueling. We have talked in this book about building up endurance and fighting the good fight, but one person can't do this work unabatedly. It's no wonder that when we feel outmanned we allow more time for watching TV or playing video games, or we relent to our kids' demands, or we separate siblings to get peace and quiet rather than let them attempt to resolve their own conflicts.

Many fathers feel they have little choice and want desperately to be more of a part of the regular family life. I suggest that those who can should adjust their schedules to have more morning or evening time

i do not mean to imply that single parents will inevitably come up short. But they are more likely to be successful if they find a partner to share their load. An ex-spouse can still play that role, as can a seasoned babysitter, an aunt, uncle, or grandparent. Many married couples opt for these alternative arrangements. I know many mothers whose husbands are rarely home and who feel more connected to their nannies or sitters when it comes to child rearing, and work hard to identify and play off each other's strengths.

with their kids during the week, and that they consider what values they hold dear and want to communicate to their kids. When armed with this new agenda, men are more likely to assert their authority, and to tell themselves (if not their bosses) that they are needed at home and that they have to make a change for their family's sake.

Other dads take a wait-and-see approach, and contend that they will be more active and make more of an effort to set aside time for their kids when they are older, when they *really* need their fathers. It will come as no surprise that I challenge them on this point, and argue that the time to teach their kids about life is in the first few years. By age seven or eight kids will have developed many of the traits that, for better or worse, they will carry with them for years to come. Sometimes I appeal to men's sense of pride in how hard they work. If we want to teach that to kids we have to start now, to show them how to persevere in the face of challenges, even if today's battle is how to tie your shoes. I also know that if we wait "just a few more years" to slow down the work schedule, to spend more time with the kids and take more vacation, that day may never come.

Family Leisure Time

I just mentioned vacation, and that was no accident. The typical worker in this country takes on average about two weeks' vacation per year. Many companies offer little additional time off, and short of feigning sick days or taking unpaid leave, many adults have to make do with the limits of their benefits. Plenty of workers also fear that taking additional time might jeopardize their financial stability or their job status. If the boss sees that one employee is less devoted than his colleagues, he or she might subtly or not so subtly deliver a message that company loyalty and being on the job establishes one's place in the pecking order.

This code is not just applied in manufacturing jobs, skilled trades, or the hourly wage segments of the economy. Many of the best-paid employees in business and professional positions are subject to the same rules. Despite their relatively high salaries and expensive perks (or because of them), many men and women feel that they have little control of their schedules, and the idea of extensive time off with their families can feel like a pipe dream. The stories of workers in Europe and elsewhere who enjoy four to six weeks' paid vacation does little to assuage the feeling that this luxury is truly a foreign concept.

Besides giving adult workers a well-deserved break, vacations are pivotal times for families and allow an annual or semiannual opportunity for families to establish rituals of the road. Some of these are not too pleasant, and the packing, driving, fending off crowds, and getting caught in expensive tourist traps can make us wish we opted to stay home. These parts of vacation aren't always fun for kids, either, but they don't have to be dreadful. Vacations are the one instance a family has extended time together without interruption (as long as the kids can successfully hide Mom and Dad's BlackBerrys), and the novelty of having their parents to themselves is often the part of a trip they cherish most.

Visiting new places, exploring ruins or historical buildings, and hiking new trails give kids a sense of adventure and discovery. On the best trips, kids and parents feel like they are in it together, and even the negatives (a cramped hotel room or bad food) become fodder for the toughing-it-out memories, a sort of family Outward Bound image that gets created even if they're far from any real wilderness. Snapshots and mementos can help conjure up these moments, and the stories we tell after we return home are in many ways just as important. Vacations help make family memories and give kids a sense that they are part of a unit, one that on occasion gets to relax, have fun, and head out into the larger world.

Not that it is all a piece of cake. The constant togetherness of a trip can grate on the happiest of families and exaggerate tensions that lie dormant when parents and kids don't see each other as much. Whether it's a kindergartener's whining, Mom's obsession with cleanliness, or Dad's need for control, vacations don't always bring out the best in us. They do present a kind of trial by fire, and if we can survive and get along for a week or more on the road without clawing each other's eyes out, that says something. If we manage to have some fun and laugh at our foibles and make light of the arguments, we can actually teach the kids a lesson that despite the odds, we can all learn to cooperate and have a good time.

To many parents with young kids, that may not sound like a ringing endorsement of family vacations. Some might start to wonder if only two weeks off is not so bad; work is definitely a lot more predictable. Plenty of mothers and fathers will choose a less painful route, and save the exploring for when the kids get older. They might plan a getaway for a week to a beachside resort, and take advantage of minicamp programs for kids that allow them time to relax and recoup. I can't really argue with that; we all need to do what we can to de-stress in our limited time off. But despite the natural appeal of water slides, limbo dances, and hair braiding, separating kids from parents for significant chunks of vacation time limits the chance for them to experience their dads and moms as full-time caretakers. Given the little extended time most parents have with their kids, it's worth considering how to balance our needs and theirs on vacation. No question, parents need downtime. Yet we also want to take advantage of one of the few chances we have to show children how to behave and belong to a family.

Why don't we save those adventure vacations or sightseeing tours for when the kids are a little older, when they'll really understand and appreciate what they're seeing? That's what schools do. Seventh and eighth graders routinely take minitrips for a night or two to the not-too-distant history-rich cities or towns. In New York, that usually means a trip to Boston or Philadelphia, or maybe colonial Williamsburg. I always enjoy talking to kids when they return from these visits, and I usually ask them what they liked most about the trip. Almost all roll their eyes at the mention of anything remotely cultural or historical, and I hear much more about the pillow fights, late night TV, the food, and if they're really lucky, the side trip to a local amusement park (inserted no doubt to calm the rabble and prevent a riot).

This should come as no surprise. Taking a group of preadolescents anywhere is apt to turn into an exercise in crowd control and curtailing hormones. As long as the kids have fun and stay out of trouble and soak up a little of the local ambience, these trips do no harm. But just as we don't want to wait to teach kids to respect others or become independent, we shouldn't hold off on teaching kids about exploring and absorbing different cultures and places. From the age of four or five kids can tolerate longer travel, and they are usually much more interested than they will be in a few years in learning from us and spending time with the whole family. Younger kids may tire more easily, but they tend to relish novelty and adventure, and may actually find that their parents know a few things about the world and how to have fun.

Vacations away from home are not the only leisure time options. Summer day trips to beaches, amusement parks, and ball games offer many of the same opportunities for family time as a week at the shore or a national park (and at a much more affordable price). Many parents with young kids avoid these places because of concerns over traffic or crowds or the heat, which are all legitimate worries. I confess to being a driving enthusiast, but I also believe that teaching kids to play games, sing songs, and otherwise pass the time in the car goes a long way toward showing them the value of mindfulness and frustration tolerance. Fending off people and the elements can be part of a family ad-

When I was a kid living outside Boston, my mother used to drive my brother and me into town and we would take a ferry to Nantasket Beach to spend the day in the amusement park there. Getting there really was half the fun, and that one day a year felt like an exotic adventure into otherwise uncharted territory.

venture, albeit one that the kids may endure more easily than their mothers and fathers. The day-trip adventures we take once and those that become part of our regular rituals can make a lasting impression on our kids, and imprint family memories that last long after they shake the sand out of their shoes.

eleven

A Brave New Town: Finding Neighborhoods, Forming Communities

new parents find themselves confronted with a whirlwind of choices when their children arrive. What names should we choose for the kids? Who will be their guardians? Should they have a formal religious affiliation? How will we pay for college? Some are immediate concerns; others are longer-term questions. One dilemma for couples usually rises above the others and is almost always fraught with anxiety: Where should we live?

It is tempting to link this worry to rapidly escalating housing prices, but parents have fretted about where to settle down long before the boom in the real estate market. For young adults who have come of age in rural areas or small towns, staying put is no longer the obvious or desirable choice, largely because of shrinking job opportunities in their hometowns. More Americans than ever before have flocked to metropolitan areas, and 80 percent of us now live in the cities or their adjoining suburbs. Urban parents, at least those in the middle- and upper-middle class, have a more difficult decision to make. Should they stay or should they go? In the end, most choose to move to the suburbs, attracted by the lure of good schools, safe streets, and perhaps a romantic vision of a quieter, more neighborly existence.

When they get there, many parents find that the reality of suburban living is more sobering. The anonymity of large cities can be disquieting if not unexpected, but the lack of regular contact with neighbors and other people in the surrounding towns can be no less distressing. In *The Geography of Nowhere*,[1] James Howard Kunstler argues that the suburbs can leave people feeling they have been cut off from the public realm and find them longing for more casual discourse with friends and acquaintances. He lists a number of factors that contribute to this sense of disengagement: the lack of sidewalks in most neighborhoods; streets designed to ease traffic flow, not to be pedestrian friendly; the lengthy distance between homes and between housing clusters and shopping areas; longer commutes to work and increased amount of time spent alone in the car.

This description of suburbia may not jibe with our own experience, and many of us can recount tales of local townspeople reaching out to help each other and of friendly gatherings and block parties. These do exist, of course, and planning group events can be the best antidote to suburban isolation, but the general trend has been in the opposite direction. As Robert Putnam points out in *Bowling Alone*,[2] his detailed analysis of the decline of community life in this country, all regions have experienced significant dips in civic engagement in the last thirty to forty years (as measured by membership in local grassroots organizations like the PTA and political groups, attendance at religious service, volunteering, and so on). The decline has been swiftest and most extensive in the suburbs.

Putnam has amassed an impressive array of statistics, but not merely to measure the impact on these groups themselves. He is more concerned that the fade in membership represents a huge loss of *social capital*. In his estimation, we are no longer as bound by "social networks and the norms of reciprocity and trustworthiness that arise from them." Many Americans do not hold to the old belief that their neighbors are good and caring people whom they can rely on for help or to return a favor. In many cases, people don't know their neighbors at all, and don't see people in collective settings enough to develop a sense of kinship and faith in the local townsfolk. Putnam offers a range of plausible explanations for this trend, including increasing time and money pressures, longer commuting distances, suburban sprawl, and the lure of

i n studies and surveys we see consistent and marked differences in the responses of young adults in the current generation and those who came before them. Robert Putnam cites one poll that asked respondents to define the elements of a "good life." In 1975, 38 percent of adults chose "a lot of money," and an equal number picked "a job that contributes to the welfare of society." By 1996, the numbers were skewed; 62 percent mentioned making money, and only 32 percent were interested in a job that could impact society.

television and other electronic media that keep adults and kids comfortably entertained indoors.

According to his research, these factors play a role but pale in comparison to the biggest contributor, the change in values from the generation that came of age in the midtwentieth century to those of the baby boomers and their offspring. Putnam's conclusions echo many of the recent declarations that World War II produced the Greatest Generation, one in which self-sacrifice and devotion to country was the norm. For the younger generations, the traditional civic virtues—patriotism, contribution to a war effort, volunteering—have largely been replaced by heightened self-interest and a quest for more material comforts. As a whole, Americans have turned inward in the last few decades, and we have become more bent on gratifying our own needs than contributing to the larger society.

The Truth About Towns

It is easy to dismiss these arguments as overly sentimental and out of touch with the demands of modern suburban living. After all, most of the adults I know care deeply about their friends and neighbors, and many are happy to lend a hand when the occasion arises. There are plenty of opportunities for parents to connect with each other on the ball fields and playgrounds. These venues have in some ways become the new main streets and the best place for catching up on local news. We may be more wedded to our cars these days, but car pooling has become one of the primary ways we practice reciprocity and share the load with other moms and dads. School bake sales continue to thrive in many communities, and the hard work of the class moms and other school volunteers runs counter to the image of the self-interested modern parent in sociology texts.

Still, there is something that rings true about the then and now comparisons. For many parents, the struggle to find the right towns with the best schools and the best neighborhoods has become a competitive pursuit, fueled by the whispers and serenades of local real estate agents. Is this enlightened self-interest and doing right by their kids or is there something a little darker afoot here? In many communities the best has become synonymous with more exclusive and elitist, and certain towns are available only to the relatively few families that can pay the high-priced entry ticket. Typically they are relatively homogeneous places, with little ethnic, racial, or economic diversity. One social critic dubbed this phenomenon "crowding into the winner's circle," a chance for adults to display their financial success and burnish their image.

I have no issue with parents who have worked hard and gained a measure of success, or those who want to offer their children advantages that they did not enjoy as kids. The problem with the most desirable towns is that they are chock-full of equally competitive and ambitious adults who put their families' needs first. Their proximity and clustering can help accomplish big things, but, inevitably, their needs and desires will clash, and things can become combustible. (Just check the minutes of the local zoning or school boards for a sampling of the squabbles that can ensue.) Although battles may be waged for the good of the town, the hard edges and sharp elbows often suggest a more personal struggle with defined winners and losers. Any notion of civic virtue can get buried in the process.

Competitive people usually make competitive parents, and it is hard to escape the fact that all the scheduled activities and classes for children often have more meaning for the adults involved than for their children. Parents who live in a hard-charging town but have more modest goals and expectations for their kids are likely to face a disconcerting reality. They either buck the tide alone (at least it *feels* like they are alone), or give in and put their kids on the same treadmill as everyone else. The subtle and explicit pressure to keep up—with the hot clothes, the right gear, the latest electronics and computer games, the best swim classes—can be exhausting, particularly when their children are old enough to demand the same privileges their friends enjoy.

Soon enough these pressures trickle down to the kids. A kindergartener may enjoy her ballet and gymnastics and swimming classes, but there will come a day when she says no to going. These replies sometimes draw blank stares from parents who are used to their kids complying with fast-paced local norms, and forget that their young children can get tired, cranky, or fed up with expectations that are not really age appropriate.

At an early age, children may sense that they are not measuring up academically, at least not according to the standard set by their peers. Kids who are sailing along reasonably well, but are not off the charts in early measures of their math and reading skills ("He only reached the 70th percentile in the suburban norms") may be steered toward additional interventions they don't really need. As we have seen, the athletic demands on young kids can be just as daunting in many communities, and the selection process for travel and elite teams can lead to bitterness and sniping among parents. These competitions and the jockeying for position are exaggerated by the specter of future successes, as if an early leg up will pay dividends during the college selection process that is ten or more years away.

Going Against the Grain

Though still relatively rare sightings, there are a few examples of communities that have decided to fight the tide of competition, alienation, and family splintering. Ridgewood, New Jersey, received a lot of press in

2002 when it organized its first Family Night with no extracurricular activities or homework assignments. Spurred on by a recent talk about overscheduling, one local mother approached the town leaders and asked them to consider canceling all activities for children and parents for one night. Parents were encouraged to stay home and have dinner with their kids, and not plan much of anything else to do. The success of this evening and resulting media coverage has led other towns to follow suit, and helped ignite a movement to create a national family night.

One evening does not represent a sea change, of course, but we shouldn't underestimate the symbolic value of the family night campaigns. They have heightened awareness about the chronic lack of family time and the rampant scheduling clashes that leave lots of parents and kids feeling like Sisyphus, struggling mightily to keep up but never quite getting over the hump. These one-night events also underscore that going further and really getting people to rethink their schedules or cut back is an altogether different game. Only a few towns have given that a shot.

Wayzata, Minnesota, a fast-growing desirable suburb of Minneapolis, has led the charge. With the help of William Doherty of the University of Minnesota, an impassioned advocate of preserving family time, the townspeople have created their own grassroots organization, Putting Families First (PFF). The group puts an emphasis on finding ways to increase family time and shared meals, and its mission statement is a concise call to raise "awareness about finding balance in our overscheduled lives." The leaders of PFF have gone a step further, getting the local coaches on board and establishing priorities that place family time and obligations (and schoolwork) ahead of organized sports and other activities. They also issue a seal of approval to local sports leagues, religious groups, arts programs, and other activities that agree to family-friendly scheduling and allow kids to balance their participation with their obligations at home. Eight years into this grand experiment, PFF is still going strong, and its ideas are now woven into the fabric of everyday life in Wayzata, something like a well-oiled conscience getting everyone to think twice before adding in one more game or practice or dance recital to the schedule.

Skeptics might wonder how to connect the PFF experience to their own towns or communities. Wayzata is a pretty small town (a population of just over four thousand) with a strong tradition of community cohesiveness and involvement. Many of the current town leaders have local roots and are at ease working together. Parents on both coasts are probably inclined to chalk up much of Wayzata's success to old-fashioned midwestern values, a homegrown friendliness, and spirit of cooperation that the rest of the country can only dream about.

Our communities may be different, but the fact remains that the people of Wayzata have made a commitment to stem the tide of overly intense commitments and packed schedules that were pulling kids and families in all directions. I would imagine that the people who are moving there now are influenced in part by the appeal of a place where the adults have decided to stake their claim to a more balanced family life. Maybe this is the real lesson here. Maybe it would help parents who live far from Minnesota to have a Wayzata *mind-set* when they are evaluating where they want to live.

For educated, hardworking, and upwardly mobile parents, this may sound funny. Do I mean they should look for a town that has de-emphasized activities and competitive sports? I suppose I could counter with a positive reframe. No, I might offer, I want them to look for places that have reemphasized family life. Home is not just where the heart is; it's the place to teach kids how to live in a thoughtful and meaningful way. In Wayzata and a few other places, parents recognize that to do this they need time with their children; they need to have dinner together and hang out and talk and read together more. As one of the leaders of PFF described it, "The family structure is the essence of democracy. If families don't take time to share their values and beliefs, those tenets of our being get lost."[3]

These are not absolute distinctions. Wayzata has not exactly packed it in on the playing field. Their local high school football team produces a lot of outstanding players who go on to receive Division I or II scholarships. That's not likely to change. But PFF has helped start a local dialogue about keeping things a little more in check, especially for younger age groups. They have coaches and program directors who know that pushing kids too hard too early is likely to lead to burnout and a diminished enthusiasm for sports and the arts. Wayzata is also lucky enough to have community leaders who have forged a consensus among parents, educators, religious leaders, and those who run local activities for children.

Finding Diversity and Adversity

Parents in the suburbs of New York and Atlanta and Boston and Chicago and San Francisco would do well to think long and hard about the values of a place when their children are young. Rather than relying solely on advice of their college friends or following the recommendations of colleagues or relocation specialists about the best towns, they might define their own criteria for the ideal place to live. If they take the time to consider their own priorities, parents may choose to add family balance, community ties, and quality of life to a list that includes good schools, ease of commute, and safe neighborhoods.

Finding the right mix may not be easy and these priorities may clash. It's worth talking to parents in different communities. Ask about homework and school pressures, Little League schedules and the pace of life. Travel around; look for sidewalks and street traffic. Visit the local parks and playgrounds. Are there places to hang out and relax? Is there a town center? Are there walking and bike paths? A town pool? Ask yourself, do folks look like they enjoy living there?

This is more art than science, a little like visiting a few leafy college campuses for an hour and making a decision about where to spend the next four years. Giving some thought to the values and expectations of a community where we might choose to settle should not be an afterthought. I have seen lots of cases of buyer's regret in my office from people who didn't take an exacting look at their town before moving in. After a few years, a couple can look around and feel like things are out of whack and that they have few kindred spirits nearby who share their desire for a more relaxing pace. I can only sympathize when they blurt out, "Why, for God's sake, did we move *here?*"

The search for a locale where they can give their kids every advantage sometimes leads parents to a place they never thought they would be. Welcome to Spoilsville, U.S.A. Living with kids who have become accustomed to a properly indulged life can grate on any parent, but is especially irksome for parents who were raised in more modest circumstances. Lots of people feel blindsided by this development. How did our kids come to want and expect so much? Usually after some soul-searching, parents point to two root causes: (1) We are a little softer than our own parents were with us when it comes to rewarding kids, but what are we to do, when (2) they are surrounded by so much luxury?

This is not just the idle chatter of the upper class. As Dan Kindlon points out, a full 85 percent of Americans in one survey feel that kids in this country are spoiled.[4] There are degrees of indulgence, however, and families that are grouped together in relatively affluent communities are more likely to feel the sting of their kids' comparisons with the junior Joneses next door. Living among successful, well-heeled people has its benefits, both personally and professionally, for many parents. But when kids are exposed only to high-income families they are inevitably going to have a distorted vision of what it means to lead a regular life, and have a limited concept of the struggle it takes to get there. Yes, Dad might work long hours, but the path to success can feel like a natural, predestined certainty for kids who grow up without knowing anything else.

In these settings, parents may feel it is more of a challenge to teach kids how to persevere and cooperate with others. If everyone seems blessed with good fortune, why not just kick back and enjoy the fruits of the family's labor? Kids who see supercharged adults successfully competing for their share of the pie may inherit some of that ambition, but they may also learn to look out for their own interests above all else. Some of their parents make a point of teaching kids about charity and doing good, but it is a little harder for kids to integrate these values if

economic diversity can help parents feel better. Happiness researchers tell us that feeling content is a relative state, and we can't help but compare our successes and lifestyles with those of our immediate neighbors. In affluent communities this can leave some parents feeling impoverished, even if their family income is well above the national average.

they don't see anyone in need, or if their concept of deprivation is based primarily on the size of one's home ("You really live in an apartment?").

Parents who choose to settle in communities with more diversity, in income as well as race and ethnicity, are less likely to find that their children have constantly inflated expectations. In these towns kids meet other kids who are different from them. They have a chance to learn from one another and discover that there are many different ways for families to live and play together. When kids of different backgrounds go to school together and get to know each other, they have a broader sense of the world, and are less likely to feel intimidated or out of place when people don't look or act just like them.

In theory diversity sounds good, but for many adults it can feel a little like spoon-feeding medicine, necessary but not that enjoyable when it comes right down to it. For parents who seek out towns that pride themselves on incorporating difference (think Montclair, New Jersey, for one), diversity implies something different, more laid-back, less intense, more interesting. After living in multicultural urban enclaves, some of the parents fleeing to the suburbs don't want to sacrifice the richness and flavor of their old neighborhoods. They want their kids to see that there are lots of different people who have many types of jobs and practice many beliefs and traditions.

Not all of us want to live in towns where everybody has the same background or works in the same field. Yet many of the sought-after suburbs have become havens for one or more ethnic groups or professions (financial sectors and attorneys this exit, doctors the next, academics and artists, one more stop) that are not separated in the cities they emerged from. Grouped together in this way, many people can start to feel like home is no longer a refuge from the workplace and that their neighborhoods are too insular and familiar. They may yearn to form their own less formal ties with people who feel the same way they do, at least when it comes to family life and the values they want to teach their kids.

The Neighborhood Nexus

I admire people like the residents of Wayzata who try to make big changes in their towns, and stick with their cause until they see tangible results. Many of us share their passion, but find the thought of initiating large-scale change in our communities more than a little daunting. Partly it's a question of time and energy. How many parents with little kids have enough left over to take on the local Little League cartel or the school board? Faced with the prospect of complicated logistics and entrenched politics, many of us shrink back and end up feeling powerless and pessimistic about our ability to start a new dialogue regarding the place of families in our harried communities.

Maybe we should set more modest goals in our own homes and our neighborhoods. If we can't have an impact on the amount of homework (often way too much) our second grader gets, we can let him have a relaxed afternoon after he is finished. We can talk to his teacher about giving us a weekly schedule of homework that we can plan around. If the soccer coach schedules two practices a week, we could ask him if they're both mandatory, and explain that the Sunday schedule conflicts with set-aside family time. We can set rules in our own homes about activities; maybe one during the week and one on the weekend for each child is enough. These efforts are designed to give the kids more freedom to explore and more time at home with their siblings and their parents.

Setting family rules and expectations are the first steps. The next is to try to establish connections with other families who are also fighting the good fight. This is easier said than done, I realize. Time and again I hear parents say, "Nobody in this town seems to feel the way I do." They are out there, believe me, but the search for kindred spirits can be a long and disheartening one.

Nursery and elementary schools can be a good place to start. Look for the moms (and those few dads) who want to hang out in the park after school, who aren't rushing to get to gymnastics or ballet or the daily playdate. Kids are the natural connection, of course, but it can be refreshing to strike up a conversation about something completely different, and it's a good way to see if you like someone as a person, not just as a parent. The town park and the local playground are other good places to meet other mothers and fathers, and some churches and synagogues have their own methods for getting young parents together.

Finding confidants when children are still young can bring relief to parents on several levels. People who move to a suburban neighborhood from somewhere else don't always have a lot of friends or relatives nearby whom they can rely on for help and support. It can be great to have someone close by to bounce ideas off, and to use as a reality check when the "normal" thing to do in town is to sign four-year-olds up for the T-ball league. Discussing values for kids, attending lectures or support groups together, and sharing stories of being wiped out and overwhelmed can go a long way toward cementing friendships between parents with little kids.

We have to be careful not to have too many illusions about our friends and neighbors. Not everyone is going to do things just like us (life would soon be pretty boring if they did). Parents will have different rules about TV and video games and have their own mealtime and bedtime rituals. They may expect their kids to work harder at home or do less. They may keep them closely supervised or allow more freedom. Some parents expect their kids to be home a lot. Others are more inclined to encourage playdates and other avenues for socializing.

When thinking about which families are a good fit with our own, we will inevitably come down to a few bottom-line questions. Are these good people who pretty much share our values? Do the kids treat other people, especially adults, with respect? Are they good at taking turns and playing nicely? Do the parents know how and when to step in if their kids get out of line? At the end of the day, do we feel comfortable that the parents will be able to handle our kids and act the way we would want adults to behave around them? Do they feel the same way about us?

I don't mean to imply that to become family friends our neighbors have to pass an elaborate screening process or extensive interview. Much of our assessment is really a gut reaction to the kinds of people we want to hang out with. Having children does change things somewhat. People can be great fun, witty, and entertaining, but that doesn't always mean they will be the best role models for kids. Conversely, I know adults who may be more staid and reserved but have solid core beliefs (and a little mirth beneath their seriousness) that I admire, and that they have passed along to their kids.

Adult Time

These neighborhood relationships are not just good for the kids, of course. We all need time to hang out and relax and have fun with other adults. Parenting and life in general are not easy. We need this respite as much as our kids do. Laughing, dancing, eating, and drinking together are all great antidotes for world-weary adults. Finding friends who like to walk or run together, or play tennis or basketball, can be crucial to our mental health and well-being, as well as our ability to maintain our energy and our focus with our children. Joining book clubs or discussion groups can help keep our minds sharp and provide a necessary intellectual outlet.

Becoming a parent does not mean total self-sacrifice or completely giving over to other people's needs. We still have a right (and perhaps an obligation) to maintain an active mind, and to have room for conversations about politics, the economy, and the environment. My wife will sometimes jokingly cut short discussions of school at dinner parties with our neighbors and remind them that we are there for adult time, not just to talk about the kids. She and others tend to steer the discussions into literary or spiritual territory. These grown-up preoccupations can be a lesson to our kids that everything does not revolve around them, and that we do not have to share all of our thoughts and ideas with them.

At the same time we don't need to ignore our children. Part of the fun in having strong neighborhood ties is getting families to hang out all together. Block parties, barbecues, pool parties, holiday and year-end celebrations, and impromptu dinners are all terrific venues for adults and kids to relax and play with each other. If we are fortunate enough to live on a street where we actually know and like our neighbors, the informal gatherings in front yards or down the block give kids a regular sense that they are part of a community where people care for each other. They also can see that it's not just their parents who expect them to play nicely or be respectful or work hard. Other adults can look out for and model this behavior, often in a more casual or less preachy manner than we manage to do at home.

The best of neighbors are also available to do neighborly things. The list of the small and not-so-small things that local parents can do to help each other is a long one: pitching in at school together; car pooling; picking up a friend's kids when they're running late from work; babysitting in a pinch; borrowing tools and the occasional cup of milk; sharing advice about sitters or house painters, roofers, and other local service people. The possibilities for helping are endless, but most of these favors are no great bother, especially if they come with the implied understanding that the next time we need a hand, our neighbors will be there for us (remember Putnam's notion of reciprocity).

As relationships deepen, being there can take on new meaning. Neighbors may come to rely on each other during more trying times, when they are battling illness or confronted with the death of a loved one or coping with a community disaster. Parents who struggle with a child who has a chronic illness or serious learning or emotional diffi-

t he events of September 11 had a profound affect on our neighborhood, and cemented ties between families that have not faded. Many of our friends were directly affected by the tragic events of that day and we grieved together. Feeling like we could all use a break, one couple was gracious enough to open up their family beach home to five families just two weeks later. Every year since then we have all spent a weekend in September together, commemorating the events of that day and giving thanks for what we have with each other.

culties need a different and less tangible kind of support from their close friends. They may need practical help identifying specialists and relevant professionals, but it may be just as important to have someone there to listen, to not turn away from them when they are struggling most. These days, with the threat of terrorism and global warming and war constantly on our radar, we all need that kind of support, whether we want to admit it or not.

Forming these kinds of bonds takes time and can't always be rushed. It may take five years or more for parents to feel like they are well integrated into a neighborhood and to have a support network in place. But families who are new to town can jump-start the process. Hanging out at the local playground, being visible at school, and walking the local streets can go a long way toward helping parents meet other mothers and fathers with young children. Some towns have newcomer clubs that serve the same purpose.

Neighborhood connections can run deep, and many people form relationships that last long after they have passed through the struggles of the early years. Surviving the chaos and exhaustion of the baby and nursery school years is a rite of passage for parents, and close friends during those years can feel like sisters and brothers in arms forever after. If families are forced to move while their children are preschoolers or in the early elementary grades, it may be difficult for parents to re-create these bonds in their new towns. Kids are pretty resilient and more likely to bounce back and make new friends, but their mothers and fathers may long for the not-so-old days when they could let their hair down with their neighborhood pals.

Kid Stuff

In addition to offering each other practical help and emotional support, local parents can create more relaxed and informal outlets for their kids. One of the reasons parents feel compelled to sign their children up for organized activities is the lack of available playmates. Nobody is playing or riding bikes on the street. Nobody is hanging out.

We can change that if we get together and stake a claim for free-wheeling kid time. In our neighborhood, there is a "hang out Fridays" group that includes my wife and several friends. Usually by the end of the week, one of the mothers or fathers will volunteer to have four or five families over on Friday after school. The kids know what to do when given the chance, and they run wild outside for a few hours. As they have gotten a little older (mainly ages four to ten now), they need only light supervision. They manage to have endless games of "capture the flag" and running bases (or hide-and-seek inside when the weather is colder) and they travel freely between two or three backyards. The parents meanwhile have their own opportunity to unwind and share a pot of tea or glass of wine, and de-stress after a long week.

These groups can take a while to evolve, but parents can make a more concerted effort to get things going. Wendy lived on a quiet cul-de-sac and loved the fact that her two-year-old daughter and four-year-old son could play outside safely. I suggested she try to organize the other moms on her block and find a day or two that could be just for backyard fun or street games. Little kids need more help organizing their games and playing together, but starting things off when they're young can help ensure that in a few years they will be more independent and able to run around and do their own thing. Getting these informal days on the schedule can also convince parents that they don't have to provide structure every day after school when the new season comes along.

Parents without sufficient backyard space or quiet streets, and their urban counterparts, might choose to use the local park or playground for the same purpose. Carrie jumped at my advice to organize playtime for her kids, and proclaimed that she would be a natural, since she was already "mayor of the park," and hung out there every day after school. Having buddies to run with lets kids feel like they are more independent and can inspire them to be explorers. It can also give mothers a break to be with each other, even if they have to keep one eye cocked for the youngest members of the group. In this way, parents can inspire each other to relax, to not fret so much over their kids, and to leave them more to their own devices.

As neighbors get comfortable with each other and feel more confident about organizing their kids, they may get more ambitious. For many little kids, baseball, football, and basketball leagues are too time-consuming and too focused on skill building (and thus, too boring). Many of them like the games but want to play them on their own without all the rules and drills. We don't all need to be Joe Torre to teach them how to play. Dads and moms with basic understanding can organize a baseball or football game for kids. The trick is getting enough kids to show up on Sunday afternoons in the spring or fall to play.

In my experience, lots of kids, even those who play on teams, want the chance to play ball in a less stressful setting. Given the opportunity, older kids can also be great teachers and get into the spirit of helping the little ones. In our local family baseball game, we have no strikes and no outs for kids under eight. Everybody gets to bat every inning, and they all get a chance to hit the ball, run the bases, and field. Dads and moms take turns pitching and catching and keeping things moving. The goal is to keep it fun and fair. Miraculously, the game always ends in a tie. Even the most competitive eleven- and twelve-year-olds get it, and they relish the chance to strut their stuff and be admired by their younger siblings and the other kids in the neighborhood. After five years, we now have twenty to twenty-five boys and girls, ages four to twelve, playing every Sunday in May and June.

There are plenty of other options for getting kids and families together. Skating parties, movie nights, and family game nights are just a few of the ways we can join in and entertain kids. Although not the main reason for organizing these events, each of these venues gives us a chance to model what it means to be part of a group. If we get together with people who are fun but also helpful, respectful, and cooperative, kids get a fuller sense of what our values are all about. They can also see that our actions pay dividends in the real world. People like to be treated well, and if we are kind and polite and grateful to our hosts, chances are we will be invited back again.

Though a rare breed, some parents have the creativity and energy to go even further. We have friends who organize their own minicamp for local kids age four to nine the last two weeks of June every year. In a short two hours, the moms (and one very helpful dad) plan a range of fun things with the kids, from Mardi Gras parties (complete with coins and beads from the Big Easy) to treasure hunts to craft projects and "silly pet tricks." The leaders take pains to keep the kids engaged and having fun, but they also realize that the novelty of being together in a relaxed backyard setting and calling it "camp" is half the fun for the kids. The simplest games—tag, water balloon fights, hide-and-seek— are usually the ones they remember most.

We may not be so creative or so organized, and parents shouldn't feel additional pressure to be über moms and dads. We should strive instead to have solid networks where we can tap into each other's strengths. The mothers who arrange car pooling and school pickups are just as important to neighbors as the parents who organize dinners and other fun events, and those who are active in the PTA. In a well-functioning community, we all have a role and can find distinct ways to make a contribution. The key is not discovering our inner clown or hidden talent, but joining with other people who share our goal of raising balanced, thoughtful, and well-meaning children.

twelve

The Zen of Parenting

i n the past decade, much has been written about the culture of competitive parenting in America. Journalists, historians, educators, and psychologists have all taken aim at this new rat race and the toll it has taken on mothers and fathers and their children. Judith Warner and others have pointed out that family life has come to mirror the business world, with clear winners and losers and kids who make the cut and those who don't.[1] As we have seen, the cuts start early, from the travel soccer teams for eight-year-olds, the advanced reading groups in second grade, the popular girls' clubs in kindergarten. The divisions and gradations only get worse as children get older: kids pigeon-holed as honors or average students by middle school; the elite athletes in town, well known before they enter high school; the members of the A social group that forms in middle school; the gifted and talented musicians, dancers, and thespians who shine brightly before they reach their teens. Throughout the years all eyes remain squarely on the finish line and the dream of the thick envelope announcing admission to an elite college.

Much of the recent criticism has focused on the intense pressure that kids and parents feel as they try to keep up with rising expectations. In many places, the push to sign up for multiple activities, to jump-start the learning process, and to establish a place in the social hierarchy begins in earnest in the preschool years and continues unabated through high school. The frequent reports of kids who burn out, who tire of organized sports and other activities by the sixth or seventh grade, tend to get buried under the avalanche of come-ons and enticements by local leagues and after-school programs looking to fill their ranks. Many parents feel compelled to keep up with their neighbors, and despite a nagging sense that their kids are doing too much, they feel they have little control over their schedules and no real opportunity to give their kids more downtime.

The cost of these hectic schedules goes beyond the strain and exhaustion of managing multiple practices and competing demands on children's time. Kids living in fast-paced communities can resemble mini-adults, dutifully toting their bags and their books from school to enrichment classes and from activity to activity. In many families, the weekend offers little respite, and having two or three or four commitments on a Saturday or Sunday is no longer considered out of the ordinary. The notion of childhood as a time of freedom and exploration can sound quaint but so yesteryear in many towns where the parents tally who scored the most goals in the first grade soccer league and who is the first in their class to read chapter books. Many educators wonder what will become of these kids down the road, when all they have known is structure, competition, and adult-organized activities.

There is a more subtle but perhaps more troubling result of the push for early achievement. The quantifying of childhood—the grades, the medals, the elite teams, the advanced classes—has done more than turn kids into winners and losers or successful competitors and slackers. In our culture children have become objectified, and in many cases they have become showpieces for their families. Their trophies and their travel team jackets may be theirs to own and wear, but the public display of their success is acknowledged by the adults in the community as a sign of parental achievement. "Boy, you must be doing something right; he's such a good little athlete" can be understood as a friendly and innocuous comment from another parent, and often it is. However, in it lies a clear message that kids' accomplishments (especially their prowess on the playing fields and in the classroom) reflect directly on their parents and their child-rearing abilities.

I n his oft-cited essay in *The Atlantic Monthly*, "The Organization Kid" (April, 2001), David Brooks offered a frightening glimpse of just what the future might hold for the mini-adults of today. He spent time with a number of students at Princeton, and was floored by their adherence to rules and routines, their single-mindedness, their obsession with maximizing their time and their output, and their unwavering ambition.

There's a fine line here. We all take pride in our efforts as parents, and if our kids compete and do well we have a right to feel good about it. As long as we are not boastful nor take too much credit for their work, what harm is done? It comes down to a question of orientation and outlook. If we expect our kids to work hard and to be independent, and they learn to push themselves and get good grades or positive feedback from their teachers, it is reasonable to salute them for a job well done. But we have to remember that although we may have helped them develop the tools, they did the work. I firmly believe that kids' achievements are theirs alone. As parents, we have to be careful not to have too much of our own self-esteem invested in how our children perform in their activities.

Sub-Zero Kids

It's not just a matter of who gets the credit. If the adults around them all have their measuring sticks out, kids are sure to follow suit. Who's the strongest, the biggest, the fastest, the smartest, the fairest of them all? These are age-old questions, but in many towns the competitions to determine the answers start a lot earlier than they ever did before. Kindergarteners know that the grown-ups are watching and giving extra attention to the kids who can read and write, so they try to make the grade. Soccer-playing second graders are quick to learn that the A team gets the goods, and the battle for the limited places on the elite squad can become fierce. The struggling artist who takes years to perfect his craft is a well-worn type for us adults, but seven- and eight-year-olds can feel the pressure to stand out in the school art show right now.

What's the takeaway message for kids? It's the *product* not the process that matters. We want bang for our buck. If you get a little extra coaching, we want to see it turn into goals. If we're going to buy a phonics game or spring for a tutor, well, you just better be ahead of the pack when it comes to reading. That summer cartooning class and the basement art room should be paying dividends. With the best advice and tools and training at their disposal, we want performance!

I know I'm getting carried away here. Few parents would actually *say* these things to their kids. But how many of us will admit to wishing for a little more output, after all the effort we have expended preparing our children? If we have bought the right educational videos, the latest software, the cutting-edge toys, shouldn't we see a return on our investment? With all the time and energy parents have devoted to their kids' education and physical development in the early years, it's not surprising that many moms and dads are disappointed when their children fail to shine right away.

The fantasy that the right stuff—the perfect stroller, the latest electronics, the coolest clothes—will somehow guarantee success for our kids is prevalent among parents in this country. It's not unlike the dream of the perfect kitchen, where the extra counter space, the immaculate center island, and the Sub-Zero fridge will suddenly turn all of us into outstanding cooks and entertainers. (Those of us who struggle to boil water know full well that no matter what appliances are close at hand we will never be auditioning for a job at Emeril's. Still we can't help but wonder what if . . .) At the very least we would *look* more accomplished in such a setting, and surely all that shiny stainless steel could work some magic. Few people want to spoil the fantasy by taking the next logical step: the pressure to deliver the perfect meal to our guests would be immense if everything looked so good in the kitchen.

After all the time and money spent on design and materials we would have no trouble, one might naturally assume, whipping up a divine soufflé. The risk of disappointment, of not measuring up to our own and others' expectations, is that much higher if we have all these great tools at our disposal.

The same logic can be applied to our kids. If they have every advantage—a spot in a top school, excellent coaching, access to the latest technology, and exposure to the arts and other culture—we might be forgiven if we expect them to measure up to some pretty high standards (especially if we never had it so good). But just like high-end appliances, these are all *external* features of their lives. An expensive range does not guarantee that the person who uses it will develop a flair for cooking, and a premier music teacher will not turn every young violinist into a virtuoso. The instructor may have much to offer a child, but only if she has the focus, the determination, and the willingness to practice what she has learned. These core internal traits are ultimately what matter most in determining future success. In our culture we often confuse the two, and parents can come to believe that it's the look or prestige of an activity or school that matters, not the substance of their child's experience in it.

Mini Grown-Ups

Chapter 8 began with the story of a mom who worried that her young son only wanted to play in the woods and ride his bike after school with a gang of neighborhood friends. I think she felt as if she had entered a time warp, a strange world that looked vaguely familiar, but so out of place compared to the rest of her experience with the kids and families around her. It was an inviting image and reminded her of her own forays as a child, but somehow it all felt so wrong. After all, she wondered, shouldn't these kids be doing something more productive?

Many of us have fallen prey to the same thoughts. The old adage we often heard as kids, "Leave well enough alone," hardly seems to fit our lifestyle or do justice to the goals we have for our children. More in-

h istorians rightly caution us to not fall prey to overly nostalgic images of childhood as a period of whimsy and play. The freewheeling suburban kids' life that many of us recall represented a brief period in our history (roughly the 1950s through the 1970s), when children had relatively few responsibilities and were given the freedom to roam and make do on their own. Prior to that time families tended to enlist their kids in work in or out of the home as early as possible, especially during the depression and in the years leading up to World War II. By the mid to late 1980s, the fears about children falling prey to strangers and the movement to provide them with more stimulation combined to limit the amount of free time in childhood, and parents turned to organized after-school activities to keep kids safe and give them enrichment.

evitably feels like better, and when in doubt, most parents choose to add on that one more music lesson or art class or sport and cross their fingers and hope it is not too much. I don't think there are too many parents who purposely set out to overschedule their kids, but there are plenty who want to push the envelope and see how much enrichment their children can take in over the course of a week and how many activities they can fit into a school year.

Part of the motivation for signing kids up is to give them a competitive advantage or help them keep up with their friends and neighbors. But the biggest stumbling block to getting parents to rethink their kids' schedule is overcoming their perceptions of the alternative to the busy life. Sure, downtime sounds good, and even kids need time to unwind; most of us will grant them that. Letting the kids relax fits with our own adult efforts to find stress relief and time for ourselves. Beyond that, it's hard to know what all the fuss is about. Why not keep them organized and out of trouble and stimulated by adults?

This question, which almost always comes up either explicitly or indirectly in my discussions with parents, goes a long way in explaining how much things have changed. The idea that childhood is a time unto itself for play and exploration has been replaced by a miniversion of adulthood in which kids learn a range of skills and how to apply them in different settings. As Steven Mintz explains, the enduring image of Huck Finn roaming the Mississippi getting into scrapes and adventures along the way and learning to fend for himself has largely been forgotten.[2] (Today, no doubt, Huck would not leave home without his cell phone, and his pal Jim would be reported to the appropriate authorities). Few kids in suburban enclaves are encouraged to find their inner Huckleberry, unless they are led by expert guides or warned of all the dangers they might encounter in the wilds of their neighborhoods. The notion that kids can make do without adult instruction or supervision and learn some valuable lessons along the way sounds sentimental at best, and risky and subversive at worse (What about that peer pressure to do bad stuff?).

The idea of a more relaxed and less structured childhood may evoke wistful and pleasant memories for parents, but it can also conjure up an image of backwardness and a lack of sophistication. This thinking can be summed up in this imagined conversation: "Sure sounds nice somewhere in the hinterlands, but here in _____ that's not how it's done. We live in a fast-paced, competitive town and you either keep up or you lose." It's as if the kids who do run free *are* the modern versions of Huck Finn, barefoot and illiterate, with a piece of straw stuck between their teeth. Nobody will say that in polite conversation, but having heard about the looks parents get when they talk about slowing down, and having been on the receiving end myself a few times (that *Little House on the Prairie* comment in chapter 3 comes to mind), it's clear that many parents have an adverse reaction to the idea of childhood as a time of self-discovery and freedom from adult intervention.

Who Writes the Script?

A few years back I worked with a boy named Matt, a lanky sixteen-year-old. Matt had some learning and organizational issues, but he was a brilliant thinker and one of the brightest people I knew at the time. He walked into my office one day looking perturbed. I asked him what was the matter and Matt pointed at the book he was reading, a hot new title that was the follow-up to a bestseller that had been made into a successful movie. "This is nothing like his first book," Matt complained. "All he cares about is the screenplay, setting the scenes and everything; it doesn't even feel like a novel." I was impressed that Matt cared so deeply about what he was reading, but he wasn't finished. "You know, it reminds me of the kids in my high school. None of them are interested in leading a life, of having a narrative. All they care about is writing the screenplay, and building a portfolio to sell to colleges."

Matt's metaphor was rich and insightful, and opened a window into his own struggle to define his narrative and identify his core values. I often refer to it when working with other teenagers, as a way of getting them to think about how they are leading their lives. Matt's reflections have profound implications for parents as well, and raise a number of questions. What, after all is said and done, do we really want for our older kids? For them to build the perfect résumé, to take honors classes, and learn all the right stuff? Are we training them to put all the pieces in place to build that portfolio, or are we encouraging them to think, to be curious, and to follow their inclinations? Is it okay if they make choices about how they spend their time if these do not conform to our expectations or match our dreams for them?

These questions are not only relevant for parents of high schoolers. They merit consideration when our children are little and before they can make their own choices or protest too loudly. There are a few more to ask: Do we have to follow the script and the expected pathways to success? Do our second graders need after-school math booster sessions and two or three sports a season? Are we forced to enroll our three-year-olds in the right nursery schools in the right towns where they can be certain of making friends who can be of help down the line? Should we sign our eight-year-olds up for fencing because we've heard there's scholarship money available in *that* sport?

I'm not suggesting that we drop everything and move to a remote Shangri-la where our kids can run free in the wild all day. I am talking about rethinking our choices in light of the bigger picture. If we view childhood as a period of self-discovery, as a journey that may take our kids to unknown places, both real and imagined, we might not feel so beholden to keep up with the typical expectations in town. If our goals include getting our kids to think for themselves and to act independently, we have to be careful how much preplanning and scheduling we do. In the end, I firmly believe that kids need the time to be kids and to be with other kids, free from the constraints of adult structure and skill-building activities (but not from reasonable expectations about their behavior).

Let me be clear on this point. I am not against all organized activities, enrichment classes, or sports for kids, but I do think we have to be more judicious about how we schedule their time and more cognizant of what they can accomplish on their own. By kindergarten or first grade, most of our kids are spending six or seven hours a day in school, which does not leave much time for them to be pursuing their own interests. Given these time limits, parents should think carefully about whether a particular activity makes sense for their child.

If a family has a strong musical tradition and parents want their kids to experience the joy of making music, it is reasonable for them to give each child exposure to an instrument at a fairly young age. This is a little different from forcing an eight-year-old to practice piano when he shows little inclination or interest in music and nobody in his family can play alongside him. A family that has worked hard to preserve its ethnic and religious traditions may reasonably require the children to learn their native language and have some organized religious instruction. Certain physical activities have more meaning for parents, and teaching kids how to play tennis or basketball may be important to moms and dads who continue to enjoy these games as adults, and want their kids to learn sports they can play their whole life. This is different from compelling kids to participate in organized soccer in third grade if they have tried it for a season or two and found it's not for them.

Zen and the Art of Parenting

Inevitably we are drawn into a discussion of how much is too much for our kids. We can easily spend pages debating this, and I could offer my own prescriptions for the right mixture of structured time and free periods. Ultimately this would do little good if we remain stuck in the same parenting paradigm. If we believe that young kids are open vessels who need as much filling up as we can give them, it is unlikely that we will stop fretting over their schedules or fine-tuning their lives. If, however, we can redefine our role as parents, and determine what skills our children need to learn from us in the early years in order to make their own decisions later on, we might be able to relax with our kids and feel more content about our efforts to raise them well.

In a way, this is what this book has been all about. I believe that if we can overcome our fears and muster the confidence to teach our kids a few key lessons when they are young, we have a right to feel that we have done our job. In these pages, we have focused on six essential lessons for children: to be independent, to persevere, to cooperate with and respect adults, to be mindful, to imagine and explore their world, and to develop compassion for others. As we have seen, these are no small tasks, and they require that parents have the endurance and strength to match their children's energy and wits, and the courage to resist imitating many of the models of family life around them.

This is not the end of the line for parents. It's not as if by eight or nine years old our kids have internalized these values and no longer need our guidance. Far from it. Children continue to need their parents to provide them with support and love, and to be their mentors and their guideposts well through their teen years and beyond. But if we have helped to lay a foundation that they can draw on when the time comes, say, when homework becomes more demanding or when they have to decide if they will join in taunting their peers, we may be more at ease letting them struggle to complete their work and put *their* values to the test.

At some point, all parents need to practice letting go. I mean this more as a mindfulness exercise than a real break from our day-to-day responsibilities (though I wish I had a cure for the chauffeuring blues). Letting go means giving up our fantasies of control over how things will turn out for our children. Despite our best efforts at tinkering and planning, we can't write the endings of our kids' narratives. And we have less editorial control over the middle than we may think. We can, at best, help set the pace and direction of some of the early scenes, or at least give the little writers something to think about as they push ahead.

Beyond that, our kids will make their own way. We can care about them, stand by them, and be their touchstones for some time to come, but we would do well to give them a wide berth, to let them go where their minds and dreams will take them without undue concern about whether they are disappointing us or not fulfilling our expectations. It takes a good deal of faith in them to let them be explorers, to trust that we have served them well and given them a firm home base and steady launching pad. If we can look back and see that we have worked hard to meet our goals as parents, and recognize that we have done what we could to set them in good stead, we might be able to whisper to ourselves: "Good luck, godspeed, do your best."

NOTES

CHAPTER 1

1. Sandra Scarr, "American Child Care Today," *American Psychologist*, 53, no. 2 (1998): 95–108. My kids thought I was a dinosaur when they heard that I started school in first grade. They had four years of education under their belts by then.
2. Tatiana Boncompagni, "Baby Shall Enroll: Mommy Knows," *The New York Times*, May 11, 2006.
3. Alvin Rosenfeld and Nicole Wise, *The Over-Scheduled Child: Avoiding the Hyper-Parenting Trap* (New York: St. Martin's Press, 2000); David Elkind, *The Hurried Child: Growing Up Too Fast Too Soon* (Cambridge, MA: De Capo Press, 2001), still a timely read more than twenty years after it was first published.
4. Christie Mellor, *The Three-Martini PlayDate* (San Francisco: Chronicle Books, 2004); Muffy Mead-Perro, *Confessions of a Slacker Mom* (Cambridge, MA: De Capo Press, 2004).

CHAPTER 2

1. To read more about the bonding controversy, see David Anderegg, *Worried All the Time: Overparenting in an Age of Anxiety and How to Stop It* (New York: Simon & Schuster, 2003); Frank Furedi, *Paranoid Parenting: Why Ignoring the Experts May Be Best for Your Child* (Chicago: Chicago Review Press, 2002).
2. Bruce Gellin, Edward Maibach, and Edgar Marcuse, "Do Parents Understand Immunizations? A National Telephone Survey," *Pediatrics*, 106, no. 5, (2000): 1097–1102.
3. Leaflet, *Step Safely with a Helping Hand* (London: Child Accident Prevention Trust, 1999).
4. Judith Warner, *Perfect Madness: Motherhood in the Age of Anxiety* (New York: Riverhead Books, 2005). See also Jonathan Alter, "Who's Taking the Kids?" *Newsweek*, online edition, July 29, 2002.

5. *Child Care: Overview* (Public Agenda, 2006). Available online at www.publicagenda.org.
6. Wendy Mogel, *The Blessing of a Skinned Knee: Using Jewish Teachings to Raise Self-Reliant Children* (New York: Penguin Compass, 2001).
7. Ann Hulbert, *Raising America: Experts, Parents, and a Century of Advice About Children* (New York: Knopf, 2003).
8. Benjamin Spock, *The Common Sense Book of Baby and Child Care* (New York: Duell, Sloan & Pearce, 1946).
9. Daniel McGinn, "Why TV is Good for Kids," *Newsweek*, November 11, 2002.
10. Sandra Blakeslee, "Video-Game Killing Builds Visual Skills, Researchers Report," *The New York Times*, May 29, 2003.
11. Judith Warner, *Perfect Madness: Motherhood in the Age of Anxiety* (New York: Riverhead Books, 2005); Susan Douglas and Meredith Michael, *The Mommy Myth: The Idealization of Motherhood and How It Has Undermined Women* (New York: Free Press, 2004).
12. Jeanne Muchnick, "The Importance of Being Ivy," *Scarsdale Magazine*, May 2006.
13. To read more on this topic, see Linda Carroll, "Smart Toys Aren't All They're Cracked Up to Be," *The New York Times*, October 26, 2004.

Chapter 3

1. National Center on Addiction and Substance Abuse (CASA) report, "The Importance of Family Dinners" (Columbia University, September 2003).
2. "Pillow Talk, Sleep, and Your Health," *Healthy Mind, Healthy Body* (Oxford Health Plans, fall 2005), 4–7.
3. Daniel Nettle, *Happiness: The Science Behind Your Smile* (Oxford: Oxford University Press, 2005).
4. William Sears, "Solve That Sleep Problem" *Parenting*, November 2005.
5. Jon Kabat-Zinn and Myla Kabat-Zinn, *Everyday Blessings: The Inner Work of Mindful Parenting* (New York: Hyperion, 1997).

Chapter 4

1. Michael Sokolove, "The Thoroughly Designed American Childhood: Constructing a Teen Phenom," *The New York Times*, November 28, 2004.
2. This is an idea I borrowed from my colleague Ellen Wachtel. She provides a more elaborate description of "baby time" in her book *Treating Troubled Children and Their Families* (New York: Guilford Publications, 1994).
3. Daniel Nettle, *Happiness: The Science Behind Your Smile* (Oxford: Oxford University Press, 2005).
4. "Tasks Children Can Do to Learn Responsibility," *Brown University Child and Adolescent Behavior Newsletter*, 1999.

CHAPTER 5

1. To read more about trends in twentieth-century parenting, see Peter Stearns, *Anxious Parents: A History of Modern Childrearing in America* (New York: New York University Press, 2003).
2. Judith Warner, *Perfect Madness: Motherhood in the Age of Anxiety* (New York: Riverhead Books, 2005), 21.
3. Ann Hulbert, "The Prodigy Puzzle," *The New York Times*, November 20, 2005.
4. Andrea Duckworth and Martin Seligman, "Self-Discipline Outdoes IQ in Predicting Academic Performance of Adolescents," *Psychological Science*, 16 (2005): 939–44.
5. As quoted by Peter Doskoch in "The Winning Edge," *Psychology Today*, May 30, 2006.
6. Lenore Terr, "Childhood Traumas: An Outline and Overview," *American Journal of Psychiatry*, 148, no. 1 (1991): 10–20.
7. Norman Garmezy and Michael Rutter, *Stress, Coping, and Development in Children* (New York: McGraw Hill, 1983).
8. E. J. Anthony, "Risk, Vulnerability and Resilience: An Overview," in E. J. Anthony and Bertram J. Cohler, eds., *The Invulnerable Child* (New York: Guilford Press, 1987).
9. Lois B. Murphy and Alice E. Moriarity, *Vulnerability, Coping & Growth* (New Haven: Yale University Press, 1976).
10. Daniel Tarplin, ed., "Optimal Struggle," *Thinking Children*, 2, no. 3 (New York: Jewish Board of Family and Children's Services, 2004).
11. Peter Stearns, *Anxious Parents: A History of Modern Childrearing in America* (New York: New York University Press, 2003), 109.
12. As summarized by Martin Seligman in *The Optimistic Child: A Revolutionary Program That Safeguards Children Against Depression and Builds Lifelong Resilience* (New York: Houghton Mifflin, 1995).
13. Robert Brooks and Sam Goldstein, *Raising Resilient Children* (Chicago: Contemporary Books, 2001), 181.

CHAPTER 6

1. See Cecelie S. Berry, "Who's in Control Here," *Child Magazine*, July 2004, for a well-considered first-person account of this struggle.
2. Judith Warner, "Kids Gone Wild," *The New York Times*, November 27, 2005.
3. Peg Tyre, Julie Scelfo, and Barbara Kantrowitz, "The Power of No," *Newsweek*, September 13, 2004.
4. Robert Fulghum, *All I Really Need to Know I Learned in Kindergarten* (New York: Villard, 1988).
5. Ross Thompson, "The Roots of School Readiness in Social and Emotional Development," *Set for Success: Building a Strong Foundation for School Readiness Based on the Social-Emotional Development of Young Children* (Kansas City: Ewing Marion Kauffman Foundation, 2002).

6. See the description of indulged adolescents in Dan Kindlon, *Too Much of a Good Thing: Raising Children of Character in an Indulgent Age* (New York: Hyperion, 2001).

7. Research has shown that young children who lash out at adults, especially their teachers, are in danger of developing more serious behavior problems later on. See Richard Tremblay, "Predicting Early Onset of Male Antisocial Behavior from Preschool Behavior," *Archives of General Psychiatry*, 51 (1994): 733–34.

8. Eric Slade and Lawrence Wissow, "Spanking in Early Childhood and Later Behavior Problems: A Prospective Study of Infants and Young Toddlers," *Pediatrics*, 113, no. 5 (2004): 1321–30.

9. Martin Seligman, *The Optimistic Child: A Revolutionary Program That Safeguards Children Against Depression and Builds Lifelong Resilience* (New York: Houghton Mifflin, 1995).

10. Thomas Phelan, *1-2-3 Magic: Effective Discipline for Children 2–12* (Glen Ellyn, IL: ParentMagic, 2003).

11. Peter Stearns, *Anxious Parents: A History of Modern Childrearing in America* (New York: New York University Press, 2003).

CHAPTER 7

1. Victoria Rideout and Elizabeth Hamel, *Electronic Media in the Lives of Infants, Toddlers, and Preschoolers* (Henry J. Kaiser Family Foundation, October, 2003).

2. Randall Patterson, "Empire of the Alpha Mom," *New York* magazine, June 20, 2005.

3. Stephanie Saul, "Record Sales of Sleep Pills Cause Worry," *The New York Times*, February 7, 2006.

4. Daniel McGinn, "Guilt Free TV," *Newsweek*, November 11, 2002.

5. Sandra Blakeslee, "Video-Game Killing Builds Visual Skills, Researchers Report," *The New York Times*, May 29, 2003, based on the original study by C. Shawn Green and Daphne Bavelier, "Action Video Game Modifies Visual Selective Attention," *Nature*, 423 (2003): 534–37.

6. Steven Johnson, *Everything Bad Is Good for You: How Today's Popular Culture Is Actually Making Us Smarter* (New York: Riverhead Books, 2005).

7. Family discussions about the values depicted on the screen might mitigate these effects, but the research suggests that few parents actually try to explain the content of shows to their children when they watch together. These findings are summarized by Jane Rankin in *Parenting Experts: Their Advice, the Research, and Getting It Right* (Westport, CT: Praeger, 2005). With reports that as many as 25 percent of *two-year-old* children have a television in their room (Kaiser Foundation, October, 2003), we also have to face the fact that most young children are watching TV on their own much of the time.

8. Claudia Wallis, "Does Kindergarten Need Cops?" *Newsweek*, December 15, 2003.

9. Centers for Disease Control and Prevention (CDC), *Mental Health in the United States: Prevalence of Diagnosis and Treatment for Attention Deficit/Hyperactivity Disorder–United States* (2003).

10. Marie Winn, *The Plug-In Drug: Television, Computers, and Family Life* (New York: Penguin Books, 1977).

11. T. Berry Brazelton and Stanley Greenspan, *The Irreducible Needs of Children: What Every Child Must Have to Grow, Learn, and Flourish* (Cambridge, MA: Perseus, 2000).

12. Daniel Anderson et al, "Early Childhood Television Viewing and Adolescent Behavior: The Re-Contact Study," *Monographs of the Society for Research in Child Development*, 66, no. 1, serial no. 264 (2001). Also see David S. Bickham, John C. Wright, and Aletha C. Huston, "Attention, Comprehension and the Educational Influences of Television," in Dorothy G. Singer and Jerome L. Singer, eds., *Handbook of Children and the Media* (Thousand Oaks, CA: Sage Publications, 2001).

13. To read more about the research on the relationship between TV and aggressive behavior in children, see Jane Rankin, *Parenting Experts: Their Advice, the Research, and Getting It Right* (Westport, CT: Praeger, 2005), and Brad J. Bushman and Rowell Huesmann, "Effects of Televised Violence on Aggression" in Dorothy G. Singer and Jerome L. Singer, eds., *Handbook of Children and the Media* (Thousand Oaks, CA: Sage Publications, 2001).

14. The research on television viewing and attention has been pretty limited. Only two large-scale studies have been conducted in recent years. One found that there was a link between the amount of early television viewing, specifically time spent watching at ages one and three, and attention problems at age seven: Dimitri A. Christakis et al, "Early Television Exposure and Subsequent Attentional Problems in Children," *Pediatrics*, 113, no. 4 (2004): 708–13.

In the second study, there was no meaningful relationship between television exposure and symptoms of Attention-Deficit/Hyperactivity Disorder: T. Stevens and M. Muslow, Pediatrics, 117 (2006): 665–72. The researchers reported that there was a modest but not significant relationship between TV viewing and symptoms of ADHD in kindergarteners.

In one smaller study of fourth and fifth grade students, children who spent more time watching television were rated as having more attention problems by their teachers: Laura E. Levine and Bradley M. Waite, "Television Viewing and Attentional Abilities in Fourth and Fifth Grade Children," *Journal of Applied Developmental Psychology*, 21, no. 6 (2000): 667–79.

There is some data to suggest that early viewing, before age three, is linked with depressed scores on measures of cognitive development: Frederick J. Zimmerman and Dimitri A. Christakis, "Children's Television Viewing and Cognitive Outcomes: A Longitudinal Analysis of National Data," *Archives of Pediatric and Adolescent Medicine*, 159, no. 7 (2005): 619–25.

15. As quoted in Mireya Navarro, "Parents Fret That Dialing Up Interferes with Growing Up," *The New York Times*, October 23, 2005.

16. Abigail Johnson Dodge, *The Kids' Cookbook* (San Francisco: Weldon Owen, 2000).

17. Malcolm Gladwell, *Blink: The Power of Thinking Without Thinking* (New York: Little, Brown, 2005).

CHAPTER 8

1. *Internet Safety*, from the office of the Westchester County (N.Y.) District Attorney.
2. Kathy Hirsh-Pasek and Roberta Golinkoff, *Einstein Never Used Flash Cards: How Our Children Really Learn and Why They Need to Play More and Memorize Less* (Emmaus, PA: Rodale, 2003).
3. Bob Bigelow, *Just Let the Kids Play: How to Stop Other Adults from Ruining Your Child's Fun and Success in Youth Sports* (Deerfield Beach, FL: Health Communications, 2001).
4. Marek Fuchs, "Van Gundy's Sideline Rules," *The New York Times*, February 9, 2003.
5. Peter Cary, "Fixing Kids' Sports," *Newsweek*, June 7, 2004.
6. David Halberstam, *Summer of '49* (New York: W. Morrow, 1989), 68.
7. Richard Louv, *Last Child in the Woods: Saving Our Children from Nature-Deficit Disorder* (Chapel Hill: Algonquin Books, 2005).
8. This work has been pioneered by a colleague and mentor of mine in Boston, Sebastiano Santostefano, and is described in his recent work *Child Therapy in the Great Outdoors: A Relational View* (Mahwah, NJ: Analytic Press, 2004).
9. Howard Gardner, *Intelligence Reframed: Multiple Intelligences for the 21st Century* (New York: Basic Books, 1999).
10. Read about the benefits of play in the following sources: Jennifer A. Connolly and Anna-Beth Doyle, "Relation of Social Fantasy Play to Social Competence in Preschoolers," *Developmental Psychology*, 20, no. 5 (1984): 797–806; Greta Fein, "Pretend Play in Childhood: An Integrative Review," *Child Development*, 52 (1981): 1095–1118; E. Saltz and J. Brodie, "Pretend Play Training in Childhood: A Review and Critique," *Contributions to Human Development*, 6 (1982); 97–113.
11. Steven Mintz, *Huck's Raft: A History of Childhood in America* (Cambridge: Belknap Press, 2004).

CHAPTER 9

1. Robert Brooks and Sam Goldstein, *Raising Resilient Children* (Chicago: Contemporary Books, 2001).

CHAPTER 11

1. James Howard Kunstler, *The Geography of Nowhere: The Rise and Decline of America's Man-Made Landscape* (New York: Touchstone, 1993).
2. Robert Putnam, *Bowling Alone: The Collapse and Revival of American Community* (New York: Touchstone, 2000).
3. As quoted by Miriam Weinstein in *The Surprising Power of Family Meals: How Eating Together Makes Us Smarter, Stronger, Healthier, and Happier* (Hanover, NH: Steerforth Press, 2005). She includes extensive interviews with the leaders of the movements in Ridgefield and Wayzata as examples of local groups trying to reassert the power of dinnertime rituals.

4. Dan Kindlon, *Too Much of a Good Thing: Raising Children of Character in an Indulgent Age* (New York: Hyperion, 2001).

CHAPTER 12

1. Judith Warner, *Perfect Madness: Motherhood in the Age of Anxiety* (New York: Riverhead Books, 2005), 215–20.
2. Steven Mintz, *Huck's Raft: A History of Childhood in America* (Cambridge, MA: Belknap Press, 2004), 382–84.

INDEX

ABOUT THE AUTHOR

Paul J. Donahue, Ph.D., is the director of Child Development Associates in Scarsdale, New York. He is the coauthor of *Mental Health Consultation in Early Childhood*, and a frequent lecturer to parents, teachers, and community groups throughout the country. Donahue has served as a consultant to the Georgetown University Center for Child and Human Development and the National Head Start Association. He lives in Westchester County with his wife and three children.

To learn more about his work, visit www.drpauldonahue.com.